HOW THE
POST OFFICE
CREATED
AMERICA

HOW THE POST OFFICE CREATED AMERICA

A HISTORY

WINIFRED GALLAGHER

PENGUIN PRESS

New York

2016

PENGUIN PRESS
An imprint of Penguin Random House LLC
375 Hudson Street
New York, New York 10014
penguin.com

Illustration credits
Chapter openers:
National Postal Museum: pages 7, 29, 47, 63, 91, 105, 113, 129, 141, 159, 201, 217, 239;
Wikimedia Commons: page 79; Rural Free Delivery © 1996. United States Postal
Service. All rights reserved. Used with permission: page 181; Forever Stamp © 2007.
United States Postal Service. All rights reserved. Used with permission: page 255.

Insert:
Office of War Information, Wikimedia Commons: page 1 (top); Wikimedia
Commons: pages 1 (bottom), 3 (bottom); Library of Congress: pages 2 (top), 6 (top),
11 (bottom); The U.S. Democratic Review, 1838: page 2 (bottom); Thomas Nast,
Wikimedia Commons: page 3 (top); Art and Picture Collection, The New York
Public Library: page 4 (top); National Postal Museum, Curatorial Photographic
Collection: pages 4 (bottom), 5 (top), 7 (top, bottom), 8 (bottom), 9 (top), 13 (top,
bottom), 14 (bottom), 15 (top); National Postal Museum: pages 5 (bottom), 6
(bottom), 10 (bottom), 11 (top), 12 (top), 14 (top), 15 (bottom); Harry T. Peters
"America on Stone" Collection, National Museum of American History,
Smithsonian Institution: page 8 (top); National Archives: page 9 (bottom); Minne-
apolis Newspaper Photograph Collection: page 12 (bottom); African American
Employees' Photo © 1963. United States Postal Service. All rights reserved. Used
with permission: page 16 (top); CSBCS Machine © 1996. United States Postal
Service. All rights reserved. Used with permission: page 16 (bottom).

ISBN 9781594205002 (hardcover)
ISBN 9780399564031 (ebook)

Printed in the United States of America
1   3   5   7   9   10   8   6   4   2

Designed by Marysarah Quinn

IN MEMORY OF BENJAMIN FRANKLIN
AND BENJAMIN RUSH,

MY FELLOW PHILADELPHIANS

CONTENTS

WHY THE POST OFFICE MATTERS

THE HISTORY OF ITS POST OFFICE is nothing less than the story of America. Of the nation's founding institutions, it is the least appreciated or studied, and yet for a very long time it was the U.S. government's major endeavor. Indeed, it *was* that government in the experience of most citizens. As radical an experiment as America itself, the post was the incubator of our uniquely lively, disputatious culture of innovative ideas and uncensored opinions. With astonishing speed, it established the United States as the world's information and communications superpower.

After the Revolution, America needed a central nervous system to circulate news throughout the new body politic. Like mail service, knowledge of public affairs had always been limited to an elite, but George Washington, James Madison, and especially Dr. Benjamin Rush (a terrible physician but a wonderful political philosopher) were determined to provide the people of their democratic republic with both. Their novel, uniquely American post didn't just carry letters for the few. It also subsidized the delivery of newspapers to the entire population, which created an informed electorate, spurred the fledgling market economy, and bound thirteen fractious erstwhile colonies into the *United* States. For more than two centuries, the founders' grandly envisaged postal commons has endured as one of the few American institutions, public or private, in which we, the people, are treated as equals.

The America of the Early Republic desperately needed physical as well as political and economic development. The government quickly mapped this terra incognita with post routes that connected towns centered on post offices; it also subsidized the nascent transportation industry, then dominated by the stagecoach, by paying its owners to carry the mail. By 1831, French political philosopher and mail coach passenger Alexis de Tocqueville wondered over America's unparalleled communications system, which brought the latest national and foreign news even to the Michigan outback.

By the time of Tocqueville's visit, the founders' ideal of nonpartisan politics had faded, and the post they created to unite opinionated Americans could divide them as well. President Andrew Jackson, a slaveholder, fumed when abolitionists used the network to send their unsolicited publications to Charleston, South Carolina, where irate locals committed a federal crime by burning the mail—a conflagration that illuminated slavery as a national rather than merely regional issue. Yet Jackson himself scandalously politicized the post with his "spoils system," which allowed the party that won the White House to hire its supporters for postal jobs wrested from the defeated rival's ranks—a gold mine of patronage that cemented and sustained the country's two-party system for the next 140 years.

In the 1840s, the post faced the worst crisis in its history. Antebellum Americans, including the migrants moving from farms to cities, and increasingly to the western frontier, protested its high letter postage by turning to cheaper private competitors that contested its exclusive right to carry mail. The post responded by turning personal correspondence, historically a costly luxury, into a cheap daily staple, which both aided its recovery and transformed Americans' personal lives. The combination of postage for pennies and the Railway Mail Service—a now forgotten wonder that efficiently processed mail aboard moving trains—later enabled many people to write to a friend in the morning and receive a reply that afternoon.

The post played a crucial role in one of the nineteenth century's crowning achievements: turning the Atlantic-oriented United States into a Pacific nation as well. The transcontinental telegraph and railroad of the 1860s usually get the credit, but they followed in the tracks of a post that was already responding to the needs of history's greatest overland migration. (Most settlers got their mail at post offices in general stores, much like the one served by the young postmaster Abraham Lincoln on the Illinois frontier.) The post subsidized the Overland Mail Company's western stagecoaches but only paid the Pony Express to carry mail at the end of its short life, when the private service helped to keep distant California slavery-free and connected to the rest of the Union.

Like America itself, the post was transformed by the Civil War. When the Confederacy stole its entire southern network, Montgomery Blair, Lincoln's brilliant postmaster general, used the savings from the discontinued operations to pay for expensive new services, including Free City Delivery, which brought mail to urban doorsteps, and the postal money order system, which initially enabled Union soldiers to send their salaries back home safely. The post had been the first, and was for a very long time the only, institution to give jobs to disenfranchised women that offered them rare entrée into public life. Most had been small-town postmasters, but Blair went further, hiring women for prestigious positions as clerks even at the department's august headquarters in Washington, D.C. The post had long been prohibited from using enslaved workers, lest they learn from publications circulated in the mail that all men were created equal. After the war, the victorious Republicans underscored their politics by employing significant numbers of African Americans. As a black woman, sharpshooting, cigar-smoking "Stagecoach" Mary Fields, a former slave who transported the mail by wagon in the wilds of Montana, broke both barriers.

Around the turn of the twentieth century, the post became a progressive champion for Americans who looked to the government to protect them from the Industrial Revolution's dark side, notably the powerful new monopolies that deprived them of affordable, competitively priced services. Their fearless if improbable spokesman was Postmaster General John Wanamaker, the Republican merchant prince. Critics accused him of running his department like his legendary namesake department store in Philadelphia, but he used his business genius on behalf of average Americans to fight for Rural Free Delivery and broaden the meaning of "postal" to include parcel delivery and even savings banking.

Despite the austerity imposed by two global wars and the Great Depression, the undernourished post nevertheless supported, for many years single-handedly, the infant aviation industry required for its Air Mail Service (an unknown Charles Lindbergh was among its pilots). It also linked citizens at home with their loved ones fighting abroad—in World War II with microfilmed Victory Mail letters (no lipstick kisses allowed). Deprived of funds and stuck with long-obsolete equipment and facilities, the post even managed to cope with the booming middle class's quadrupling mail volume until 1966, when, amid riots, protests, and burning cities, the institution faced its second crisis, famously illustrated by the weeks-long shutdown of Chicago's post office.

By 1970, America increasingly looked to business rather than government for problem-solving strategies, and Congress, now accustomed to focusing on the post's bottom line, transformed the tax-subsidized Post Office Department into the self-supporting United States Postal Service. This odd government-business hybrid was finally allowed to modernize its facilities for handling traditional mail. Within a decade, however, the post—ruled by a fiscally conservative Congress and hampered by its own mismanagement—failed to join, much less lead, the revolution from paper mail to email that was its next logical development. In 2007, reeling from onerous new regulations as well, the USPS began to report huge deficits and entered its third and ongoing period of crisis.

Since 1775 until recently, the post has responded to the nation's changing needs—indeed, the institution's advances had often helped precipitate them—but crises and budget-driven policy decisions have gradually, almost imperceptibly, erased America's collective memory of what this dynamic institution has been and vision of what it could be. The people and their elected representatives, who must soon decide the post's future, now know very little about the post, past or present. Indeed, the most widely read academic history was published in 1972, and the best popular one in 1893. Most of the scholarly literature focuses on the nineteenth century, and there has been very little study of the period after the 1930s. It is time for Americans to learn more, particularly about the post's modern history, which this book bases on extensive primary research, including interviews with scholars and postal professionals as well as explorations of libraries, museums, and archives.

Most histories of the United States focus on military, political, and socioeconomic matters, but *How the Post Office Created America* tells the nation's story from the perspective of its communications network. Restoring the record of how the post made us the people we are is important, both for this misunderstood, underappreciated institution and for the insights into the country's past and current affairs that it provides. After all, recurrent themes in the post's story—including the respective merits of public service and private enterprise, the limits of federal power and states' rights, the complex relationships between government and business, the fruits of bipartisanship, the value of national infrastructure, and the country's regional and political polarization—echo through the history of the United States to this day. The post deserves the effort to remember, because just as the founders had envisioned, it created America.

1

INVENTING THE GOVERNMENT:
B. FREE FRANKLIN

THE POST BEGAN TO CREATE the United States long before the Declaration of Independence. In the summer of
1754, Benjamin Franklin, one of the Crown's two postmasters general for North America, traveled to Albany,
New York, to represent Pennsylvania at a highly unusual
political assembly. Great Britain's thirteen scattered colonies were not
yet a unified bloc but instead quarrelsome competitors for their mother
country's favor. The prospect of the bloody Seven Years War—the first
round in the struggle between England and France and their respective Native American allies over control of North America—had forced
officials from the seven northernmost fiefdoms to gather for the first
time in search of a common defensive strategy. Franklin took advantage of the rare opportunity posed by this "Albany Congress" to present a larger, bolder vision of familial unity, which reflected his nearly
unique experience of running the rudimentary postal network that
strung the otherwise fractious siblings together.

Franklin could be sure of his fellow delegates' close attention. At
forty-eight, he was a bright star in the Crown's colonial constellation
and a celebrated personification of what would become the American
up-by-the-bootstraps success story. The fifteenth child of a pious Puritan candlemaker had had barely two years of schooling, yet he had
gone on to become a postmaster and the editor-publisher of the *Penn-*

sylvania Gazette, the colonies' best newspaper, and the popular periodical *Poor Richard's Almanack*. His fortune secured, he pursued his passions for science, technology, and music; mastered chess; read in German, French, Italian, Spanish, and Latin; and became an influential political philosopher and government official.

Franklin's provocative essays on relations between the Crown and its colonies ranged from "Observations Concerning the Increase of Mankind, Peopling of Countries, &c.," which offered an American perspective on British trade policy, to the droll "Rattlesnakes for Felons," which suggested exchanging reptiles for English convicts transported to the colonies. His ideas excited intellectuals on both sides of the Atlantic, including a young Harvard student named John Adams. Eminence notwithstanding, Franklin thoroughly identified with the eponymous Coopers, Chandlers, Smiths, Wrights, and other average countrymen and their down-to-earth view of the world and its ways. One of his saucy satires of official hypocrisy, published in 1747, was entitled "The Speech of Miss Polly Baker, before a Court of Judicature, at Connecticut near Boston in New-England; where she was prosecuted the Fifth Time, for having a Bastard Child: Which influenced the Court to dispense with her Punishment, and induced one of her Judges to marry her the next Day."

Franklin's wide-ranging accomplishments bespeak a wonderful convergence of a dazzling intellect and the extroverted, pragmatic, industrious temperament later associated with America's "national character." A great believer in self-improvement and the active pursuit of personal virtue, he cultivated thirteen qualities meant to counter his own peccant inclinations, including overeating and unseemly jesting. Despite his lapses, he observed that he "was by the Endeavour made a better and a happier Man than I otherwise should have been." Moreover, he was equally devoted to the development of civic virtue, upholding Aristotle's view that "though it is worth while to attain the end merely for one man, it is finer and more godlike to attain it for a nation." His tireless efforts to promote the commonweal in his adopted

Philadelphia included helping to found lofty institutions, such as the University of Pennsylvania and the American Philosophical Society, but also practical ones, such as the city's fire department, public library, and premier hospital. Indeed, one of his first public services, in 1727, had been organizing the Junto, a club devoted to the uplift of men from all social classes. Franklin is best remembered for the clever aphorisms that made him a household name: "If man could have half his wishes, he would double his troubles," and "To-morrow, every fault is to be amended; but that to-morrow never comes." Many others, however, are earnestly altruistic: "The noblest question in the world is, what good may I do in it?" and "Well done is better than well said."

Much has been made of Franklin as the quintessential postmaster general, and he was certainly a very good one. At a time when overland travel was a grueling ordeal, he personally surveyed and strengthened the sketchy system that connected, albeit erratically, the widely scattered, culturally diverse provinces from Falmouth, Maine, to Charleston, South Carolina. He made many improvements, from plotting more efficient routes marked with milestones to speeding up delivery; round-trip service between Boston and Philadelphia was cut from six weeks to three, and one-way service between Philadelphia and New York City to a mere thirty-three hours. His colonial post was more efficient—and, for the first time, profitable—but it remained a conventional mail service, based on Britain's, that was primarily designed to advance an imperialistic power's interests, serve a narrow elite, and produce some revenue for the Crown.

The real importance of Franklin's postal career would have far more to do with the creation of the future United States and its government than with the uniquely American post that would only emerge two years after his death. Like his experience as a colonial media mogul, running the fragile communications web that linked the fragmented colonial world had given him an unusually big picture of it, which had inevitably affected his views about its greater potential. Writing of the closely affiliated Iroquois tribes, Franklin wryly observed that "It would be a very strange Thing, if six Nations of igno-rant Savages should be capable of forming a Scheme for such an Union, and be able to execute it in such a Manner, as that it has subsisted Ages, and appears indissoluble; and yet that a like Union should be impracticable for ten or a Dozen English Colonies, to whom it is more necessary, and must be more advantageous; and who cannot be sup-posed to want an equal Understanding of their Interests."

The Plan of Union that Franklin boldly unveiled at the Albany Congress before the colonies' major leaders, including Thomas Hutchin-son, the future royal governor of Massachusetts, was an outline for an American quasi-government. He had not yet become the "first Amer-ican" and was not proposing that the colonies should unite in declar-ing independence from Great Britain. Rather, he asserted that they should join together to deal with important external matters that con-cerned all of them, including trade as well as defense against the threat from the French and Indians to the west of their seaboard. According to his plan, each colony would elect its own representatives, rather than having them selected by the Crown. These delegates would reg-ularly gather in an assembly, presided over by an executive chosen by Britain, to discuss and devise solutions for problems they shared. His wary peers listened, debated, and then, surprisingly, adopted a modi-fied version of his plan for consideration by their colonial assemblies. These jealous provincial bodies recoiled from the idea of such a cen-tralized authority, and the Crown from anything that smacked of colonial independence. Still, the right man had appeared at the right moment to present major politicians of the day with a new political vision.

Franklin went on to serve the Crown for twenty more years, and one of his sons would remain a prominent loyalist. Nevertheless, in the winter following the Albany Congress, he spurned a proposal for a colonial union put forward by the Crown's own Board of Trade on the grounds that it enabled Parliament to tax Americans without their consent—a violation of their rights as Englishmen—and without even allowing them to pick their own representatives, as his Plan of Union had. James Madison later cited Franklin's correspondence with Massachusetts colonial governor William Shirley on this subject, observing that the prescient argument made in his letters "repelled with the greatest possible force" the Crown's authority over America and did so "within the compass of a nut shell."

Just a month before the Albany Congress, Franklin's *Pennsylvania Gazette* had debuted America's first political cartoon. The simple drawing showed a snake that had been cut up into pieces, signifying the colonies, and the caption read JOIN, OR DIE. The immediate reference reflected Franklin's concern over the need for the English provinces to unite against the French in the looming colonial wars. On a subtler level, however, the sketch invited a provocative question: Why stop there? Within a generation, Franklin and the post would be at the center of a revolution.

AN APPRECIATION OF THE POST'S foundational role in the creation of the United States requires a little knowledge of the systems that preceded it. The term comes from *positus,* Latin for "position" or "station," and a postal system carries information from one place to another, preferably with dispatch. ("Posthaste" first appeared as an instruction on the cover, or outside, of a letter but soon became a synonym for "hurry up!") Mail is now one of many media, but for all but a recent sliver of history, it *was* the media. Letters were the only means of communicating over distance, and delivering them required reliable transportation. Boats could carry mail over water, but until the 1790s, when the optical telegraph relayed coded messages via towers, spaced ten to twenty miles apart, that were equipped with telescopes, a man on a horse was the fastest means of delivering information overland.

Some four thousand years ago, Middle Eastern monarchs established the first postal systems, which were designed to transport official government communications. Herodotus famously praised the ambitious 1,600-mile-long system of the Persian emperor Darius I (r. 522–486 BCE), which used "post riders," or mounted couriers, to carry communiqués etched on clay tablets: "It is said that as many days as there are in the whole journey, so many are the men and horses that stand along the road, each horse and man at the interval of a day's journey; and *these are stayed neither by snow nor rain nor heat nor darkness from accomplishing their appointed course with all speed* [italics added]." Centuries later, the network established by the Roman emperor Augustus (27 BCE–14 CE) was similarly reserved for officials, who often traveled in carts along with the mail on the post roads that also helped to spread imperial hegemony and civilization. Indeed, Rome's post was called the *cursus publicus,* or "public road."

After Rome's fall, communications links in the West were largely limited to kings, monks, and scholars until the thirteenth century, when European businessmen began to sponsor services that were commercial rather than governmental. (The word "mail" derives from Middle English *maille,* or "metal link," for the woven-metal bags carried by the armed couriers of the Hanseatic League, an organization formed at that time to protect the business interests of member German towns and merchant communities.) By the sixteenth century, the German Thurn und Taxis dynasty had begun to expand on the Holy Roman Empire's imperial system to create the first public post, which transported correspondence for paying customers as well as officials throughout much of Europe.

Adam Smith, the eighteenth-century Scottish social philosopher and political economist, said that a post is "perhaps the only mercantile project which has been successfully managed by, I believe, every sort of government." Like sound currency, decent civil service, and efficient transportation, a mail system gradually became a sine qua non of nationhood. By the early seventeenth century, France and England had opened the royal mails to their general populations—that is, to the segment able to pay the high postage. A century later, the combination of the Industrial Revolution and the Enlightenment, which encouraged the exchange of ideas in a so-called republic of letters, had induced other European nations to follow suit. These posts, however, were not public services in the modern sense of amenities provided by a government for its people's good—usually because no profit-minded business would do so. These imperial systems were designed for official communications, producing revenue for the state, and, not least, espionage and surveillance.

By the time Europe's powers got around to providing public postal service, at least to the well-off, some of the requisite bureaucracy and infrastructure, such as roads and shipping routes, was already in place. The New World was a tabula rasa, and even mighty Great Britain struggled to impose a rudimentary postal template on its North American territory. By the mid-eighteenth century, however, this primitive communications chain had helped the colonists to develop an identity that had less to do with Great Britain, whose citizens they were, than with America, where they had now lived for generations.

COLONIAL AMERICA'S FIRST POSTMASTER—then, as afterward, a prestigious position—was Richard Fairbanks, a respected Bostonian appointed in 1639. He also had a monopoly on selling alcohol in the city, and following English custom, his tavern near the great port's bustling Long Wharf became the colonies' first post office. Fairbanks presided over a minimal mail service, however, that was narrowly designated for "all letters which are brought from beyond the seas, or are to be sent thither."

As this transatlantic emphasis suggests, the Crown's North American post was not designed for communications among average colonists. Government officials had the franking privilege—a valuable perquisite that enabled them to use the mail gratis. Otherwise, the service was meant to produce revenue for the king, and its high fees limited its use to the very wealthy and to businessmen and lawyers who had no other way to conduct their affairs or transfer money over distance. Common folk communicated informally through written or, more often, spoken messages sent via obliging friends, shipmasters and other travelers, servants, and Indian runners, such as the man cited by John Endicott, first governor of the Massachusetts Bay Colony, in a letter to John Winthrop, a wealthy lawyer: "Your kinde lines I received by Mascanomet."

Few colonists could afford to use the Crown post, but its mere presence was another proof that they belonged to a widely dispersed community that the historian Ian Steele calls the "English Atlantic." For generations they understood themselves not as Americans but as members of a sprawling commonwealth whose capital was London. They regarded the vast gray ocean less as an obstacle than as a bridge to Great Britain and considered it far more important, and less fearsome, than the vast inland wilds. They had little interest in neighboring colonies, which they considered rivals, and looked to transatlantic trading ships and mail packet boats to bring much of what they considered most valuable: exciting newcomers, the latest consumer goods, and especially news from the distant center of their universe. When a ship from abroad arrived at Boston's Long Wharf, the city's male elite gathered to share their letters and news from Europe in the rarefied precinct of their "merchants' exchange." The hoi polloi gleaned the tidings secondhand, then headed to a nearby taproom or coffeehouse to discuss the latest goings-on.

Geography as well as an Anglocentric worldview greatly restricted colonial communications. Even the simplest postal network requires some sort of transportation system, but such was the difficulty of simply getting from point A to point B, especially overland, that it was easier for residents of Massachusetts and the Carolinas to sail to Great Britain than to visit each other. Whenever possible, colonists and their communiqués floated to their destinations on the boats and rafts that plied the rivers and the convoluted coast. Otherwise, they traveled by foot or horseback along trails unfit for wheeled vehicles that had been blazed by game animals and the Indians who hunted them. In a vicious circle, the awful roads hampered intercolonial communications, which further developed the provinces' sense of isolation and autonomy, only worsening the chances of unified transportation and postal networks. Pennsylvania's enterprising governor William Penn established a local mail service based in Philadelphia, and Virginia's planters devised a "tobacco post" that imposed a fine of a hogshead of the lucrative leaves for neglecting to pass the mail along to the next-door neighbors, usually via enslaved servants. Such systems were extremely limited, however, and the colonies had no centralized network that could transport mail across their borders.

Great Britain's gradual, modest improvements to the colonial post were primarily motivated by the need to inspire some political esprit de corps among her quarrelsome children, whose culture clashes threatened her struggle with France over control of North America. In 1650, the Crown optimistically ordered its provincial governors to start building a "King's Highway" between Boston and Charleston, South Carolina. In 1673, Francis Lovelace, the governor of New York, responded to King Charles II's wish that his American subjects "enter into a close correspondency with each other" by establishing a monthly mail route on the Boston Post Road, as the highway between New York City and Boston would be called; this service was interrupted just six months later, however, when the Dutch briefly retook the large territory along the Hudson and lower Delaware Rivers that they called New Netherland. In 1691, Britain finally recognized that the lack of an intercolonial postal system greatly hindered trade and authorized a centralized network that linked New Hampshire, Massachusetts, Connecticut, New York, and Pennsylvania on a weekly basis. Thomas Neale, a favored courtier who never even visited America, received a monopoly to run the system for his own profit, but it was a financial failure, and in 1707, the Crown assumed control.

A witty journal kept by sharp-eyed "Madam" Sarah Kemble Knight, an important chronicler of colonial society in the early eighteenth century and America's first postal historian, suggests the obstacles that traveling conditions still posed to mail delivery, even on the Boston Post Road. Marked only by axe notches hacked into trees, this dubious "highway" had first consisted of old Indian paths that were frequently broken by mountains and rivers. Over time, towns along the route had grudgingly widened, straightened, and minimally upgraded their own sections of the road. Certain adjacent taverns, inns, and print shops became post offices and informal community centers, and their proprietors, postmasters.

In 1704, the thirty-nine-year-old Knight—a merry widow who worked as a kind of colonial paralegal, speculated in real estate, and was once indicted for selling liquor to Indians—set off from her native Boston for New York City. She had no choice but to do the 268-mile business trip on horseback, as the rough highway could not accommodate carriages. She frequently rode in the company of a Crown post rider who, according to Governor Lovelace's original job description, was to be "a stout fellow, active and indefatigable, and sworn as to his fidelity." In addition to carrying the mail about twenty-five miles per day, these doughty couriers were expected to guide travelers, watch out for runaway indentured servants and slaves, and avoid confrontations with hostile tribes. Just seven months before Knight set out, Indians attacked the English settlement at Deerfield, Massachusetts, killed fifty-six colonists, and captured more than one hundred prisoners.

Knight's observations about the roads—"very bad, Incumbered with Rocks and mountainous passages, which were very disagreeable to my tired carcass"—are the more noteworthy for occurring in the colonies' most populous, settled region on their best approximation of an interstate. On a typical day of traveling with the post, she choked down a dismal meal in an inn on the route ("what cabbage I swallowed serv'd me for a Cudd the whole day after"), then followed the mail courier to a roaring river. There being no bridge, he dutifully "got a Ladd and Cannoo" to ferry her across, then raced off toward his next relay stop some fourteen miles away. Knight forded another raging stream, then struggled to catch up with the post rider, who had left her to make her own way on the dark, narrow trail that passed for the road. She spent a sleepless night at another inn, disturbed by the "Clamor of some of the Town topers in [the] next Room," then set out again with the courier at about 4:00 a.m. Transporting the mail from Boston to New York City required seven such long, bone-rattling days on horse-back in all weather, although Knight took breaks that spread the ordeal over two weeks. Considering the conditions, it's not surprising that even in clement weather, a letter sent from Boston took at least a month to arrive in Virginia.

As Knight's complaints about noisy topers "tyed by the Lipps to a pewter engine" suggest, the multitasking post offices where Americans of high and low degree sent and picked up their mail before the distant advent of letter boxes and home delivery were lively social hubs. The proprietor-postmasters of these taverns and businesses passed along juicy tidbits from the mailbag to their customers, who in turn were expected to read aloud from their own letters and publications. Many could oblige in what was already a surprisingly literate society, particularly in the New England colonies and among men, largely because of the dominant Protestant culture's stress on Bible reading.

The Massachusetts General School Law of 1647, wonderfully known as the "Old Deluder Satan Law," made the case for education on moral grounds:

> It being one chief project of that old deluder, Satan, to
> keep men from the knowledge of the Scriptures . . . It is
> therefore ordered that every township in this jurisdiction,
> after the Lord hath increased them to fifty households
> shall forthwith appoint one within their town to teach all
> such children as shall resort to him to write and read. . . .
> And it is further ordered, that when any town shall

increase to the number of one hundred families or
householders, they shall set up a grammar school, the
master thereof being able to instruct youth so far as they
may be fitted for the university.

Such laws meant that many colonists for whom letters were a rarity
could at least share whatever newspapers and pamphlets (leaflets containing timely essays) that circulated with the mail at the postmasters'
discretion.

The Crown's post was expensive, slow, erratic, and limited in scope.
Many colonists also resented the fact that what revenue it produced
went back to Britain, and some, notably Virginians, even tried to equate
postage with taxation. Nevertheless, this rudimentary network and the
social and physical development it spurred gradually helped civilize a
wilderness and push thirteen quarrelsome provinces toward developing
a new, independent-minded, egalitarian culture more American than
British.

THE IMPORTANCE OF THE LINK between the post and publishing in
shaping a distinctive American mentality, personified by Franklin, is
hard to overstate. Britain initially forbade the publication of domestic
newspapers on the prescient grounds that they could incite sedition.
As time went on, however, the publication of shipping news, public
notices, and the advertising essential to commerce became practical
necessities. In 1690, Benjamin Harris, a Boston printer who published
the works of influential Puritan minister Cotton Mather, announced
that he would offer *Publick Occurrences, both Forreign and Domestick,* on
a monthly basis, "or if any Glut of Occurrences happen, oftener." The
authorities almost immediately shut down his news sheet, however,
because Harris had had the temerity to refer to the Mohawks, who
were the Crown's ambivalent allies, as "miserable Savages." Then, in
1704, John Campbell, not coincidentally also Boston's postmaster,

received the government's imprimatur for his *Boston News-Letter,* the colonies' first real paper, which had perhaps three hundred readers. The popular two-page weekly covered news from the English Atlantic world and within the colonies, as well as sermons, believe-it-or-not yarns, poetry, obituaries, accounts of natural wonders and grisly crimes, and, in 1718, a riveting report of the killing of the pirate Blackbeard, word of which had already circulated by mouth.

In 1721, James Franklin, a cantankerous Boston printer, became the publisher of the *New-England Courant,* which featured more domestic political news than its predecessors and even critiques of the Massachusetts authorities, who would later imprison the outspoken journalist for his antiauthoritarian views. In 1717, he had indentured his twelve-year-old brother, Benjamin, a voracious reader who had dreamed of becoming a sailor. The apprentice learned to set type, peddle papers, and compose essays. As he later recalled, he had to write his popular, sarcastic "Silence Dogood" letters on the sly: "But being still a boy, and suspecting that my brother would object to printing any thing of mine in his paper, if he knew it to be mine, I contrived to disguise my hand, and writing an anonymous paper I put it at night under the door of the printing house."

At seventeen, Franklin staged his first act of rebellion by fleeing Puritan Boston and the irascible James, who had beaten him. He settled in Quaker Philadelphia, the broad-minded "City of Brotherly Love," which was the colonies' unofficial capital and postal center, and soon attracted the attention of Sir William Keith, then governor of Pennsylvania. The grandee urged Franklin to start his own printing business and even offered to supply letters of credit so he could buy the necessary equipment in London. The penniless Franklin traveled to England, only to find that no such letters had preceded him, and he never forgot the British official's betrayal and broken promises. Stranded abroad, he had to work for months to earn his passage back home.

Franklin went on to open his own print shop on Philadelphia's bustling Market Street and prosper. (One notable client was George

Whitefield, a celebrity evangelist of the era's "Great Awakening" Protestant revival, whose sermons the deist published despite his own beliefs, because the tracts both sought to improve the public's morals and turned a nice profit.) In 1737, Britain recognized the enterprising printer's merits by appointing him Philadelphia's postmaster, and in 1753, he was promoted to the important position of joint postmaster general for all the North American colonies.

Franklin's service in the Crown's colonial post exemplifies his flair for doing well while doing good. Many colonial printers, particularly those who also published newspapers, were eager to serve as postmasters, less for the position's modest financial rewards than for its perquisites. The job put them on the inside track for lucrative official printing jobs and also gave them privileged access to both the news and its circulation. Their valuable franking privilege enabled them to send their newspapers to one another through the mail for free, and articles recycled from these "exchange papers" helped to pad their broadsheets' profitable ads and notices for little trouble or expense. Moreover, once the costly, top-priority letters and government documents had been locked in the portmanteau, as the secure official mailbag was called, postmasters selected which newspapers could also travel with the post, though informally, in saddlebags, and pending the courier's approval as to bulk. This was an easy decision for postmaster-printers who were eager to increase the circulation of their own publications, and at no cost.

No one was more assiduous in exploiting a postmaster-publisher's privileges than Franklin. His print shop–post office became the locus for the latest news and gossip, which he published, along with his own trenchant commentaries, and circulated for free. The Crown position's remuneration per se was small, he wrote, but the job "facilitated the correspondence that improv'd my newspaper, increas'd the number demanded, as well as the advertisements to be inserted, so that it came to afford me a considerable income. My old competitor's newspaper declin'd proportionably."

It was not a coincidence that Postmaster General Franklin waited until 1758, after he had made his fortune, to order that *all* the newspapers the post riders agreed to carry could travel in the mail for the same uniformly low rate. This egalitarian change encouraged the fledgling field of journalism, made it more competitive, and motivated ambitious publishers to expand their readership by offering, along with the still dominant foreign news, a less provincial, more broadly American perspective that transcended colonial boundaries. Few newspapers traveled all the way from Boston to Baltimore, but by the early 1760s, the *New-York Mercury* could claim readers in Connecticut, New Jersey, and even Rhode Island as well as its home colony.

As their intertwined postal, transportation, and publishing systems increasingly enabled colonists to share information that went beyond Anglocentric or purely parochial interests, they could not fail to draw sharper distinctions between Great Britain and America. Whether the issue was trade or taxation, agriculture or education, it gradually seemed more practical for a Bostonian to discuss it with a New Yorker or a Philadelphian than with a Londoner.

A change in the use of Boston's elegant Old State House offers a bricks-and-mortar illustration of the colonists' gradual shift from a European to an American identity. The building was constructed in 1713 to be the seat of the Massachusetts Assembly and nerve center of the northern colonies, and its main entry, spectacularly adorned by Great Britain's royal lion and unicorn, faces east, to the Atlantic and the mother country. The western, inland façade is not nearly as grand. Instead of looking toward mighty Britannia, this entry opened onto the Boston Post Road and the wild territory that sprawled west to the Appalachian Mountains and beyond. As the colonies moved into closer relations with one another, however, the reports that passed through this door began to eclipse Europe's news in importance. By the 1760s, the Old State House was the incubator of the independence movement, and its modest western door to the American interior was its main entry.

. . .

FOR MOST OF COLONIAL HISTORY, Britain had been too preoccupied with its own internal affairs to pay much attention to its distant American subjects. More than a century of this benign neglect, compounded by the inherent complexities of transatlantic communications, had fostered the colonists' strong streak of self-reliance. John Smith, a founder of the Jamestown colony in 1607, had yoked the values of industry and liberty early on, writing sternly: "You must obey this now for a Law, that he that will not work shall not eat" and also "Let all men have as much freedom in reason as may be," because "the very name of servitude will breed much ill blood, and become odious to God and man." Anne Bradstreet, his contemporary in Massachusetts, was no less hardworking and independent-minded. America's first published poet and woman writer, as well as the mother of eight children, ridiculed the critics who condemned her for daring to assert her views in print:

> *I am obnoxious to each carping tongue*
> *Who says my hand a needle better fits;*
> *A Poet's pen all scorn I should thus wrong,*
> *For such despite they cast on Female wits.*

By the time Franklin addressed the Albany Congress in 1754, his countrymen were a confident people who no longer lived in their grandfathers' America. They had made significant progress in the gargantuan task of creating a modern civilization in the wilderness. Their inland transportation, though still poor, had improved, and their excellent sailing ships roamed the seas to Europe, the West Indies, South America, Africa, and Asia. Skilled artists and artisans were turning their cities into capitals of culture and fashion as well as politics and commerce. Wealthy Americans took the Grand Tour of the Continent, and at home they enjoyed imported delights, from elegant Georgian architecture to tea and its paraphernalia. Most important, the colonies were producing the homegrown intellectuals who would create the American Enlightenment. Franklin and the much younger philosopher-statesmen, including John Adams, Thomas Jefferson, James Madison, and Benjamin Rush, were determined to bring the Age of Reason's lofty principles down to earth and put them into practice. This desire was rooted in the robust conviction, shared by America's Protestant divines and France's philosophes alike, of the individual's right—indeed, obligation—to know, think, and do for oneself, which European governments still regarded as a wild idea.

For a long time, Britain and her increasingly self-sufficient colonial subjects had mostly avoided conflicts over just who was in charge of what on American soil. In the 1750s, however, Franklin's postal improvements and the Crown's fast, light mail packet boats, which began regular service between England and the colonies, increased the king's ability to supervise his feisty children. Then, in 1765, an activist Parliament seriously perturbed the relationship by passing the Stamp Act, which levied a new tax on the colonists that was meant to defray the cost of maintaining ten thousand British troops to defend the Appalachian frontier. The law's name derived from the fact that the tax often took the form of so-called revenue stamps that had to be affixed to the pages of newspapers and legal and commercial documents, including licenses, wills, and even playing cards; specially embossed paper was also used for the purpose. Britain added insult to the economic injury by passing the law without the colonial legislatures' approval, which violated the Englishmen's constitutional rights. When the colonists furiously objected, the Crown made things worse by maintaining that it had long taxed them without discussion or complaint by charging them for mail service.

Americans had long chafed at the high cost of postage, which even Postmaster General Franklin had initially tried to rationalize as a fee for a service. Now Britain itself invited them to consider it as taxation without representation—a form of tyranny, as the rallying cry first voiced in Virginia nearly fifty years before had put it. That same year, angry delegates from nine colonies followed the precedent set by the Albany Congress and met in New York City to participate in the so-called Stamp Act Congress. These representatives soon found that they had much more in common than this latest grievance and began to develop a broader, more unified political consciousness.

The fracas over the hated Stamp Act was also a personal turning point for Franklin. Since 1757, he had been a mostly absentee postmaster general while also working in London as a lobbyist for several colonies, and the bon vivant had relished life abroad. In addition to his official duties, he conducted scientific experiments and tinkered with inventions, including a more efficient chimney damper and a glass "armonica." He met David Hume and Adam Smith and was awarded honorary degrees from Oxford and St. Andrews universities, after which he was customarily addressed as "Dr. Franklin." As much as he loved London's social and intellectual tumult, however, he had grown increasingly disenchanted with Britain's corrupt politics and egregious socioeconomic inequities. He had initially opposed the Stamp Act and fought successfully for its repeal a year after it was passed, but for him as well as the "Sons of Liberty," a colonial group of nascent rebels riled by the hated tax, Parliament's ameliorative gesture was too little, too late. Asked if the Crown should send military forces to suppress colonial dissent, he said, "They will not find a rebellion; they may indeed make one."

The visionary apologist for an American union, initially within the British Empire, now saw no alternative to true independence. In 1772, Franklin forwarded to some Massachusetts firebrands letters that had been written by Thomas Hutchinson, the colony's governor, in which he advocated "an abridgment of what are called English liberties" in America. Scandal ensued on both sides of the Atlantic when the letters were published, although for different reasons. The mischievous Franklin had already been known to tweak his postmaster's frank from "Free. B. Franklin" to "B. Free Franklin," and in 1774, he was heaped with official opprobrium and fired from his Crown position. In 1775, he sailed for Philadelphia just as the battles of Lexington and Concord signaled the beginning of hostilities, and he was soon appointed the Pennsylvania Assembly's delegate to the Second Continental Congress. Despite his age—Franklin was seventy, George Washington forty-four, and John Adams and Thomas Jefferson only in their thirties—he became one of the founders' most radical voices for American independence.

The former postmaster general returned to a seething revolutionary milieu in which a new, underground postal system was evolving into the backbone of a new government. Many colonists had already been boycotting the Crown's mail or bribing its couriers to carry their letters separately for a cheaper, if illegal, fee. (The latter practice was so common that Hugh Finlay, a British postal surveyor, wrote: "Were any Deputy Post Master to do his duty, and make a stir in such matter, he would draw on himself the odium of his neighbours and be mark'd as the friend of Slavery and oppression and a declar'd enemy to America.") Thousands of patriots, including Samuel Adams, Patrick Henry, and Jefferson, had joined so-called committees of correspondence in order to exchange information and ideas about the growing political crisis, and they had good reason to fear using the Crown's post. Like France, England intercepted mail and searched it for seditious content; indeed, surveillance had been one of Henry VIII's motivations for establishing a state-run post in the first place. Even previously neutral colonists were outraged by Britain's interference with their letters and newspaper delivery, which heightened their sense of estrangement and determination to enjoy the free exchange of ideas, no matter how controversial—a radical principle intrinsic to both the post and the government about to emerge.

The patriots desperately needed their own secure, independent communications network so that they could talk treason and circulate the latest news without fear of arrest. In 1774, William Goddard, a temperamental but gifted Baltimore publisher-postmaster fed up with the Crown post's efforts to obstruct his patriotic newspapers' circulation, created the independent "Constitutional Post," which was quickly adopted by the committees of correspondence, financed by subscriptions, and managed by a group that nominated postmasters and set routes and rates. (Its couriers included Paul Revere, a talented silversmith and engraver later celebrated in Henry Wadsworth Longfellow's stirring if inaccurate poem "Paul Revere's Ride.") When running the system became a full-time job, Mary Katherine Goddard, William's capable older sister, assumed his duties in Baltimore, later becoming America's first woman postmaster in her own right.

The patriotic circles that supported the committees of correspondence and the Constitutional Post became the incubators for the new government that would wage the revolution and create the United States. These rebel groups increasingly ignored the local British authorities and ran their own public affairs, including the elections of the delegates to the Continental Congress, convened in Philadelphia in 1774. That same year, William Goddard asked the assembly to officially adopt his independent post, warning that otherwise "letters are liable to be stopped & opened by ministerial mandates, & their Contents construed into treasonable Conspiracies; and News Papers, those necessary and important vehicles, especially in Times of public Danger, may be rendered of little avail for want of Circulation." At first, the delegates were too distracted by the battles at Lexington and Concord to take action. Finally, however, they saw that the war's outcome would depend on a secure network that could both sustain popular support and allow communications between politicians and the military. On July 26, 1775, the Continental Congress voted to transform the short-lived but crucial Constitutional Post into the Post Office Department of the United States—a nation rooted in a communications network that promoted the free exchange of ideas.

The effort and cost of operating the post was a tremendous burden, especially during the war, yet the founders considered its importance so obvious that their entire authorization for the department was just two sentences long. Congressional delegates and military officers received the franking privilege, which encouraged them to write the many letters that have been a tremendous boon to historians. Franklin was appointed postmaster general and empowered to hire a secretary, a comptroller—he chose Richard Bache, his son-in-law and mediocre successor—and the necessary deputies. Goddard was chagrined when he, who had created the system and influenced the much older Franklin's thinking about postal matters, was passed over for the top job. However, he agreed to serve as the department's first "riding surveyor," or inspector, charged with making sure that service was reliable and secure. By Christmas 1775, the Crown's mail, long starved for business, shut down for good.

On July 4, 1776, the founders signed the Declaration of Independence from Great Britain. (The Smithsonian National Postal Museum, in Washington, D.C., owns the only existing piece of mail from that day: a dated "cover," or a folded letter's addressed outermost surface, sent via the Constitutional Post, that's addressed to John Hancock, a delegate to the Continental Congress and signer of the declaration.) Franklin sailed to France as the new nation's ambassador and secured the alliance that was essential to America's victory in 1783. He returned home to sign the Constitution in 1787, and when he died three years later, at the age of eighty-four, his status was second only to George Washington's.

As John Adams later wrote of the first American, "His name was familiar to government and people, to kings, courtiers, nobility, clergy, and philosophers, as well as plebeians, to such a degree that there was scarcely a peasant or a citizen, a *valet de chambre*, coachman or footman, a lady's chambermaid or a scullion in a kitchen, who was not familiar with it, and who did not consider him as a friend to human kind." His gravestone read only "Benjamin and Deborah Franklin, 1790," but one of Poor Richard's aphorisms would have been a suitably earthy epitaph:

If you would not be forgotten
As soon as you are dead and rotten,
Either write things worth reading,
Or do things worth the writing.

BEFORE THEY HAD EVEN WON their War of Independence, the found-ers had set a powerful precedent for the government's financial and political support of the postal network that had helped to create it. That almost all of the revolutionary era's mail concerned politics and defense had already underscored the post's civic nature, and by the time the Constitution was ratified, in 1788, Washington, Rush, Madi-son, and other future-minded leaders were ready to expand upon it. These founders were no longer content with Franklin's limited, con-ventional, revenue-oriented system, which had been inherited from Great Britain. They wanted a radical, thoroughly American institution that would help to unify and expand their new republic, in which the people were sovereign, not the king, and in which information about public affairs was not a privilege but a right.

2

BUILDING THE POSTAL COMMONS

THE BIRTHDAY OF THE United States may be July 4, 1776, but its federal government was not established until 1789, a year after the Constitution had finally been ratified. The period after victory in the War of Independence had been a difficult, dangerous one for the tenuous union of the thirteen former colonies, which were only loosely bound by the Articles of Confederation of 1777, ratified in 1781. Their differences were no longer muted by the shared goal of securing autonomy from Great Britain, and after more than a hundred years of developing their individual identities, each was protective of its own sovereignty, prerogatives, and culture, as well as broke. Congress appeared to be little more than an assembly of partisans pursuing their own states' provincial interests, and even Thomas Jefferson wondered about the point of maintaining it once the common British enemy had been vanquished.

The post was essential to this experimental new union. Other than conducting foreign affairs, the federal government's power was minimal at best and, within the prickly new states, so volatile an issue that it had jeopardized the signing of the Constitution. Indeed, until the Civil War officially settled the matter, many Americans would say "the United States are" rather than "is." (For the same reason, many modern historians prefer to speak of the "union" or "republic" rather than the "nation" when referring to the country during the antebellum era, on the grounds that although America was a state, a self-governing political entity, it was not yet a nation, a tightly knit people who embrace a common culture.) No sooner had independence been won than George Washington was confiding his fears regarding the preservation of the hard-won, jittery union in a letter to Benjamin Harrison, a Virginia planter:

> The disinclination of the individual States to yield
> competent powers to Congress for the Federal
> Government—their unreasonable jealousy of that body
> & of one another—& the disposition which seems to
> pervade each, of being all-wise & all-powerful within
> itself, will, if there is not a change in the system, be our
> downfall as a Nation. This is as clear to me as the
> A.B.C.; & I think we have opposed Great Britain, &
> have arrived at the present state of peace & independency,
> to very little purpose, if we cannot conquer our own
> prejudices.

Those biases were rooted in the former colonies' very different origins. Puritan Massachusetts's high-minded vision of a virtuous society clashed with the pragmatic view of the Dutch traders who set the tone for New York. The culture of the tolerant, egalitarian Quakers and other religious refugees who settled the mid-Atlantic region contrasted sharply with that of the South's elitist, slave-owning planters. Maintaining a sense of unity was further complicated by the Northwest Ordinance of 1787, which sent the first wave of pioneers flooding into the territory that would become Ohio, Michigan, Indiana, Illinois, Wisconsin, and part of Minnesota—a vast wilderness that also had to be incorporated into the new country somehow. Washington knew that it was by no means certain that any single government, much less the brand-new republic—then the largest of the world's few—could preside over the sprawling, diverse, thinly populated United States, to say nothing of the adjacent territories still claimed by mighty European rivals. He would brood over the challenge throughout his presidency, even raising the question in his farewell address: "Is there a doubt whether a common government can embrace so large a sphere?" His own answer was surprisingly equivocal: "Let experience solve it. . . . It is well worth a fair and full experiment."

Washington and other founders, notably Benjamin Rush and James Madison, believed that the success of that risky experiment required a postal system the likes of which the world had never seen. For thousands of years, both knowledge of state affairs and mail networks had been privileges of a chosen few. The infant United States, however, was based on an idea that was anathema to history's great powers: if a people's republic were to work, the people had to know what was going on. As Washington said, "The importance of the post office and post roads on a plan sufficiently liberal and comprehensive . . . is increased by their instrumentality in diffusing a knowledge of the laws and proceedings of the Government." A physician and public intellectual as well as a politician, Benjamin Rush used more poetic language, describing the post as "the only means of carrying heat and light to every individual in the federal commonwealth."

Officially an arm of the Treasury Department and run on a shoe-string budget, Franklin's old post was not up to the formidable task that Washington and Rush envisioned. In 1790, the system consisted of just seventy-five post offices and 1,875 miles of post roads and still catered to merchants and businessmen along a narrow band of the East Coast. Newspapers were still not classified as official mail, and their distribution largely depended on private arrangements among postmasters, publishers, and post riders; this uncertainty regarding delivery discouraged the kind of high-quality, competitive publishing that feeds democracy. Mail service was erratic and slow (a letter sent from Maine to Georgia took more than a month to arrive), thefts were frequent, and private competitors were numerous. After surveying the department, Samuel Osgood, the first postmaster general under the

Constitution, concluded that postage fees were too high, the volume of letters was too low, and the population was too widely dispersed. Moreover, foreign mail was poorly handled, politicians abused the franking privilege, and many transportation contractors and even postmasters were more interested in serving themselves than in serving the public. (Something of the department's financial constraints comes across in Osgood's plaintive appeal for enough money to hire someone to lay the fire at its headquarters.) His dire assessment notwithstanding, Osgood underscored the egalitarian aspirations of America's post by stressing that even remote parts of the country must have ready mail access to wherever Congress might choose to convene.

Transforming Franklin's limited post into an information and communications dynamo was a wildly ambitious proposition for the fledgling government of a country much of which was wilderness. As soon as the Constitution took effect, Washington asked an anxious Congress three times to assuage his anxieties about the country's inadequate network, but the nervous politicians had good reason to delay and temporize. Complying with the president's request would resurrect incendiary issues regarding the central government's authority *within* the states that had almost derailed the Constitution.

The rather vague language regarding the post in previous legislation had not resulted from mere carelessness. A mail system is a so-called network enterprise, which by definition is both centralized and local and becomes more valuable as it grows. Politicians of all stripes understood that the expansion Washington desired would put a post office—a federal outpost—in every town and village, thus greatly increasing the federal government's footprint at a time when, compared to the powerful states, it had few functions. The question of the national government's right to build post roads was particularly inflammatory, because the states regarded the prospect as an invasive threat to their sovereignty.

Legislators had hitherto dodged these federal-versus-state sensitivities by not getting too specific about the nature of the post and what it could and couldn't do. The Articles of Confederation simply gave Congress "the sole and exclusive right of establishing or regulating post offices from one state to another, throughout all the United States, and exacting such postage on the papers passing through the same as may be requisite to defray the expenses of said office." This careful phrasing glided over the touchy question of Congress's postal authority within the states, several of which, notably Vermont and Maryland, had even established their own posts during the 1780s.

The Constitution, too, had been evasive regarding the structure and prerogatives of what was then also called the General Post Office. It merely said that Congress would "establish Post Offices and post Roads." Interestingly, the post was not specifically given the exclusive right to operate a mail system, either because such a monopoly was assumed or was associated with Britain and political patronage. Lest its ratification be jeopardized, the Constitution's framers preferred to keep things simple and left many postal particulars up in the air, presumably to be settled at a later, ideally less fraught time.

Complying with Washington's requests to clarify and update postal policy would force legislators to revisit the state-federal conundrum at another particularly tricky moment. A proposal that Congress—the government's legislative branch—should delegate its constitutional authority to establish post offices and post roads to the postmaster general—the executive branch—had set off a heated debate about control of the network's design. The Senate supported the idea on the sensible grounds that the system would grow in a more efficient, orderly fashion under the charge of a single able administrator, as was the case in Great Britain. At the time, however, senators were not directly elected by the people and were considered less knowledgeable about local districts than members of the House of Representatives. The mere thought of congressmen surrendering their power to designate new post routes to a federal mandarin struck many of them as unconstitutional and undemocratic, to say nothing of politically unwise, as it would diminish their clout with their constituents.

Political minefields notwithstanding, Congress finally rose to the president's challenge. After much heated argument, the legislators passed the comprehensive Post Office Act of 1792, which laid down important policies that would affect the country's political, social, and physical development for generations to come and help expand the founders' provincial East Coast into the transcontinental United States. Just as the republic truly came into its own with the signing of the Constitution, the post assumed its permanent status and open-ended, truly American character with this landmark legislation.

THE POST OFFICE ACT helped turn the abstract idea of democracy into a concrete reality by authorizing mail service for the entire population rather than just the privileged few or the conveniently located. This huge expansion, however, required some jesuitical phrasing to get around thorny federal-state conflicts. The Constitution had authorized Congress to establish post "Roads"—a very contentious term from the states' viewpoint. The act used less precise, more diplomatic language to empower Congress to establish postal "routes," based on the close reasoning that a route was merely a commitment to deliver the mail by whatever means available, perhaps a river. (Washington and Jefferson favored federal road building, and the latter brooded over the meaning of "establish": did it suggest that Congress could actually make post roads or only select among existing ones?) The need to appease the ornery states resulted in America's poor roads and patchy overland transportation network, which appalled foreign visitors. By the time President John Adams left office in 1801, however, the country had 903 post offices and almost 21,000 miles of post routes, and just as the act's authors had planned, settlers and economic and civic development followed the mail.

The law that unified Americans as a postal people also gave them an unprecedented say in the network's design—an almost unimaginable experiment in democracy in action. Modern Americans take for granted the "universal-service mandate," which says that all citizens everywhere are entitled to mail access for the same price, but this principle was rarely discussed in such absolute terms until the twentieth century. The act didn't make it a basic right, like freedom of speech or religion, but it fostered the idea that if a group of citizens could establish their need for postal service, they could reasonably hope that the government would provide it.

Encouraging the people's expectation of a place on the country's communications grid was essential to the republic's physical and political development as well as the post's. Pioneers were likelier to venture into the wilderness if they anticipated maintaining a link to the great world and having an outpost of the federal government, a place on the map, and a civic identity. The first step in the so-called petitioning process for mail service required a community to badger the Post Office Department or their congressman for it. In many instances, the congressman then submitted the constituents' appeal to the postmaster general, who had retained the constitutional power to establish post offices. If service was deemed warranted, he authorized a new post office, and Congress, responding to the direct will of the local people, determined the route by which the mail would reach it.

Petitioning processes were very often successful, especially in the freewheeling territories, as areas under federal jurisdiction but lacking the status of an official state were called. Indeed, complaints about the overabundance of post offices created by legislators' pork-barreling were voiced by the turn of the century. Nevertheless, Americans had objective proof of their national government's responsiveness to their direct input, which not only brought them mail but also turned clusters of cabins in the middle of nowhere into villages with names, and rutted trails through dense forests into roads on a map. By the time President Jefferson left office in 1809, America had almost 2,300 post offices and

36,000 miles of routes—more than thirty times and twenty times, respectively, than in 1790, before the act passed.

IN GREATLY EXPANDING THE reach of the postal system—and the federal government—the Post Office Act precipitated what the historian Richard R. John calls "a communications revolution that was as profound in its consequences for American public life as the subsequent revolutions that have come to be associated with the telegraph, the telephone, and the computer." To Washington, such a robust post would "tranquilize" a restless, fragmented young America and unify its footloose population: "There is no resource so firm for the Government of the United States as the affections of the people, guided by an enlightened policy; and to this primary good nothing can conduce more than a faithful representation of public proceedings, diffused without restraint throughout the United States." To Rush, Madison, and others, however, the post was also a transformative agent that would ensure democracy in their new government of opinion, educate the people, and change society.

Madison is one of the best known and celebrated of the founders, while Rush, also a leading philosopher of the American Enlightenment, is among the most misunderstood. His modern reputation ironically rests on his brief service as the Continental Army's surgeon general, yet he was an inept doctor who relentlessly purged and bled his patients, not infrequently unto death. (The high mercury content of his popular Bilious Pills, laxatives also known as Rush's Thunder Clappers, later helped researchers trace the path of the Lewis and Clark expedition.) He's also remembered as America's first psychiatrist and the mediator of the late-life reconciliation of presidents Jefferson and Adams, who were, like Franklin, Madison, and Patrick Henry, his close friends. Despite his psychological insight, however, Rush could be self-righteous and judgmental. Indeed, his injudicious complaints about military hospitals had antagonized his superiors in the Continental Army, notably General George Washington, and ended with his resignation from the service.

Personality quirks notwithstanding, Rush was the quintessential humanitarian and a beloved public figure, whose widely read essays helped Americans figure out who they were and what they wanted as a people. He was an early, outspoken advocate for compassionate treatment for the poor, the mentally ill, and the imprisoned. His writings on social reform ranged from "An Address to the Inhabitants of the British Settlements in America, upon Slave-Keeping" to "An Inquiry into the Effects of Spirituous Liquors on the Human Body and the Mind." Like Franklin, his fellow Philadelphian, Rush didn't just talk about the Age of Reason's lofty principles but also practiced them. As a young man, he had joined both the cerebral American Philosophical Society and the feisty Sons of Liberty. Perhaps most important, he inspired others with his sanguine view of humankind in general and the new United States in particular. Of Rush's infectious optimism, Oliver Wendell Holmes later said, "His own mind was in a perpetual state of exaltation, produced by the stirring scenes in which he had taken a part."

Rush championed many causes, but his conviction that the post must circulate information and promote literacy among average folk— still a truly revolutionary idea abroad—was an extension of a particular passion: the government's obligation to foster public education, including free schooling from the primary grades through college. His zeal was grounded in personal experience. Only about half of the founders had attended college, and Rush, the son of a simple farmer and gunsmith, was among the many who were the first in their families to do so. When his father died, his mother was obliged to send her brilliant eight-year-old to live with an uncle who was a clergyman and schoolmaster so that the boy could have a proper education. He went on to attend what is now Princeton University, receive his medical degree at the University of Edinburgh, and then spend several years abroad studying science and languages, particularly excelling at Greek. He returned to Philadelphia and prospered as a physician, professor of medicine, and popular writer, but he never forgot that his good fortune began with the schooling that so many born in similarly humble circumstances were denied.

Rush's advocacy for newspapers as egalitarian educational tools that were "absolutely necessary" to adapt the "principles, morals, and manners of our citizens to our republican forms of government" is writ large in the Post Office Act's remarkable provisions for the circulation of information. The law essentially subsidized the growth of America's struggling press by recognizing all newspapers as patriotic enterprises that, for the first time, qualified as official mail—a marked contrast to the policy in Great Britain. As such, papers were now entitled to a place in the sacrosanct portmanteaux and the same secure handling as letters—and at a very low postage rate meant to encourage the development of an informed citizenry.

Inventing an altruistic public policy is well and good, but in a brand-new government with a very tight budget, opinion had been divided on the question of how to pay for it. Along with authorizing newspaper circulation at nominal rates throughout the entire population, the Post Office Act extended congressmen's franking privilege to enable them to communicate with their constituents about government matters for free. (Legislators quickly flooded the mails with text from speeches given less to influence policy than to impress voters back home; such material was later called "bunkum," derived from Buncombe County, North Carolina.) The money for delivering the overwhelming bulk of the mail had to come from somewhere, which had occasioned a spirited debate.

The "restrictionists," who included Secretary of the Treasury Alexander Hamilton as well as postmasters, who were paid from commissions on mail volume, believed, as Franklin had, that the post should support itself and even, like Britain's, turn a profit for the government. From their perspective, the system should remain concentrated along the cost-effective East Coast, where both the population and profitable business and commercial correspondence were centered. The restrictionists also insisted that newspapers that paid no postage could hardly be considered legitimate mail worth delivering. Taking the opposing view, Rush, Washington, and their fellow "antirestrictionists" argued that the post was no mere moneymaker for the Treasury but what Rush described as "the true non-electric wire of government," which should circulate papers for free whether the service paid for itself or not—a startling notion indeed.

In the end, the act embraced the Platonic ideal of a post that if not profitable should at least be self-supporting—a fateful decision that marked it as the rare federal agency that was expected to sustain itself on its revenue. The law also adopted a compromise, proposed by Madison, that papers would pay *some* postage, in order to ensure postmasters' diligence, but not much, because the information they carried was "among the surest means of preventing the degeneracy of a free government; as well as a recommending every salutary public measure to the confidence and cooperation of all virtuous citizens."

The legislators came up with a radical Robin Hood–style scheme to finance their ambitious new post. Revenue from populous areas, where the volume of lucrative letters was highest and service the most cost-effective, would cover the expense of supplying newspapers throughout the whole country, including the least profitable rural regions. Mailing a single-page letter would cost between six and twenty-five cents, depending on the distance traveled, but a big broadsheet could travel for one hundred miles for a mere penny, and any distance for a penny and a half. (Two years later, "periodicals," such as pamphlets and magazines, were also admitted to the mail, for slightly higher postage.) Most letters were sent by businessmen along the settled northeastern corridor, so Americans in the rustic South and on the expanding western frontier particularly benefited from this policy.

The Post Office Act set off the greatest explosion of newspapers in history. Few papers had survived the war and its tumultuous aftermath, but with the delivery problem resolved, any aspiring journalist who could afford a hand press could now set up as a publisher. The act also mandated that all newspapers were to be treated equally, so coun-try editors received the same informative exchange papers as their urban peers, which helped to decentralize journalism further. By 1794, newspapers comprised seven-tenths of the mail's volume, and their numbers kept on climbing. By 1801, America would have perhaps 200; by 1810, some 365; by 1820, about 1,200. The increased competition en-sured that the change was qualitative as well as quantitative.

Newspapers soon began to replace congressmen's bunkum-filled letters as major sources of public information, setting the stage for the great political debates of the momentous nineteenth century. Wherever Americans gathered, in Philadelphia's elegant salons or the Michigan Territory's cabins, they were able to discuss the same important events and ideas. Much of the credit for this enormous advance belongs to the man who was fittingly eulogized by two of his great peers. Thomas Jefferson wrote, "a better man than Rush could not have left us, more benevolent, more learned, of finer genius, or more honest." To John Adams, "as a man of Science, Letters, Task, Sense, Phylosophy, Patri-otism, Religion, Morality, Merit, Usefulness, taken all together, Rush has not left his equal in America, nor that I know of in the world."

THE POST OFFICE ACT OF 1792, designed to inform and bind the people, also established their right to secure, private correspondence and unfettered access to news, opinions, and ideas, no matter how con-trarian. European governments still regarded this as a heretical idea, but Americans' exposure to foreign censorship had made them allergic to such interference. Fear of the Crown's practice of intercepting and opening mail had inspired the development of the foundational com-mittees of correspondence and the Constitutional Post and fueled the fires of revolution. When abroad, Jefferson, Madison, John Jay, later the first chief justice of the Supreme Court, and other politicians had been forced to write in code lest their letters be read by officials in England's Secret Office or France's Cabinet Noir. When Franklin served as the ambassador to France, his secretary was a double agent also paid by Britain—a perfidy that the wily old philosophe may have exploited for his own advantage. More recently, Americans had witnessed some ugly partisan censorship on their own soil during the debates over the Constitution, when the post office in Boston, where ratification was widely supported, refused to release material sent from Pennsylvania that opposed it.

The Post Office Act's tough stance regarding any interference with the mail was a powerful reinforcement of the people's right to free speech, which the First Amendment had established the previous year. The law made it a crime for anyone other than the addressee to open a piece of mail. The only exceptions were poorly addressed or otherwise undeliverable letters, which were forwarded to postal headquarters, where special "dead letter" clerks strove to get any valuables that had been enclosed to the rightful recipients or return them to the senders. Just months after the act was passed, Postmaster General Timothy Pickering, who later served as secretary of the departments of war and state, encapsulated many of its reforms in his "Instructions to the Deputy Postmasters." He addressed administrative matters, such as the proper basis for postage rates and the need for accurate accounting, but his stress on postal employees' responsibility for protecting the mail's inviolability is particularly striking. They were not to open any correspondence themselves, nor "suffer any person, but such as you entrust in the execution of your office, to inspect or handle the letters under your charge."

The act also imposed the death penalty for stealing mail, which was a grave problem at a time when the post was the only means of delivering sums of money over distances. A law passed in 1799 modified this sentence to forty lashes and imprisonment, but only for a first offense. President Jefferson himself would complain not only that his opponents published material from his private correspondence but also that he daren't abolish flogging for postal theft because the problem was "so frequent and great an evil." For many years, however, the government lacked adequate resources to enforce its laws against postal crime. (Pickering recommended a British practice for thwarting thieves: "I know of but one effectual Security—To cut bank notes into two parts—send one and wait an acknowledgment of its receipt, before the other is forwarded.") Still, the act had laid the legal foundation for the security of Americans' mail, which would markedly improve in 1830 with the inauguration of the Office of Instructions and Mail Depredations—the federal government's oldest law enforcement agency.

Just seventeen years after Benjamin Franklin became America's first postmaster general, the Post Office Act utterly transformed his modest mail network. He would have been flabbergasted by the speed at which the post would become the federal government's biggest, most important department and prime the United States to become the world's most literate, best-informed country within two generations—surely one of the most significant, least appreciated developments in American history.

AMERICA'S RADICAL NEW POST both reflected and affected the lively society of the Early Republic, the variously defined period roughly extending from the Revolutionary War's end to the Civil War's prelude or outbreak. This long era between cataclysms is often overlooked, but it was a time of phenomenal physical growth and social change for the young United States. The Louisiana Purchase of 1803 doubled the republic's size to include everything from the Mississippi River in the east to the Rocky Mountains in the west and from the Gulf of Mexico in the south to the Canadian border in the north. Just a year later, Lewis and Clark's Corps of Discovery took the first steps toward America's future as a Pacific nation. This territorial growth spurt was accompanied by a matching increase in population, which surged from 3.9 million in 1790 to almost 12.9 million by 1830, and to 23.2 million in 1850.

In some ways, the society of the Early Republic was an early version of the Age of Aquarius. The old colonial class structure, derived from Great Britain's, that had distinguished people who lived off their wealth from those who earned a living was giving way to a more fluid meritocracy. The ranks of gentlemen had expanded beyond those who inherited the distinction to include, in John Adams's formulation, anyone who had a liberal education, including him. The literacy rate climbed as high as 90 percent in populous regions, and most citizens were farmers who, unlike their European peers, owned their own land. Pragmatic American geniuses accelerated the Industrial Revolution with the cotton gin (short for "engine"), mechanical reaper, steamboat, and other inventions, which also expanded employment opportunities. Merchants, skilled artisans, and others who both worked and owned property formed the new class of "middlings"—the advance guard for the later nineteenth century's huge bourgeoisie.

The Early Republic's exuberant optimism and determination to realize the Enlightenment's philosophical and spiritual principles inspired a great interest in individual rights and efforts to uplift society. The widespread Protestant revival known as the Second Great Awakening advanced a more hopeful view of the human condition and encouraged the involvement of disenfranchised groups, notably women and African Americans, which helped set the moral tone for early feminist and abolitionist movements. The old institution of indentured servitude disappeared, and slavery was outlawed by the northern states. New academies, colleges, and other educational institutions flourished. The socialist Owenites, who rebelled against industrialization by forming utopian settlements dedicated to cooperation, sharing, and respect for nature, emerged simultaneously with community-oriented, cooperative, agrarian Mormonism.

As in the 1960s, the Early Republic's brilliant, forward-looking culture had a shadow side. More young people chose their own spouses, but more sexual experimentation increased the number of out-ofwedlock pregnancies. Alcohol production and consumption rose, as did urban crime and suicide. Educated youth rioted on campus, much like young rowdies in the cities. Ominously, the new, more democratic ideas about status and the meaning of labor and leisure sharpened the distinctions between the northern states, which admired work as enterprise, and the southern ones, which associated it with slavery.

The newspapers circulated by America's democratized postal system helped to spread the Early Republic's new ways of thinking, but they also fanned the flames of the country's increasingly combustible politics. Few people hewed to Washington's original high-minded ideal of eschewing parties in the interest of unity, and most supported one of two major camps. The Federalists of the Northeast favored a robust federal government and Alexander Hamilton's vision of an economy based on business and banking. Their opponents accused them of elitism and Anglophilic, aristocratic pretensions. The Democratic-Republicans, who were first centered in the South, agreed with Thomas Jefferson on the need to keep the federal government modest in size and aspiration, beware of bankers ("more dangerous than standing armies"), and cleave to an agricultural economy of independent, literate farmers and artisans. They were criticized as rabble-rousing, Francophile anarchists.

Both political parties had mouthpieces in highly partisan newspapers, which served up vitriolic opinion and patriotic poetry along with material from exchange papers, franked documents, and even the occasional interesting private letter. (Confronting a news lull in 1800, the editor of the *Palladium*, in Frankfort, Kentucky, published George Washington's will.) Noah Webster's bruising experiences as a journalist and founder of the Federalists' *American Minerva*, New York's first daily newspaper, surely helped inspire the great lexicographer's efforts to clarify and standardize the country's speech with *An American Dictionary of the English Language*. He objected to the Early Republic's over-the-top rhetoric, in which a political rival might be referred to as a "prostitute wretch," "spiteful viper," or "maniacal pedant," because such language was not just uncivil but also imprecise: "metaphysical abstractions that either have no meaning, or at least none that mere mortals can comprehend." (Not surprisingly for a publisher, Webster had a personal connection with the post, albeit not the usual one: he had once served as a postal surveyor, or inspector, charged with arresting mail robbers between New York City and Hartford, Connecticut.)

THE POST HAD EXISTED on the East Coast in some form since colonial days, but the Post Office Act of 1792 extended it to the frontier's constantly moving western edge. As Timothy Pickering, who expanded mail service as far west as Louisville, Kentucky, rather grandly put it, "Our fellow citizens in the remote parts of the Union seem entitled to some indulgence." To keep growing, however, the countrywide communications system required a countrywide transportation network. The post was prohibited from actually building the necessary roads, but it did the next best thing by subsidizing the transportation industry that would spur their development. This vast public-private venture further shaped the can-do national character and enabled increasingly peripatetic Americans to experience the almost mystical entity called the United States through the post that was both its most localized and its most universal enterprise. Indeed, the postmaster was the only federal employee whom most citizens would ever meet.

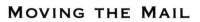

3

MOVING THE MAIL

MANY CITIZENS OF THE Early Republic exhibited the restlessness that was already an American character trait. In 1800, only about 10 percent of the people lived west of the Appalachians, but by 1824, that figure had jumped to 30 percent. As Chief Justice of the Supreme Court John Marshall, who was born in a log cabin on the Virginia frontier, put it, Americans were "an infant people, spreading themselves through a wilderness occupied only by savages and wild beasts." Morris Birkbeck, an early Illinois pioneer and social reformer who was born in England, described his new countrymen as "great travellers; and in general better acquainted with the vast expanse of country, spreading over their eighteen states . . . than the English with their little island. They are also a migrating people; and even when in prosperous circumstances, can contemplate a change of situation, which under our old establishments and fixed habits, none, but the enterprising, would venture upon, when urged by adversity."

In the first half of the nineteenth century, more than half the population moved from one place to another over the course of ten years, including a surprising number who ranged far indeed. Extending the young republic's central nervous system to circulate information to settlers in the Wild West that began on the other side of those mountains was no easy task. Yet just as Washington and Rush had intended, the postal and transportation networks worked in tandem to enable an increasingly diverse population spreading across a vast landscape to feel and function like Americans. Mail service drew settlers into the daunting frontier with the promise of providing both newspapers and the letters, albeit infrequent, that were an emotional lifeline to loved ones perhaps never to be seen again. Supplying it, however, required forging a transportation system in the bush. This phenomenal physical challenge was complicated by fierce political opposition, especially in the South, to federal road construction within the states. Nevertheless, the public-private collaboration between the post and the independent carriers it paid to move the mail caused dirt roads to shoot through dense forests, turned remote hamlets into centers of civic life, developed the market, and supported the sense of an American identity.

ONCE THE CONSTRAINTS IMPOSED by the Revolution had lifted, the demand for better means of travel exploded along with the mail volume, which caused many post riders to lead a second horse burdened with overflowing, often soggy mailbags. Both transportation and the post were still largely limited to the East, along the major North–South axis from Maine to Georgia, but the new, technologically advanced stagecoach at least allowed more people and mail to be carried there much more reliably than by horse or canoe. These modern, enclosed carriages, recently perfected in Britain, were drawn by two to six horses along set routes at set times, periodically stopping at "stages," or relay stations, where passengers could rest while the teams were changed.

America's wretched roads had practically ruled out the use of carriages well into the eighteenth century, particularly in the countryside. Most wheeled vehicles had been rough, open carts or wagons whose passengers, seated on straw, bounced along on dirt lanes that were little more than granitic ruts and often impassable in wet or frozen weather. By 1761, however, John Stavers, a resourceful innkeeper from Portsmouth, New Hampshire, was among the first entrepreneurs to grasp that transportation's future lay with the stagecoach. He advertised a "large stage chair, with two good horses well equipped," that would carry four persons from his inn to Ipswich, Massachusetts, where they would spend the night before proceeding to the Charlestown ferry and on to Boston. His enterprise attracted the attention of Hugh Finlay, the Crown's postal inspector, who observed that Stavers's drivers, who illegally transported letters for a fee, were "so artful that the postmaster cou'd not detect them." This sensible bureaucrat decided that it was "proper to take this man into the pay of the office . . . because the mails brought by the Stage Coach did rather more than pay the 10 pounds of Staver's [*sic*] yearly salary."

Travelers soon took to the high-tech stagecoach, which would play a vital role in American life for much of the nineteenth century. Compared with the wagon, it offered more protection from the elements and highwaymen, and its "shock absorbers," in the form of leather strapping, gave a more comfortable ride. The coach also functioned better in poor weather and darkness and thus was more predictable. Passengers leaving Boston on Monday morning could reasonably plan, barring blizzard or flood, on reaching New York City by Saturday night, and far more easily and safely than Madam Knight had managed astride her horse. Stagecoach lines soon sprang up to connect important cities, followed by local branches radiating from these hubs.

In 1785, barely two years after the Revolution ended, the post made the first of its greatly underappreciated contributions to America's transportation network by subsidizing stagecoaches to carry the mail, starting on certain major routes. The coaches were slower and much more expensive than the post riders, but they could carry much more mail, particularly the bulky newspapers, and do so more securely and dependably. Moreover, as Congressman Charles Pinckney of South Carolina emphasized, the government's investment improved both mail service and transportation by encouraging "the establishment of stages to make intercourse between different parts of the Union less difficult and expensive."

Postmaster General Ebenezer Hazard, who succeeded Richard Bache, Franklin's lackluster son-in-law, in 1782, seemed like the ideal executive to navigate the major technological transition from post rider to stagecoach. He was an experienced bureaucrat who had worked first for the Constitutional Post in New York City, then as a postmaster during the Revolution. Hazard was also a publisher, a scholar who had collaborated on a Greek translation of the New Testament, and a member of the American Academy of Arts and Sciences. A humanitarian, he expressed his deep concern about the fate of Native Americans in an 1816 essay entitled "Remarks on Mr. Schermerhorn's Report Concerning the Western Indians" and also belonged to the New York Society for Promoting the Manumission of Slaves, and Protecting Such of Them as Have Been, or May Be Liberated. History was a particular passion, and Hazard had used his travels during an earlier stint as the post's surveyor general to gather rare materials that documented the republic's founding, which were later published in his two-volume *Historical Collections; Consisting of State Papers and Other Authentic Documents; Intended as Materials for an History of the United States of America.* (More volumes had been planned, but poor sales ended the project.)

Hazard threw himself into what was already one of the federal government's most demanding jobs. His small staff in the capital (then still Philadelphia) was charged with everything from the oversight of postal finances in an era of pen-and-ledger accounting to returning undeliverable valuables to their senders. In addition, Hazard reorganized the department and its already characteristic plethora of rules and regulations. He also restricted mail censorship to wartime or when specifically ordered by certain high officials, adjusted postage rates, and improved the erratic service that had caused cracks about "hazarding a letter."

Hazard was a former businessman, and he was also determined to run his department as a profitable enterprise. In 1782, the Congress of the Confederation, which governed the United States between March 1781 and March 1789, had strengthened his hand by restricting to the post the "carrying and delivering of any letters, packets or other despatches from any place within these United States." This reinforcement of its tacit monopoly on transporting letters for payment, which Great Britain had previously imposed on the Crown's colonial mail, prevented private carriers from snatching up the most cost-effective, lucrative routes. Without protection, the post would have been left scrambling to provide mail service at uniform rates to all parts of the country, including the unprofitable remote areas.

Like his six successors, Hazard achieved what would become the nearly impossible dream of future postmasters general: making the post support itself, and even run a surplus. Despite his many accomplishments, however, he was the first to battle with the combative transportation contractors on which the post depended. He complained that the stagecoach proprietors illegally carried private letters on the sly—indeed, he sued one man for doing so—missed connections between mail coaches, and were even known to speed up slow trips by leaving heavy mailbags behind. Worse, they routinely tweaked the mail coaches' schedules to please their passengers, who liked to depart in the morning and arrive in the evening—the opposite of the timing preferred by the post's lucrative business customers.

The highly principled, devoutly Presbyterian Hazard was outraged by the crafty proprietors' unpatriotic duplicity. If the post were to subsidize the stage system, he reasoned, the department had the right to make the rules and set the schedules for mail coaches. He also maintained that unlike the post riders, the proprietors also made money from carrying passengers and freight, and thus should charge the post less for their services. The independent, entrepreneurial stagecoach owners, however, were just as determined to maximize their profits at their federal patron's expense, and they loudly protested the postmaster general's assertions.

Hazard was a poor politician by his own admission, and he failed to grasp the importance of the post's relationship with the transportation industry and publishing—another emerging special interest, already antagonized by the limits he had imposed on the circulation of bulky newspapers in order to save money. The inevitable crisis occurred in 1788, when Hazard returned the major mail route between Boston and New York to the post riders. The ferocious labor-management dispute that ensued disrupted newspaper delivery at the very moment when Americans were desperate for the latest reports regarding the new Constitution's ratification.

The postmaster general had acted on the assumption that a country of avid newspaper readers cared more for businesslike principles than for timely information, but his tough ploy backfired. The public was infuriated, and so was Washington, the incoming president. He feared that interference with newspaper delivery at such a sensitive time would strike some as a dirty trick by the Federalists, and he expressed his annoyance in a letter to John Jay: "It is extremely to be lamented, that a new arrangement in the post office, unfavorable to the circulation of intelligence, should have taken place at the instant when the momentous question of a general government was to come before the people."

Criticized, overworked, and underpaid—another major grievance—Hazard took refuge in an early retirement in 1789. Despite his travails, he left behind a more secure, efficient department and a network that had expanded upon Franklin's old North–South coastal axis with more East-West routes into the rapidly developing interior, including Pittsburgh, the gateway to the western towns along the Ohio River.

The stagecoach proprietors were the first of a long progression of transportation contractors to exasperate postmasters general. Joseph Habersham, a Georgian who served presidents Washington, John Adams, and briefly Thomas Jefferson, became so fed up with some proprietors' shoddy performance that he started a government-run mail coach line between Philadelphia and Baltimore. This service, which ran from 1799 to 1818, operated so well that Congress actually considered expanding it from Maine to Georgia before abandoning the idea as too ambitious and competitive with private industry—an increasing concern. In 1802, Gideon Granger, Habersham's successor, became the first postmaster general to pay more for a route's stage service than its revenue could cover, which reified the principle of using profits from populous regions to expand and support service in underdeveloped ones. (For a sense of just how lucrative letter postage could be: sending a two-page letter from Ohio to Virginia cost fifty cents in 1815, which is more in both real and cost-adjusted terms than the cost of mailing a one-ounce letter from Hawaii all the way to Alaska in 2015.)

American history has slighted the importance of the post riders who carried the overland mail for more than a century and the stagecoaches that succeeded them. From before Washington's presidency through Martin Van Buren's, the coaches dominated America's roads in the East, and they prevailed much longer in the wilder West. Without the government subsidization that accounted for a third to a half of the industry's revenue, this vital transportation network could not have expanded into the remote places that no private, profit-driven enterprise would have invested in—a crucial factor in developing the highways, crossroads, and settlements that turned a wilderness into the *United* States.

THE SHEER SPEED OF the post's growth during the Early Republic is hard to comprehend. Before the Post Office Act of 1792 was signed, mail was transported from Maine to Virginia just three times a week; south of Virginia, only once a week in winter, twice in summer. There were no postal facilities at all west of Pittsburgh and Albany. That same year, however, the department began its ambitious expansion, particularly into the underserved West and South. By 1810, America had 2,300 post offices and 36,000 miles of post roads; by 1830, approximately 8,400 and 115,000.

The post's development in Ohio, which was initially part of the wild and woolly Northwest Territory, suggests the challenges of extending the network into a frontier. The ranks of its adventurous pioneers, who numbered just 45,000 in 1800 but almost 938,000 by 1830, included East Coast farmers already looking for greener pastures; François D'Hébécourt, a French former classmate of Napoleon's and postmaster of tiny Gallipolis, on the Ohio River; and Rufus Putnam, a Revolutionary War general who set out to make a fortune as a real estate developer. Postal service was essential to the expansionist dreams he shared with his enterprising partners in the Ohio Company of Associates. They purchased a million and a half acres of the Northwest Territory and, in 1788, established its first U.S. settlement at Marietta. The settlers who ventured there wanted to maintain connections with the East Coast and also to replicate it as fast as possible. (One of their first projects was building a fort, called the Campus Martius, to protect themselves from the understandably aggrieved Native Americans they sought to displace.) Marietta got a post office in 1794, but by the time of statehood in 1803, it was one of just eighteen in all of sprawling Ohio.

Delivering a letter from the East Coast to Ohio required heroic efforts from the post. In 1800, Postmaster General Habersham inaugurated the "hub and spoke" circulation system, in which large, centralized "distributing post offices" sorted an entire region's mail, then dispersed it to the spokes, or local "common" post offices, where the recipients retrieved it. Most of the new state's postal facilities were strung along the great Ohio River or its tributaries, which were the best means of transportation in wild terrain and the inspirations for its early "river roads." A letter sent from Philadelphia, say, to Cincinnati was forwarded to the big distributing post office at Pittsburgh, then traveled west by canoe or boat on the watery superhighway of the Ohio to its destination; outgoing mail went against the river's current and took twice as long. The complexity of scheduling such aquatic service comes across in a notice announcing that a boat carrying the mail would leave Marietta "every Monday morning at five o'clock, or the evening before, if She chuses," reaching Wheeling "the next Wednesday Evening unless a very extreordinary [sic] Fresh in the river shall render it empracticable [sic] which will very seldom if ever happen."

Ohio's increased development and need for better communications with the outside world soon required decent overland transportation as well. Its first "highway" was aptly called Zane's Trace, because initially that's all it was. This glorified trail for horseback riders was hacked through the wilderness by Colonel Ebenezer Zane and his sons, who didn't bother to ask Congress's permission until 1796, after they had already begun the task. The road proceeded through the towns of Wheeling, Zanesville, and beyond Chillicothe to reach the Ohio River opposite Limestone, Kentucky; travelers had the option of paying for the Zanes' ferry services where desirable. In 1803, the new state widened the trace to twenty feet and built the bridges necessary to accommodate wagon traffic.

The shortage of good roads meant that Ohio's overland mail had to be transported by old-fashioned post riders long after stagecoaches had taken over much of the job in the settled East. These intrepid couriers were cut from the same rugged cloth as the Zanes and the explorers and pioneers who would keep pushing America's boundaries westward. One job description for the position ordered that "in the selection of riders you must always take persons of integrity, sound health, firmness, perseverance and high ambition, and pride of character. Among these a preference is due to young men, the less the size the better." One such was James S. Totten, fourteen, who took the job when General David Sutton, his grandfather and guardian, died and left him penniless. The plucky, jockey-weight boy supported himself on his weekly route's eight-dollar monthly salary and later become a prominent local politician.

Despite Ohio's impenetrable woods and rushing rivers, the mail had to be delivered with all possible speed. Post riders carried lanterns for traveling in darkness and were allowed no more than twenty minutes for breakfast and thirty for dinner. The territory's first regular overland route was contracted in 1798 to a Daniel Convers, who was obliged to pay a stiff one-dollar fine for every hour's delay in a scheduled delivery. By 1809, the mere approach of post rider John DePue ("a small, thin, wiry man") blowing his horn brought things to a standstill, according to one account: "All teams and vehicles were prompt to give way, the carrier equally prompt to claim it. The United States mail must not be obstructed or delayed for a moment."

Ohio's postal network grew quickly despite the many and various challenges. In 1810, the seemingly amphibious Samuel Lewis, who carried the mail between Cincinnati and Chillicothe, was badly delayed after being struck in the head by a floating log when swimming across a stream while leading his horse. Another post rider was treed by a pack of wild hogs, shot a particularly aggressive boar, then proceeded on, although regrettably a bit late. Still another escaped from an Indian attack just a mile from Fort Meigs, but finding a replacement after he quit proved difficult. Even the armed crews of the mail boats that plied the Ohio stuck to midriver to avoid attacks from hostile tribes. Nevertheless, the number of the state's post offices—a good gauge of development—grew from 90 in 1810 to 301 in 1820, to 692 by 1830, and to 1,224 in 1840 before slowing down.

Not all parts of the rapidly expanding United States and its communications system grew at Ohio's breakneck pace, particularly in the rural South. Post riders struggled to get the mail from Georgia to New Orleans on a yard-wide Indian trail through swamps and streams spanned only by fallen logs. In 1815, the news that General Andrew Jackson had vanquished the British in the Battle of New Orleans, albeit after the war had officially ended, took almost a month to reach New York City. Despite the challenges, Congress doggedly continued to extend the post, notably in 1825 by authorizing routes to the courthouses of any new county seats, even in remote areas. By 1829, when Andrew Jackson became president, any community of any size—even tiny Chicago, with barely a hundred residents—belonged to America's information grid. Just as the founders had planned, the states were securely bound by major post routes that intersected with smaller ones to enable countrywide communications, if sometimes still of a poky sort.

. . .

FOR MILLENNIA, POSTAL SERVICE had been hampered by transportation's sluggish development, but the latter's stasis was ended by a major technological breakthrough in the Early Republic. Water was the best way to get around in wild country, but rivers and the sea were also subject to currents, tides, and weather that interfered with postal celerity and reliability. Then, in 1807, Robert Fulton's steamboat, gloriously impervious to Mother Nature's variable ways, revolutionized transportation afloat. In 1813, Congress authorized the steamers to carry mail, which they did more speedily than the overland alternatives, and ten years later declared all waterways to be post roads. Some canal boats also received mail contracts, and even steamboats that lacked them accepted mail along their routes. (Such letters were marked "steam" or "steamboat" when the ship's master delivered them to a post office, where they were assigned the postage due at their places of origin. Through this public-private process, the steamer's officer got a fee for his trouble, the correspondents got faster service, and the post got full postage while saving on transportation.)

The new ships were the harbingers of the transformative age of steam. Combined with the railroad—the first real advance over the horse in overland transportation since antiquity—they would by 1835 enable Americans and their mail to travel by water and rail from Washington, D.C., to Boston in a miraculous thirty-seven hours. Once the "Tom Thumb" steam locomotive chugged down the Baltimore & Ohio (B&O) Railroad's tracks at a dizzying eighteen miles per hour in 1830, railways quickly began to web the country east of the Missouri River. Most were smaller lines, such as the Saratoga & Schenectady and the Boston & Providence, that were backed by local entrepreneurs eager to improve transportation for their major businesses. (Later, the more ambitious Missouri-Kansas-Texas Railroad, nicknamed the Katy, would inspire the blues song "She Caught the Katy [And Left Me a Mule to Ride].") The government didn't directly fund the railroads, which were privately owned, but it encouraged the new industry's growth, not least by reducing by some millions of dollars the protective tariffs on the imported iron required to build tracks. The companies had to ask the states in which they operated for the right of eminent domain, which prevented landowners from blocking their progress; then they had to buy the right of way from the landowners. In exchange for these considerations, the rail companies were required to promote the public good, which was soon translated to mean speeding up postal service.

The railroad's postal potential was immediately clear to William Barry, President Andrew Jackson's first postmaster general, who authorized mail to travel by train in 1832 on a limited basis. Almost immediately, contract negotiations between the post and its new carriers grew heated. By 1835, the B&O was flexing its muscles by demanding $250 a mile per year to carry mail between Washington and Baltimore, which was several times the sum offered by the infuriated Amos Kendall, Jackson's second postmaster general. (His pique inspired his choice of a galloping post rider—often mistaken for a later Pony Express courier—as the post's insignia rather than a steaming locomotive.) Once other rail companies sensed their industry's clout, they were similarly demanding, which drastically reduced competition for mail contracts.

The post's long relationship with the railroads, as with its other transportation contractors, was plagued by more serious versions of the same problems that it had experienced with the stagecoach proprietors. The government, like any buyer, wanted to pay less for more service than the seller had in mind, particularly considering that the transportation in question was underwritten by passengers' fares. The post also wanted to control the scheduling of mail trains, as it had finally been able to do with mail coaches. The railroad owners, however, insisted that, as private companies, they were neither obliged to lower their rates nor inconvenience the customers who were their primary business. Their bargaining position was strong, as both parties knew that the industry that could transport mail the fastest had a lock on postal contracts. Both also knew that the railroads' economic survival, unlike that of the stagecoach lines, didn't depend on the desirable but not essential portion of their revenue supplied by the post. The choleric Jackson was so incensed by the railroads' effective monopoly on carrying the mail that he considered forcing them to accept whatever compensation the post offered.

In 1838, Congress acknowledged that the post's future was tied to the railways despite the cost and made them post roads; a year later, the government also established steep rates to compensate the companies for what was already lackluster service. (Kendall had had the foresight to propose government ownership of mail cars to limit costs, but Congress refused his request.) The two great monopolies—the public post and the private railroad—went on to collaborate, if contentiously, in sending bright steel threads of civilization into the dark wilds, stitching the widely distributed states and territories closer together.

DESPITE THE RAILROAD, the stagecoach remained the dominant means of transportation in less developed regions for a long time, and it continued to carry the mail over more miles until the Civil War era. Alexis de Tocqueville, the French philosopher-historian who famously toured America in 1831, was astonished by the scale of the young country's post, which was already the world's largest, boasting twice as many post offices as Great Britain and five times more than France. Of a stagecoach trip through the Michigan boondocks, where the population had already climbed from 4,700 in 1810 to some 32,000 by 1830, he wrote:

> I traveled along a portion of the frontier of the United
> States in a sort of cart . . . which was termed the mail . . .
> along roads which were scarcely marked out through the
> immense forests. From time to time we came to a hut in
> the midst of the forest; this was a post-office. The mail

dropped an enormous bundle of letters at this isolated dwelling, and we pursued our way at full gallop, leaving the inhabitants of the neighboring log houses to send for their share of the treasure.

Tocqueville's amazement at America's post was matched by his incredulity at the abysmal state of its roads. The federal government subsidized the mail coaches, but the states' sensitivity prevented it from funding the highways and byways on which they traveled. In a typical observation, Gustave de Beaumont, Tocqueville's traveling companion, wrote of their trip from Louisville to Memphis: "Frightful roads. Perpendicular descents. Way not banked; the route is but a passage made through the forest. The trunks of badly cut trees form as it were so many guard-stones against which one is always bumping. Only ten leagues a day." The Frenchmen were ruefully amused by Americans' seeming indifference to such conditions. Beaumont recounts one example of the natives' sangfroid: "'You have some very bad roads in France, haven't you?' an American says to me. 'Yes, Sir, and you have some really fine ones in America, haven't you?' He doesn't understand me. American conceit."

Washington, Jefferson, and other forward-thinking politicians had wanted to create a system of decent highways to promote settlement as well as postal service and weave the frontier into the fabric of the mother country. Their commonsensical desire was almost always thwarted by the states' concerns over sovereignty. In 1806, President Jefferson and an obliging Congress authorized a rare exception to the rule: the construction of the tellingly named National Road. This trans-Appalachian highway, also known as the Cumberland Road and later as Route 40, eventually extended from Maryland through Pennsylvania to the Ohio River and nearly to St. Louis; it doubled as Main Street in many of the towns and villages it bisected. (The popularity of the celebrated "pike"—short for "turnpike," a toll road—peaked twice: first with increased westward settlement in the mid-1820s, then again in the 1840s, when Americans in covered wagons and stagecoaches began the great cross-country migration.) In 1817, John Calhoun, the prominent southern senator and later vice president, proposed that Congress could "counteract every tendency to disunion" by funding more such highways if it would simply reinterpret the postal "routes" as "roads," but President James Madison, also a southerner, vetoed the bill.

America paid a steep price for the sovereign states' touchiness in the form of its patchwork of poor-to-terrible highways, but so did the imperious minirepublics. In most cases, the states and their local governments were stuck with the bill for providing any roads that were needed for mail service, and congressmen's habit of wooing constituents with new routes regardless of physical conditions made this a constant trouble and expense. Officials had to levy taxes or tolls to pay contractors to build or improve roads or assemble crews to do the work. Moreover, once a post road was established, locals were obliged to keep it in good condition, and even to improve it if they wanted better, more frequent service.

Living near a major mail route conferred many benefits, from higher real estate values to proximity to a multitasking stagecoach tavern. This venerable institution, which combined the services of a hotel, a barroom, a restaurant, a stable, and often a post office/community center, was vitally important to public life. Washington himself had frequented Georgetown's Fountain Tavern, where he transacted much business, including the purchase of land for the new "federal city," as the capital later named for him was first called. John Fowler, an early travel writer and contemporary of Tocqueville's, described the barroom of one such inn as a bustling information center, its walls "covered with advertisements of elections—fares of stages and steamboats . . . auctions—sales of land—sales of stock . . . sales of everything that can be sold—quack medicines without end—the most prominent being specifics for dyspepsia." True to America's egalitarian ethos, everyone dined family style at one long table. This democratic practice surprised

European travelers, as did the facts that innkeepers were important, well-informed persons likely to be postmasters and politicians, and that servants were not disposed to cater to fussy guests.

Tocqueville had the chance to discuss the perplexing state of America's roads with Joel Roberts Poinsett, a distinguished South Carolina politician and the first U.S. minister to Mexico (where he encountered the festive flower that was renamed "poinsettia" in his honor). Congress was then debating responsibility for the maintenance of the National Road, which it later decided to upgrade, then hand over to the states to operate as toll roads. When Tocqueville asked him to explain the government's philosophy on road building and upkeep, Poinsett gave a thoughtful reply that's particularly interesting coming from a southerner: "It's a great constitutional question whether Congress has the right to make anything but military roads. Personally, I am convinced that the right exists; there being disagreement, however, practically no use, one might say, is made of it." He admitted that, generally, "our roads are in very bad repair" because Washington, D.C., lacked "the central authority to force the counties to do their duty. The inspection, being local, is biased and slack," and "no one wants to have a suit with the local authority." Anticipating the federal government's ambitious national highway policy of the next century, Poinsett added, "The turnpike system of roads seems to me very good, but time is required for it to enter into the habits of the people."

While traveling on the Mississippi River in more comfort than the roads afforded, Tocqueville underscored the connection between improvements in America's postal and transportation systems: "There isn't anyone who does not recognize that the discovery of steam has added unbelievably to the strength and prosperity of the Union, and has done so by facilitating rapid communications between the diverse parts of this vast body."

4

THE POLITICIZED POST

 ALEXIS DE TOCQUEVILLE AGREED with Washington, Rush, and Madison that the only "infallible" means of producing a strong, thriving country was "to increase the ease of communication between men." He added that America,

> which is the country enjoying the greatest sum of
> prosperity ever yet accorded a nation, is also the country
> which, proportional to its age and means, has made the
> greatest efforts to procure the easy communication I was
> speaking of. . . . In America one of the first things done
> in a new State is to have the mail come. In the Michigan
> forests there is not a cabin so isolated, not a valley so wild,
> that it does not receive letters and newspapers at least
> once a week; we saw it ourselves.

By the time of Tocqueville's trip, the post circulated 1,200 newspapers offering a wide array of political views. Many were small-town weeklies that were coddled and protected by local congressmen who depended on their partisan editorializing, but some were more ambitious urban journals meant for a wider readership. (A New York City paper could be sent to, say, New Orleans for 1½ cents, while a two-page letter to the same destination would cost a whopping 50 cents.) Tocqueville noted that average Frenchmen had neither the "astonishing circulation of letters and newspapers" that even Americans in the "savage woods" enjoyed nor their knowledgeable opinions about what was going on in the world.

That said, it was increasingly apparent that supplying Americans with information didn't necessarily lead them to greater understanding and harmony. Circulating uncensored news and views on public affairs may prevent a monopoly on political opinion and feed democracy, but, as Rush, Madison, and their peers had understood, it can also undermine government. They took that risk. Indeed, foreign visitors were often shocked by American journalism's irreverent, rowdy tone and questioned the value of cheap newspapers, on the grounds that they catered to the lower class's presumably lower tastes in order to expand circulation. There was no question that the founders' radical post had fostered a peculiarly American political culture that was both vital and disputatious.

THE DYNAMISM OF adolescent America's postal network in no small part reflected the prodigious talents of John McLean, one of the country's most capable postmasters general ever. Around the time of his appointment, in 1823, the system that had long clung to the East Coast now included more than 4,000 offices and almost 85,000 miles of routes spread throughout the republic. Politicians eager to woo voters kept adding more, and this tremendous growth inevitably led to big deficits. James Monroe, the last of the founder-presidents, was eager to end the resulting bad publicity for his expansionist administration, and he chose McLean—significantly, a westerner from Ohio—to reform the federal government's largest, most important, and most popular enterprise.

The new postmaster general was a little-known but charismatic former lawyer, judge, congressman, and newspaper publisher, and he quickly demonstrated that he also had that rare combination of grand vision and zeal for details required to excel at running what Americans would later call a bureaucracy. (Huge administrative offices or departments that conducted government business in an organized way had existed since ancient China and Rome, but in the United States, such institutions, notably the post, came into their glory days later in the nineteenth century.) He set about reorganizing his chaotic department and instituted sound accounting and record-keeping systems. He also established a centralized Dead Letter Office, where expert clerks dealt with inadequately addressed mail from all over the country, and took major steps toward cracking down on postal crime.

The post had long lacked the means of enforcing its own stringent laws, particularly regarding the theft of money from the mail. Such robberies had only increased as the population grew; immigrants and a decline in old-fashioned agrarian values were customarily blamed. Mail coaches often transported amounts of $50,000 or more, plus whatever money passengers carried. In 1818, the Great Eastern mail coach en route to Philadelphia had been robbed of $90,000, then an almost incalculable sum, which caused a national scandal. The thieves were caught, and the money was sent to its intended recipients, but this success was an exception to the rule. Determined to change that status quo, McLean increased the post's surveillance capabilities and cleared the way for the establishment in 1830 of the Office of Instructions and Mail Depredations, the department's investigative branch.

Speed is the hallmark of good postal service, and McLean was remarkably successful in accelerating the mail. Indeed, he even foresaw that the telegraph, although then only the optical sort employed in France and Sweden, was a logical extension of paper mail: "If it were possible to communicate by telegraph all articles of intelligence to every neighborhood in the Union," it would be "proper to do so." Expeditious delivery depended on the efficiency of the mail coach network, which was then the General Post Office's major concern. McLean's talented assistant postmaster general, Abraham Bradley, a lawyer and respected topographer, mapped every route and charted every delivery to every post office in the United States. (His popular maps hung in local post offices, which helped acquaint Americans with their rapidly expanding country's size and shape.) Mail service under McLean accelerated to the point that newspapers eager to convey their timeliness incorporated the words "post," "express," and "mail" in their titles; even "limited," which referred to fast mail coaches that offered fewer seats because of their bulky cargo, became nearly synonymous with "speed."

McLean's concern with celerity reflected his anticipation of the economy's shift from agriculture to manufacturing and trading. In 1825, he pushed Congress to expand the department's original mandate to bind the country with news about public affairs to include the latest market information. The new "express mail" service, which used round-the-clock relays of post riders between the major cities, charged much higher rates, but it expedited transactions between, say, brokers in the cotton capital of New Orleans and financiers in the economic capital of New York City. The democratized access to economic news also enabled all traders, not just big-city speculators and insiders, to receive the same information at the same time. As McLean put it, "On all the principles of fair dealing, the holder of property should be apprised of its value before he parts with it."

McLean accomplished all these feats while also greatly expanding the system westward, adding nearly four thousand new post offices, and even generating a profit. Postmasters general had traditionally kept a low profile, as befitted administrators of a revenue office within the Treasury. McLean became something of a celebrity, however, and not only because of the post's increased size and stature. He was as skilled in public relations as in management and actively burnished the reputation of Americans' favorite government institution and his own as the knight in shining armor in charge of it. He insisted that the General Post Office was every bit as important as the cabinet-level departments of Treasury and State and began to refer to it officially as the Post Office Department. (It had long been called that informally, but Congress would not make the designation until 1872.) He reported directly to the president instead of to the Treasury secretary and ensured that his annual reports were covered in the newspapers, which also publicized his long workdays, short vacations, and newly popular fervent Methodist Christianity. Attuned to the cultural impact of the Second Great Awakening, the first evangelical presidential contender went so far as to call his worldly office a sacred trust and to promise job security to dutiful employees regardless of changes in political administrations.

POSTMASTER GENERAL MCLEAN'S STATUS as a serious presidential candidate reflected his own renown, but more important, the post's centrality to American life. As the Early Republic's politics became more partisan, however, the network designed to unite the country's far-flung, ever more diverse population also helped to divide it into combative factions. By the 1820s, differences between the North and South had grown sharper, particularly regarding slavery and the economy's transition from decentralized agriculture to centralized industrialization and banking. The Federalists had evolved into the liberal-minded National Republicans, later known as Whigs. They were still based in the Northeast and stood for business, progress, moral uplift, and an activist federal government. The populist Democratic-Republicans, soon simply Democrats, had expanded their power base from the South into the West. They defended state sovereignty and the common man from what they saw as an overweening Establishment that favored federal meddling, high finance, and the idle rich.

The Democrats found a powerful leader in Andrew Jackson, the first celebrity president since George Washington. In 1828, he trounced the incumbent, John Quincy Adams, by promising to curb the banks, corporations, and federal bureaucracy that he believed were trying to wrest control of America from the people. A backwoods frontiersman of humble origins, "Old Hickory" was the very personification of the spreading of power from the established East to the developing West that the post had done so much to effect. (When his "fancy-pants" opponents sneeringly referred to him as Andrew Jackass, this master of the common touch embraced the association, and the rustic yet powerful mule became the Democratic Party's symbol.) Jackson remains one of American history's most complicated, polarizing figures—both the little people's champion against the elite's hegemony and a slave-owning oppressor of Native Americans—so perhaps it's not surprising that he was both an eloquent advocate for the post and its expansion and the president who made it an overtly partisan political tool.

True to his word, Jackson set about transforming Washington, D.C., with his "rotation in office" policy. This plan to redistribute federal jobs was officially meant to uproot ingrained corruption and give average citizens their fair share of government employment. However, Jackson was an outsider in the capital, and he needed a political base there and a way to reward his supporters. He swiftly solved the problem by firing, regardless of merit, about 13 percent of civilian federal workers who just happened to be National Republicans, then giving their positions to his Democrats.

The post, which employed three-quarters of the government's civilian workforce, was the particular target of what became known as Jackson's "spoils system." (The term refers to a remark made by New York senator William Marcy, himself a Democrat, in 1832: "They [Democrats] see nothing wrong in the rule that to the victor belong the spoils of the enemy.") The department had never been utterly free of politics, but it had functioned without too much overt interference until Jackson's mass firings, which were especially draconian among postmasters in the National Republicans' Northeast, where mail service was best. This exercise in bald-faced political patronage was all the more audacious for ignoring the department's tradition, only recently reaffirmed by Postmaster General McLean, of protecting competent employees' jobs from political shifts.

President Jefferson may have technically invented the spoils system when he replaced 10 percent of federal workers with his supporters, but Jackson took it to a new level by institutionalizing postal patronage and making it the financial engine of America's two-party system. For nearly a century and a half, the government would effectively underwrite much of the country's politics by enabling the camp that won the White House to reward tens of thousands of its supporters with postal jobs (although, as Lincoln would later observe, there were always too many pigs for the tits). The spoils system's political impact was amplified by the fact that many of the postmasters appointed were the editors of their local newspapers, who were thus rewarded for their partisan electioneering in print. These new officials were supposed to quit journalism while in office, but they had the consolations of a federal position, the franking privilege, exemption from military and jury service, and insider access to lucrative government publishing jobs.

Jackson had good reason to fear that McLean, a National Republican at heart, a moralistic former judge, and a potential rival for the White House, would regard his postal scheme as an outrageous abuse of power, as well as a personal attack. The wily president quickly solved this dilemma in 1829 by promoting McLean to the Supreme Court, where he would remain in the public spotlight but safely insulated from electoral politics for three decades.

The manifestly unjust postal patronage system became a major and enduring public scandal. Generations of Americans would share the outrage of the anonymous author of an essay called "Seven Years in the Boston Post Office" over the fact that a dutiful clerk "should be rejected from his position, conscious of no fault, not even a difference of political opinion, discharged without recommendation, without the ghost of a reason!" The popular political cartoonist Thomas Nast later captured the popular sentiment with a drawing of a mock-heroic statue of Jackson, hero of New Orleans, in full military dress but mounted on a huge hog instead of the customary charger. The caption read IN MEMORIAM—OUR CIVIL SERVICE AS IT WAS.

Unabashed, Jackson took yet another major step in politicizing the post in 1829, when he adopted McLean's view that the postmaster general should belong to the cabinet and be treated—and paid $6,000 per annum—like the secretaries of the departments of Treasury, War, and State. This decision has often been attributed to the president's desire to have even more control over the huge bureaucracy and to be able to reward his own top political fixer with a cabinet office—a juicy patronage plum. However, the post's elevation in status also reflected its ever-increasing importance in American life and Jackson's own earlier experience of it in the wilds. In a message to Congress in 1829, he declared that mail was to the body politic "what the veins and arteries are to the natural body—carrying rapidly and regularly to the remotest parts of the system correct information of the operations of government and bringing back to it the wishes and feelings of the people."

The first postmaster general to be empowered by Jackson's new policy was William Barry, a well-intentioned Kentucky lawyer, politician, and presidential crony. Like Jackson, he favored the department's ambitious expansion, particularly in the West, which had already given America a hundred times more post offices than it had when the Constitution was ratified. This phenomenal growth had come at a high price, however, and had forced even the storied McLean to run a deficit for his last two years in office. Barry decided to address the financial problem not by cutting costs but by increasing revenue through more and better service. He doubled or tripled the frequency of many weekly routes and replaced many post riders with more efficient stagecoaches. By 1833, the mail traveled more than 26 million miles, up from 13.7 million in 1829. Postal revenues rose from $1.7 million to more than $2.6 million, but so did deficits, increasing from almost $75,000 to more than $313,000.

Barry had acted boldly by increasing service but not always wisely, gullibly overpaying duplicitous transportation contractors eager to cash in on his desire to speed up the mail. In 1834, Congress began an investigation into postal finances. The National Republicans, now Whigs, were already outraged by the spoils system, not least because it had taken postal jobs from many of their partisans, and they regarded Barry as a surrogate for Jackson. They waved reports of outrageous contractors' charges and disregarded delivery schedules and declared the department to be in a state of utter disarray. Although they failed to implicate the postmaster general in direct wrongdoing, the Whigs insulted and harassed him to the point that he threatened to fight a duel. The president finally took mercy on the beleaguered Barry and named him minister to Spain, but the ill-starred future diplomat died en route.

Amos Kendall, Jackson's next postmaster general, was a very different political animal. A lawyer and former newspaper editor and Treasury auditor, he was as shrewd a backroom player in Washington's power politics as his predecessor and fellow Kentuckian had been inept. (He tellingly described Barry as too good a fellow to succeed in such a bare-knuckled job.) He quickly became Jackson's right hand, the center of his intimate "Kitchen Cabinet," and the first presidential press secretary. Though a Yankee by birth into a poor Massachusetts farm family, he had a visceral affinity for Jacksonian democracy, limited federal government, and the sovereignty of the common man. He used his Dartmouth education—he had graduated first in his class—and journalistic skill to write presidential addresses that gave Old Hickory's political philosophy a new eloquence.

Kendall was a skillful, hardworking postal administrator who quickly took the department's finances in hand and reaped the belated rewards of some of Barry's policies. Looking to the economic future, he further streamlined express mail between southern commercial capitals and northern cities by replacing bulky newspapers with paper slips containing the latest market information; he even added a western route to serve Cincinnati and St. Louis. When a massive fire demolished the post's old headquarters on E Street in 1836, just as thousands of miles of new routes were being added to the network, Kendall set up shop in a nearby hotel and proceeded to implement the important new postal reform bill just passed by a friendly Congress.

The Post Office Act of 1836 reorganized the department's finances, from mandating new bookkeeping procedures to imposing stricter rules for scandal-ridden transportation contracting to authorizing the president to appoint postmasters who earned more than $1,000 per year. The law also made it easier for legislators to monitor postal finances. The department was ordered to submit its budget for the following year to Congress and to send all of its revenue, not just surpluses, to the Treasury, which would then dispense its operating expenses and cover its deficits. Despite expanding at a breakneck pace, however, the post was still expected to bring in enough revenue to pay its costs.

One important provision in the act authorized the Office of Inspection, as the Office of Instructions and Mail Depredations was now called, to employ special inspectors ("reliable men for confidential work") in order to curb corruption, particularly in transportation contracts, and to pursue perpetrators of mail-related crimes, such as fraud and theft. These agents were assigned to different geographical regions, where they also made unannounced visits to examine local postmasters' operations and accounts, much to those postmasters' dread. The Office of Inspection developed into an elite branch that, despite some partisanship, was generally highly regarded for the honesty, intelligence, and competence of its personnel.

Like Jackson, Kendall was a complex character whose admirable and abhorrent qualities are hard to reconcile. He was a generous philanthropist, notably on behalf of the deaf, but also a key supporter of the racist president and his spoils system, as well as a brazen opportunist. Indeed, the gifted executive who managed to extend the postal network while briefly producing a surplus astutely resigned just as the department faced a grave crisis partly arising from its ambitious growth despite a troubled economy. In a characteristic move, just before he left office in 1840, Kendall sent franked notices to postmasters asking them to subscribe to the partisan publication he was about to join as editor.

. . .

JUST AS KENDALL AND JACKSON were enthusiastically wielding the post as a tool of their partisan agenda, some very different public figures were learning how to use it for very different political ends. As America's population grew larger and more various in ethnicity, religion, location, and personal interests, kindred spirits began to draw together into "voluntary associations." One of the nineteenth century's major social developments, these activist organizations promoted particular causes, from literacy to chamber music, but the most influential focused on controversial moral issues, such as temperance, women's rights, and abolition. Any group that aspired to attract support beyond the local level had to rely on the post to spread its message.

In the 1820s, the General Union for Promoting the Observance of the Christian Sabbath waged perhaps history's first direct-mail campaign, which changed American politics. These "Sabbatarians" mostly belonged to evangelical sects, such as Methodists and Baptists, whose numbers and clout had increased. They were determined to keep holy the Lord's day and were outraged that even on Sundays, the post circulated modernity's evils in the form of newspapers and their worldly advertisements. They were particularly riled by a federal law, which had seemed unremarkable enough when it was passed back in 1810, that ordered post offices to be open for business every day on which mail arrived there. Thus, by the Sabbatarians' lights, postmasters in the many places where the mail was delivered on Sundays were compelled to violate the holy day by working, perhaps joined by wayward males who, at the sound of the mail coach, would abandon their pews to read newspapers, smoke, gossip, and even drink at the post office.

The post's policy of treating all seven days of the week as the same struck the Sabbatarians as sacrilegious. Jeremiah Evarts, a prominent Congregationalist evangelical, found it "very strange, that such a provision should have crept into the law, for it was clearly a repeal of the *Fourth Commandment*." These zealots also saw the ruling as a federal attack on the long accepted right of state and local governments to exercise some moral as well as civil authority, as many did in imposing the mostly uncontroversial "blue laws" that banned commerce on Sundays. Rather than trying to repeal the federal law, the Sabbatarians tried to circumvent it by stopping stagecoaches from delivering the mail on Sundays, thus effectively closing many post offices. Not coincidentally, businessmen who were devout observers of the Lord's day, including many in the movement's own ranks, would no longer be at a disadvantage in reading Sunday's market information a day late. The Sabbatarians decided to use mass mailing to drum up support for their cause and their case against the federal government.

Many Americans disagreed with the Sabbatarians and disliked their proselytizing. The pious movement was concentrated in New England and Pennsylvania, where good mail service had been long established. Many "anti-Sabbatarians" lived in small towns and rural areas that had fought hard for the right to timely communications and information, particularly in the South. Then, too, the Democrats' stronghold was less inclined than the National Republicans' Northeast toward lofty reforms and evangelical fervor, favoring Jefferson's view that "it does me no injury for my neighbour to say there are twenty gods, or no god. It neither picks my pocket nor breaks my leg." The anti-Sabbatarian ranks also included religious dissenters and supporters of the egalitarian viewpoint of minister-postmaster Barnabas Bates: "Is it not necessary that something should be done to guard the equal rights of all, whether Jews or Christians, believers or unbelievers, whether they belong to any sect, or to no sect at all?"

The federal government ultimately sided with the anti-Sabbatarians, and mail delivery continued on Sundays. Nevertheless, a voluntary association's activism, mediated by the post, had raised enduring questions about federal versus state rights, freedom of speech, and the relationship between religion and government. Public morals had long been the concern of state and local authorities, but the Sabbatarians challenged the rectitude of the federal government itself by politicizing the post in a very different way than Jackson. Their example inspired other groups to use the mail to fuel countrywide, long-distance debates on contentious public issues that tested the founders' vision of a republic united by its information-driven post.

Arthur and Lewis Tappan were very successful, very religious brothers and business partners who were quick to use the connections between publishing, politics, and the post to influence public opinion on behalf of a particularly controversial voluntary association and cause. After securing their fortunes in the silk trade, they had divided their formidable energies between private enterprise and the moral movements encouraged by the Second Great Awakening. These dual ambitions were neatly expressed in Arthur's *New York Journal of Commerce*, a kind of early *Wall Street Journal*, which starchily rejected "indecent" advertising.

The Tappans were determined to use the post to disseminate the viewpoint of the American Anti-Slavery Society, a powerful voluntary association they helped found. In the South, slavery was increasingly regarded, at least officially, as a benign, paternalistic institution sanctioned by the Bible. In the North, opinions on the subject ranged from indifference to enthusiasm for a back-to-Africa movement to support for abolition. In 1835, the Tappans' organization sent unsolicited abolitionist tracts and newspapers, such as *The Emancipator*, to large numbers of randomly chosen southern officials, ministers, and prominent businessmen, most of whom were offended by both the Yankees' proselytizing and their use of the post to circulate it. This direct-mail campaign sparked the country's first crisis over postal content and a historic antebellum riot.

America's simmering regional differences regarding slavery reached the boiling point in July, when a load of the inflammatory abolitionist publications arrived at the post office in Charleston, South Carolina. Alfred Huger, the city's postmaster, was obligated by federal law to deliver the materials, yet public sentiment and his own native sympathies gave him pause. When he asked Postmaster General Kendall, his boss and Jackson's intimate, what he should do, that smooth politician had only temporized, vaguely citing a so-called higher law of respect for community mores. (In a characteristically paradoxical move, Kendall later supported the Union in the Civil War.) In any event, vandals took the matter into their own hands, broke into the post office, and stole the offending mailbags, which were burned by a large, enthusiastic mob. (This was not the first time that the post was blamed for bearing what the locals perceived as bad news. During the War of 1812, the residents of pro-war Democratic-Republican Baltimore wrecked the headquarters of the city's antiwar Federalist newspaper; in response, its publisher had his journal printed out of town and mailed back to the city, where the militia had to protect the post office from the rioters.)

By also raising the issues of freedom of speech and the right to uncensored mail, the Charleston postal conflagration powerfully illuminated the question of slavery for the entire country. Southern politicians protested that the post must be stopped from transmitting the Yankees' incendiary propaganda. They were already horrified by the rebellions staged in South Carolina in 1822 by Denmark Vesey, a formerly enslaved carpenter who had purchased his freedom with lottery winnings, and in Virginia in 1831 by the enslaved Nat Turner. Their sentiments were shared by Jackson, who urged Congress to forbid the mailings, and even by John Calhoun, his political enemy, who proposed at least banning them from states that prohibited such materials. The southerners' efforts to censor the mail, however, had come too late. In "Freedom's Defense," an essay published in 1836, the anonymous author, styling himself as "Cincinnatus," remarked that "tyrants" are prone to single out an unpopular or controversial issue, then "call upon the people to restrain the freedom of speech and the press so far only as is necessary to remove this evil from among them." Moreover, the idea that southern Democrats were attempting to turn the United States into a censoring "slave power" took hold and soon became a cornerstone of the post-Whig Republican Party.

The Post Office Act of 1836 reinforced the sanctity of the mail,

abolitionist materials or no. Although the southern states mostly ignored the law within their borders, members of a voluntary association
had highlighted the moral importance of slavery as a countrywide, not
merely regional, issue and the North and South's ideological divide,
and it was the post that delivered their message. An early abolitionist,
Benjamin Rush surely would have experienced mixed emotions had he
lived to see the information network meant to unite Americans across
borders also become the means of publicizing the political divide that
would tear the United States apart.

WASHINGTON, D.C.'S neoclassical General Post Office, designed by
Robert Mills, is one of the city's architectural glories and now a chic
boutique hotel. When Jackson commissioned the capital's first building to have an all-marble exterior, it seemed only fitting that the headquarters of the federal government's biggest and best enterprise should
occupy an American version of an Italian Renaissance palace, complete
with Corinthian columns, vaulted ceilings, spiral staircases, and expansive skylights. Yet by the time the building was finished in 1842, the
seemingly invincible post was facing the worst crisis in its long history
and nearly went out of business.

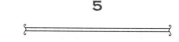

5

CRISIS AND OPPORTUNITY

MID-NINETEENTH-CENTURY AMERICA was a giant laboratory busily conducting massive experiments in social change. Census figures show that just between 1840 and 1850, the population increased by 35 percent to more than 23 million people, including many new immigrants from Scandinavia, Ireland, Germany, and central Europe, as well as more than 3 million enslaved persons. The economy's transition from farming to industrialization and capitalism drew rural men and women to cities that offered new kinds of complex jobs in modern, centralized factories and office buildings. (As Mary Paul, a young girl who fled the country for a position in the textile industry, wrote to the folks back home in 1845, "I get along very well with my work. . . . I think that the factory is the best place for me, and if any girl wants employment I advise them to come to Lowell.") As westward migration significantly increased, the era's great technological breakthroughs of the railroad and Samuel F. B. Morse's electric telegraph helped to make the vast continent seem smaller.

The telegraph was an extraordinary advance but one that primarily affected the stock market, big newspapers, and some other time-sensitive businesses. The lives of virtually all Americans, however, were changed by another communications revolution waged by a post suddenly on the brink of collapse.

By the early 1840s, the post's vast system of 150,000 miles of mail routes had unified an ever-expanding America, but the institution was one of many enterprises, both private and public, to find itself in deep financial trouble. A burst of wild economic excess and speculation had culminated in the great Panic of 1837, which set off a recession that dragged on for seven years. A third of the states defaulted on loans for building railroads, canals, and other overly ambitious projects. Many banks closed, the real estate bubble burst, businesses failed, and unemployment climbed. By 1842, the catastrophe's ripple effect had left even the U.S. Treasury nearly penniless.

Even as the economy staggered, the post had continued its exuberant expansion, abetted by its demanding new transportation contractor. That the railroads charged the post high fees for poor service was bad enough. Worse, the fast trains and their low fares had encouraged a new, semicovert industry of private express mail companies. These carriers challenged the post's monopoly and seriously cut into its revenue by illegally toting carpetbags full of letters by rail for about a third of what the government charged. The upstart rivals had plenty of customers, especially during a recession.

Increased efficiency had cut the actual cost of transporting the mail, but letter postage had remained punitively high at a time when people still had no other way to communicate over distance. According to a complicated rate system based on the number of pages and the distance to be traveled, sending a single sheet from New York City to Troy, New York, in 1843 cost 18½ cents, but a heavy barrel of flour could make the same trip for just 12½ cents. The demand for reform when the average worker made under a dollar per day fueled the American version of the "cheap postage movement" that had originated in Great Britain.

The post defended its pricing policy with the traditional argument that it needed the revenue from letters, particularly in populous, cost-effective areas, in order to serve the entire country, especially the labor-intensive, unprofitable regions in the South and West. Then, too, the post also had to deliver officials' free franked materials and the newspapers that comprised most of the mail's bulk but brought in only 13 percent of its revenue, while the private carriers had the luxury of concentrating on letters in the Northeast's profitable urban corridor. An essay by an anonymous writer identified only as "Franklin" laid out the position vigorously defended by Postmaster General Charles Wickliffe: "It is the care and duty of the Post Office Department, to provide proper mail facilities for *every* section of the country, whether thinly settled or densely peopled."

Aggrieved Americans were unmoved, particularly residents of the eastern cities, who resented subsidizing mail service in remote areas. Some correspondents economized with such tricks as writing messages both horizontally and vertically on a page or in the margins of newspapers. Many others simply turned to the private carriers, whose advertised services might include convenient home delivery. These competitors were emboldened when the government lost a lawsuit against one express company for violating the post's monopoly, and before long, they carried a very substantial portion of America's mail.

By the early 1840s, the triumphant post so admired by Tocqueville only a decade before was fighting for its life. The toxic combination of the troubled economy, the system's relentless westward growth, and competition over pricing produced a string of big deficits that further fueled the public's dissatisfaction. Beset with complaints from everyone from the man on the street to Horace Greeley, who sounded his loud laments on the so-called moral organ of his *New-York Tribune,* Congress was forced to contemplate a massive reform of postal policy.

BOTH MAJOR SCHOOLS OF thought on the subject of letter postage reflected nineteenth-century America's moralistic view of economics and politics. Members of the cheap postage movement argued that encouraging people to correspond freely would promote the values of sociability and cohesiveness—a goal equal if not superior to financial considerations, particularly at a time of tremendous mobility and migration. Senator James Simmons of Rhode Island implored Congress to eliminate any obstacle to the circulation of "a current of affection through every inhabited portion of this extended country, producing such harmony as has not been witnessed by created beings since 'the morning stars sang together.'" In a January 1845 article in the *Boston Post,* Oberlin College economist Amasa Walker similarly questioned whether the public good wasn't more important than a self-sustaining post, which was obliged to charge rates that were "exceedingly onerous and unjust" and "almost prohibitory upon the friendly and social correspondence of the people."

The cheap postage movement had an economic as well as ethical rationale. According to what was later called the "quantity production principle," the larger the volume of goods or services, the lower the cost. Henry Ford would capitalize on this idea much later, but as Clyde Kelly, an influential Republican congressman and postal historian, would observe in the 1930s, "Lower unit cost through the increased volume due to decreased prices was patiently and persistently proved by the Post Office for half a century before its implications were realized and put into practice by private industry."

Pliny Miles, a popular journalist and spokesman for the cheap postage movement, combined both the high-minded and pragmatic arguments by preaching that price slashing would bestow an important social service on America's large, footloose population and also increase the department's revenue. He asserted that the many migrants who were on the move to the cities or the western frontier in search of better lives should be able to send half-ounce letters to the folks back home and vice versa, regardless of distance, for a mere penny. (His *New York Times* obituary described this classic nineteenth-century reformer with a Dickensian flourish: "a striking figure—tall, thin, of nervous-sanguine temperament, wearing a beard that never scraped acquaintance with a razor; a rapid walker, keen observer, talking with wonderful volubility, always cordial, open-hearted, and everywhere welcome for his agreeable social qualities.")

Members of another bloc of dissatisfied Americans went further than advocates of the cheap postage movement by challenging the post's monopoly, whether in hopes of privatizing it or at least forcing it to lower its rates. They allowed that the Constitution said that the government should have a post office department and transport the mail, but they asserted that nowhere did it say that an independent firm could not offer the same service. Many Americans little concerned with legal fine points enthusiastically agreed with them that it should be possible to send a letter anywhere in the country for five or six cents. Determined to force postage reform in 1843, James Webster Hale, a swashbuckling sea captain and entrepreneur also known for promoting Chang and Eng, the famous touring Siamese twins, established Hale & Co., an independent mail service that he considered legal. At a time when the government charged almost nineteen cents to send a letter from New York to Boston, say, he charged five cents. His business boomed, and he soon employed 1,100 workers in 110 offices in major eastern and midwestern cities.

Lysander Spooner, a lawyer, philosopher, anarchist, abolitionist, labor activist, entrepreneur, and maverick by any measure, didn't merely want to force the post to reform; he wanted to privatize it. Based on an idiosyncratic system of justice that he called the Natural Law, Spooner opposed any government interference in matters of personal liberty, the free market, and the right to private property. Monopolies of all kinds, notably the post's, were the libertarian's major bêtes noir. In a pamphlet called "The Unconstitutionality of the Laws of Congress, Prohibiting Private Mails," he stated that "the constitution expresses, neither in terms, nor by necessary implication, any prohibition upon the establishment of mails, post-offices and post roads, by the states or individuals." In 1844, Spooner put his theory to the test by starting the independent American Letter Mail Company. Its offices in New York, Baltimore, Philadelphia, and other cities sold stamps and dispatched mail couriers traveling by rail or boat to various cities, where local messengers delivered the letters to their final destinations. The company, which charged just 6¼ cents for a half-ounce letter, provided good service and was a commercial success. The government fought back by plaguing both Spooner and Hale with multiple lawsuits, but Washington was shocked by the vigorous legal debates sparked by the beleaguered post's new rivals.

In what seemed like the final blow, the post was even losing its grip on the telegraph. In 1843, after Morse failed to find private funding, he secured a government grant of $30,000 to build a prototype of his transformative network, which transmitted information through electrical impulses carried by wire. On May 24, 1844, to much acclaim, he famously tapped "What hath God wrought?" on a line from the U.S. Capitol in Washington to the train depot in Baltimore. (In October, the Washington terminal was moved to the second floor of the General Post Office.) In 1845, Congress supplied $8,000 for expenses and put the postmaster general in charge of the new service, which initially was mostly used by merchants in need of speedy market information.

The telegraph dazzled the nation. One journalist rhapsodized that the technology "seizes upon the lightning itself, and endows it with flashes of intelligence. . . . The speaking lightning has no limit." The civic-minded Morse and many other influential figures, including Henry Clay, the Whig presidential candidate in 1844, regarded the technology as an obvious extension of the post's mission to speed information throughout the country. Morse envisioned a system in which the government owned the patent and licensed and regulated private companies that would provide the actual service. The case for postal control was strengthened by the argument that the lightning-quick delivery of news was a valuable asset, and that if the telegraph were in private hands, it could become both a monopoly and a tool for other monopolies. If the post were in charge, the government could ensure that everyone, not just market speculators or big urban newspapers, would get the same information at the same time.

Government policy, however, is shaped by shifts in political and cultural attitudes as well as objective technological and economic changes. The public's initial enthusiasm for the postal telegraph waned as the 1840s unfolded and attention shifted to the looming Mexican-American War. Postal reformers were far more interested in securing cheap letter rates for the entire population than in developing a new service largely for the business sector. Politicians were leery of making a huge investment in postal infrastructure when the department's deficits were already high. Then, too, the perennial opponents of a big federal government agreed with the editor of the *New York Post*, who declared that if Washington ran the system, "it would suffer as all enterprizes suffer, which are taken out of the hands of individuals." The postal telegraph that had once seemed inevitable was in jeopardy.

In 1847, Morse offered to sell his patent to the United States for a mere $100,000. As a congressman, Cave Johnson had been known as the "Watchdog of the Treasury" and the scourge of postal patronage, and he had disparaged the new technology as little more than "mesmerism," or pseudoscientific quackery. As postmaster general, however, he had come to understand its value and potential and desperately wanted to acquire it for the department. He argued that the post would be "superseded in much of its important business in a few years, if the telegraph be permitted to remain under the control of individuals."

Congress fatefully declined Morse's offer. The disappointed inventor chose former postmaster general Amos Kendall to head up a consortium of eager private investors who bought the patent, and he himself remained involved with the group. Telegraph lines were extended to New York, Boston, Buffalo, and Philadelphia, and by the early 1850s, Wall Street and other big businesses would heavily rely on the technology, although the huge discrepancy in cost compared to mail restricted its general use. The post had lost the first round in the debate over the telegraph as an obvious extension of its mandate, but the argument would continue into the next century.

THE POST HAD EITHER broken even or generated small surpluses until its expansion in the 1820s, when it generally began to report progressively greater losses. By 1844, the department was losing so much business to competitors that a reluctant Congress, fearing the political consequences of either cutting mail service or paying to support it, was forced to act, despite southern politicians' suspicion of costly federal schemes that called for tax increases and strengthened Washington's hand. As it is wont to do in such situations, Congress created a special commission to assess the crisis and make recommendations for fixing it. This group of experts took the high road, concluding that the post had not been created to generate revenue but for "elevating our people in the scale of civilization and bringing them together in patriotic affection," as well as to "render the citizen worthy, by proper knowledge and enlightenment, of his important privileges as a sovereign constituent of his government." Accordingly, starting with the Post Office Act of 1845 and continuing through 1851, Congress passed a series of reforms that would stimulate the full flowering of what the historian Wayne Fuller called "the people's post office."

The government finally abandoned the hoary principle that the post must support iself, even as it was extending all the way to the Pacific. The institution was explicitly defined as a public service that, like the military, deserved financial support, and after the Post Office Act of 1851, deficits would be accepted as a matter of course. Congress shored up the post's finances in other important ways, especially by passing legislation that reinforced its poorly defended monopoly. Known as the Private Express Statutes, these laws made it a crime for other carriers to transport mail in places served by the post, which soon put the independent competitors out of business.

The legislators also took steps to cut the steep transportation costs that constituted about two-thirds of the post's total budget. In 1845, they imposed a stricter, performance-based classification system on the railroads' compensation and also established the Star Route service to make carriers' contracts in remote areas more competitive. The work of getting the rural mail from one post office to another had traditionally been given to local stagecoach proprietors, who could charge the government for one or more horses, a wagon or coach, and a driver. Henceforth, the four-year contracts would be awarded to the lowest bidders, who might need only a mule, a sled, or a canoe to get the job done with "celerity, certainty, and security"—criteria soon abbreviated to the three asterisks that gave the Star Route service its name. Congress also tried to improve the very poor but surging international service between the United States and Europe by authorizing the building and operation of steamships to transport the overseas mail. The prospect of this government-subsidized transatlantic fleet was also generally applauded as a potential military naval deterrent to hostilities with Britain on the North Atlantic, although the lucrative postal contracts generated the predictable allegations of political favoritism and corruption.

Most important, Congress embraced the arguments for cheap letter postage. In 1845, it passed the most popular of its midcentury reforms, which enabled Americans to send a half-ounce letter of however many pages within three hundred miles for five cents, more than three hundred miles for ten cents. Then, in 1851, Congress authorized three-cent postage on prepaid mail for distances up to three thousand miles, which mostly ended the privatization debate. Spooner and Hale had lost that battle, but they had arguably won the war by seriously challenging the post's monopoly and forcing it to compete on price. (Spooner took on his next challenge: arguing for abolition on the grounds that, like the postal monopoly, slavery was unconstitutional.) Postal reformers turned their attention to securing cheap international postage and improvements in metropolitan post offices.

In 1847, a delighted America got its first stamps: tiny receipts that turn letters and parcels into official mail. (Some "postmaster provisionals" had appeared a few years before, but they could only be used locally.) Just as Great Britain had put Queen Victoria on the world's first postage stamp in 1840, the United States honored Franklin and Washington (based on the Gilbert Stuart portrait) on its five- and ten-cent issues, respectively. At first, the new stamps were mostly available at the larger post offices, but as more were issued, their sales soared along with the volume of letters and the department's revenue.

INTENT ON POSTAL REFORM, the mid-nineteenth century Congress not only gave Americans cheap stamps but also, by increasing publishers' subsidization, even more access to information. "The mail" had long primarily meant newspapers, and by the first third of the nineteenth century, postmasters general and others bemoaned the costly problem of transporting the heavy, bulky papers as well as franked matter throughout the rapidly expanding country. The freeloading materials almost guaranteed postal deficits, and postal managers and social critics suggested raising rates for publications and abolishing exchange papers and even the franking privilege. Americans were passionate news devotees, however, and the once struggling press was now a formidable industry with a built-in mouthpiece. Then, too, the politicians who relied on the frank to promote themselves and rally their bases were reluctant to relinquish it. To please the public and the press, as well as its own members, Congress *lowered* postage on most newspapers going anywhere, which would increase their circulation 166 percent between 1850 and 1860 alone.

The government's generosity particularly benefited the small-town press. Beginning in 1845, papers could circulate postage-free within thirty miles of their origin. Then, in 1851, legislators further reduced the local publishers' overhead by permitting all county weeklies to circulate free within their entire counties, which secured their status as an American institution. Greeley's weekly *New-York Tribune* still circulated widely, to be sure, but the combination of the pricing reforms, the railroad, and breaking news provided by the telegraph improved and further decentralized journalism. Regional papers in Cincinnati, St. Louis, and many other cities prospered, and the whole industry boomed. As the historian Richard Kielbowicz observes, "Far more than other government policies or actions touching the press, the routine operations of the post office shaped publications' contents, formats, and circulation."

Congress's bias toward smaller newspapers was not just a benign effort to help the little guy. The official explanation was that a robust civic life required the circulation of local as well as national and international news and opinions. That sounds reasonable enough, as does the desire to help small enterprises stay competitive. However, the rural papers were often highly partisan supporters of the local congressmen, who could be counted on to represent in Washington their constituents' deep suspicion of city slickers and their supposedly radical politics and immoral ways. In any event, when urban lawmakers tried to get lower postage rates for the larger interstate papers, they were defeated on the grounds that such a step would be undemocratic.

A Congress as passionately devoted to the diffusion of printed knowledge as Benjamin Rush could have wished also spurred the growth of two other publishing industries. In 1851, books were finally admitted to the mail, then given a lower postage rate a year later. In 1852, magazines received the same very low rate as newspapers, which inspired enterprising publishers to churn out bulky new magazine-book hybrids that anticipated the wildly popular "dime novels."

WHEN IT EMERGED FROM what remain its darkest days, the post had found new ways to enlarge upon the founders' vision of an information and communications society mediated through the mail. In 1792, the emphasis had been on circulating news about public affairs in a young, experimental democracy. In 1825, this mandate had been expanded to include market information for an industrializing economy. Now, in a more educated, sophisticated society, the post's mission extended to private communications as well, producing America's golden age of letter writing. The recently endangered institution had entered the prelude to its glory days.

6

THE PERSONAL POST

BY THE MID-NINETEENTH CENTURY, the post, long primarily a vehicle for newspapers, now also enabled average Americans to enjoy easy, back-and-forth personal correspondence for pennies, and they did so in rapidly accelerating numbers. Statistics on volume are dodgy, but around 1820, most Americans still received fewer than one letter per year; that figure rose to nearly three by 1850, to seven by 1854, and kept on rising. In what historian David Henkin calls "the postal age," their correspondence no longer had to be reserved for matters of life and death but could carry on casual written conversations between friends.

Certain social advances encouraged the epistolary explosion. "Man of letters" referred to a learned, active correspondent before assuming its modern meaning of literary scholar or critic, and by the mid-nineteenth century, about 90 percent of America's white population, male and female, was literate if not learned. Schoolchildren spent less time on rote exercises and memorization and more on asking questions and composing essays. The new vogue for writing letters encouraged adults to reflect on their experiences, sense of identity, and worldview. Even mass-produced consumer goods, such as affordable steel-nibbed pens, paper, and books, helped to raise America's general level of intellectual sophistication.

That nearly all Americans could both write letters and afford to mail them would prove to be an enormous gift to historians, because correspondence now provided personal information from all social strata, not just the elite. Something of the enormous importance that average folk placed on their mail, which still required often-futile trips to the post office to retrieve, comes across in excerpts from an 1857 letter, written by a "Jamie" from Cleveland to a young lady in Mount Vernon, Ohio:

> My dearest Ella
>
> Another week has passed I have received no letter from you, and although I wrote to you on New Years Eve, I can not let this morning pass without writing a few lines at least.
>
> Every day have I been to the office, expect to find a letter from you, but every day I was doomed to be disappointed. I at last came to the conclusion that you had been so much engaged during the past week that you could not find time to write, but I hope this day will not pass without you writing. . . .
>
> I received a letter from Mrs. Smith on New Years day, a long time had passed since I had heard from her, you can imagine I was right glad to get it.
>
> I am very fond of sleigh riding, but I can not find any one to accompany me, whose company is half so pleasant as yours. . . .

Postage for pennies profoundly affected ideas about and prospects for maintaining relationships over distances even greater than the hundred and five miles separating Jamie from his lady friend. The pioneers who could now afford to stay in touch with those left behind were the most obvious beneficiaries. Settlers wrote for and received seeds from treasured plants back home to grow in their new, faraway gardens.

Miners and loggers in the West sent money to their families in the East and got daguerreotypes of their growing children in return. Cheap postage even popularized the hobby of collecting autographs, which now could be done inexpensively by mail.

The new stamps also made correspondence far more convenient. Previously, letters of one or more sheets had been folded up, sealed shut with wax or an adhesive wafer, addressed on the "cover" side, and taken to a post office. The postmaster calculated the postage and jotted it on a corner of the cover, perhaps adding the date and name of his town or office. (Some postmasters also used hand stamps, occasionally very handsome ones, but postage rates were too complicated to standardize that technology.) If the sender prepaid the postage, that too was marked on the cover. Most of the time, however, the cost was paid by the recipient, who had to come to the post office to fetch it. He or she might well decide that, unless it was a love letter, the message wasn't worth the expense and return it to the postmaster. This labor-intensive system naturally generated a huge backlog of unwanted mail and dead letters. In one of many schemes to avoid postage, a traveler promised loved ones that he or she would send a letter upon reaching a particular destination; when it arrived, the reassured recipients would refuse it. Indeed, Zachary Taylor did not realize that the Whigs had nominated him to be their presidential candidate in 1848 because their letter to that effect sat in his local post office amid a pile of mail that he had refused to redeem.

Stamps revolutionized this cumbersome mailing process. Postage was standardized and prepaid by the sender, so recipients were no longer primed to reject all but the most important letters. (As a result, the volume of commercial solicitations, advertisements, religious tracts, and get-rich-quick promotions soared along with that of personal correspondence.) Moreover, stamps came in sheets that, although not yet perforated, were conveniently backed with adhesive and ready to stick on covers, which themselves were soon rendered obsolete by manufactured envelopes.

The correspondence craze debuted during the Victorian age, and many Americans as well as Britons embraced that fussy era's emphasis on doing things "the right way." Less educated participants in the new postal culture, along with immigrants grappling with English, could turn to popular manuals for help in refining their correspondence. These guides offered formats for terse business letters and flowery declarations of love, along with glossaries of formulaic expressions, such as "I take pen in hand . . ." Sometimes even the well educated consulted more advanced reference books for advice on, say, the propriety of writing or mailing letters on the Sabbath while a houseguest or the correct salutation for a letter to a titled person. Correspondents no longer had to cram as many words as possible onto each sheet, so they could afford to pay more attention to aesthetics. Good penmanship, or a "fine hand," long a marketable skill for clerks, was now also an indication of character, and many Americans mastered the beautiful copperplate script later associated with formal wedding invitations.

The Victorians' obsession with correctness was physically expressed in their desire for multiple accouterments for every activity, right down to different spoons for eggs, marrow, and coffee, and they were mad for stationery, pens, inks, wax, and sealing wafers. The correspondent's ultimate accessory was a handsome wooden lap desk: a small, portable office-in-a-box that could rest on a table or one's knees. The lid of this "Victorian laptop" served as a writing surface and lifted to conceal the necessary supplies, and perhaps a tiny dictionary. A lock and key, or even a secret drawer, protected ribbon-bound relics that preserved the sensory memory of a beloved person: letters sanctified by a precious signature, teardrop, kiss, or whiff of cologne.

Cheap postage was a particular boon for women. Previously, most hadn't been able to afford the luxury of mailing letters, which makes the correspondence of an Abigail Adams or Jane Franklin so relatively rare. When stamps plunged to three cents, women took up their pens in earnest. Despite the era's popular conduct manuals, which deplored the practice of women reading and writing their own letters without their husbands' or fathers' supervision, correspondence became so important a part of their daily lives that lockets designed to hold stamps were a popular accessory.

Some of the social rules governing women's correspondence were predictable. The style thought proper for their letters was more discursive and emotive than the more focused, taciturn tone considered appropriate for men's. (That said, precocious fifteen-year-old Carrie Deppen, who worked as a telegrapher, was neither windy nor sentimental. A collection of her correspondence includes flirtatious notes that she mailed to male colleagues down the line and a letter to her supervisor asking for a raise on the grounds that she was paid less than other workers, particularly the men. Her boss responded that Deppen was lucky to have a job at all and that she received a modest salary because she still lived at home.)

Many women wrote letters primarily to maintain their bonds with loved ones, but others were activists, such as suffragists, temperance advocates, and abolitionists, for whom correspondence, like meetings and marches, was a political tool. They often divided their letters into a section for news that was meant to be circulated widely in reform circles and another for personal communication between friends. In 1855, Lucretia Mott opined on women's history at some length in a letter to her colleague Elizabeth Cady Stanton, who was planning to write on the subject, but she began on an affectionate note: "Three weeks ago I received thy letter announcing thy plan of a Book,—and 3 weeks ago it ought to have been answered. Repeated absence from home, and the care of a family of 20 when at home, are not sufficient reasons." Then she added some warm encouragement for her friend's projected history: "This is the right work for thee dear Elizh., and success will no doubt attend the undertaking."

Women were now important postal customers, but their increased presence in post offices, which had always been male-dominated public spaces, posed a special challenge to prissy Victorian social mores. The era's bourgeois establishment tried to impose order on the Industrial Revolution's rapidly changing, topsy-turvy, urbanizing world by constructing social and architectural honeycombs that sorted and segregated different social groups: public and private, rich and poor, adults and children, masters and servants, and especially males and females. Middle- and upper-class Victorian women were in most ways far more restricted than their mothers and grandmothers had been in terms of the freedom to choose their own pursuits and move about in the world. Particularly in big cities, architects struggled to find ways for women to appear in public places without impropriety—an effort that among other things popularized the new department stores, which offered ladies' restrooms and restaurants for dainty luncheons safe from the male gaze.

The post reflected the larger society's ambivalence about women's public status by commissioning buildings that used separate windows, counters, and other such contrivances to segregate them from men. The architect Ammi B. Young showed a particularly Victorian zeal in designing special female entrances and even, in 1861 in Philadelphia, a "ladies' vestibule" screened by a heavy iron grille of the sort associated with cloistered convents. The San Francisco post office took delicacy to the nth degree by installing a separate window for men who were picking up mail addressed to women—an "amenity" that also encouraged keeping them sequestered at home and their correspondence under male supervision.

THE MOST COLORFUL AND engaging addition to America's great democratization of personal correspondence must be the greeting card. The ancient Egyptians and Chinese were the first to use special forms of written rhetoric to mark occasions and express good wishes, and by the fifteenth century, printed and handmade cards had become rather expensive holiday gifts in parts of Europe. America began to manufacture cards in the mid-nineteenth century, the first of which celebrated

Christmas and the New Year (as well as Jewish versions of the latter), soon followed by St. Valentine's Day.

The vogue for greeting cards that marked religious holidays might at first glance seem to be an expression of the era's profound piety. Many people did attend worship services then, but more also did so out of a desire for conformity, status, or sociability. Moreover, the dominant Protestant, low-church culture had a long-standing aversion to lavish Nativity celebrations and the popish veneration of saints. Despite the new cards' iconography, they had less to do with spiritual considerations than with worldly ones, including cheap postage, high literacy, mass production, and technological advances, such as brilliantly colored inks and cheap paper made from pulped wood. In short, certain religious holidays became secular ones as well, and the cards were the gaudy hybrid flowers of America's new industrial, postal, and consumerist cultures.

Exhibit A is the valentine. The earliest commercial ones, which were produced in England in the first half of the nineteenth century, were elaborate handmade affairs assembled in factories. Americans of that era had to make their own cards or buy the expensive imported ones. Then, in 1847, Esther Howland, a new graduate of Mount Holyoke Female Seminary, turned the British custom into a homegrown craze. While living in her parents' home in Worcester, Massachusetts, she received a fancy English valentine. Howland sensed a business opportunity, ordered some imported paper lace, trimmings, and other decorations from Britain, and made some sample cards of her own, which she hoped to sell through her father's stationery and book business. Her brother, the firm's salesman, agreed to test the market while on the road, and when he returned with five thousand orders, she got down to work. By the end of the decade, Americans were mailing some three million valentines per year.

Howland's cards were frilly, but her approach to their production was thoroughly businesslike. At first, she took over the third floor of her family's house, where a corps of women friends operated an assembly line that churned out small collage-like cards. One of her later mass-produced valentines might feature an elegant young couple surrounded by ribbons, cupids, bluebirds, and flowers and some light verse of the sort that Howland had exchanged with fellow students at Holyoke. Some were sweet and sentimental:

> *Oh, could I hear thee once declare*
> *That fond affection lives for me,*
> *Oh, could I once delighted share,*
> *The sweet return of love from thee.*

Others were saucy:

> *Weddings now are all the go,*
> *Will you marry me or no?*

Howland and her valentines were soon a great success, and by the end of the decade, Americans were mailing some 3 million of them per year. She went on to run her New England Valentine Company for forty years, which was a significant achievement for a single woman of the day; this famous merchandizer of romantic love and courtship never married.

The new greeting-card industry grew quickly. Louis Prang, a Prussian lithographer who settled in Boston, was one of its early masters. The artistry of his color process was the envy of American and British rivals alike into the 1890s, when cheap imitators put him out of business. Manufacturers in the increasingly competitive environment tried to diversify their offerings by catering to niche markets, such as valentines for children or Christmas greetings for the wealthy. The cards' imagery and messages, now produced by stables of artists and writers, grew more contemporary and, like America in general, more sophisticated.

Greeting cards were made for mass consumption, but they shaped as well as reflected public sentiments, including unsavory ones. Valentine's Day wasn't just about love and friendship but also had a mischievous, even dark, dimension. Some people cherished that one special card from a sweetheart, but others saw an opportunity for the kind of rowdy behavior that's tolerated on particular occasions, such as Mardi Gras and Halloween. Well into the twentieth century, pranksters sent a stunning number of "vinegar" or "poison" valentines. Some cards were misogynistic, mocking spinsters, childless women, and "old hags." Others featured ethnic slurs and stereotypes, such as "Aunt Jemima" and minstrel-show imagery. Many were simply mean or sarcastic:

> *Hey, Lover Boy, the place for you*
> *Is home upon the shelf*
> *'Cause the only one who'd kiss you*
> *Is a jackass like yourself!*

Or:

> *You claim you're good at anything!*
> *So come on, show some proof*
> *And let me see how good you are*
> *At jumping off the roof!*

Perhaps the most surprising thing about vinegar valentines is that so many of the bad-natured cards have been carefully saved.

NOT ALL OF THE nineteenth century's new stamps were stuck on letters and cards. The handsome miniature portraits also created the hobby of philately: the collection or study of stamps and other postal materials. The exacting pursuit was perfect for Victorians' taxonomic eye and passion for observing, gathering, and sorting all manner of things, from ferns to fossils to Britain's "Penny Blacks," which depicted the eponymous queen's silhouette in dramatic black and white. Just as their contemporary Charles Darwin examined and categorized finches' differences, the first stamp collectors peered through their magnifying glasses in search of anomalies, which they classified and catalogued. The hobby grew more interesting as the number and variety of stamps increased and their design and engraving became more intricate, mostly to foil counterfeiters. Some collectors began to specialize in technical issues, such as the errors and variations in dye color and engraving that can occur during production, and others concentrated on aesthetics. In time, however, most philatelists organized their treasures around a certain theme or subject, such as a historical era, famous persons, or particular locations.

The same economic and social developments that fostered letter writing helped to popularize philately. The Industrial Revolution had expanded the ranks of a literate middle class that had enough time and money to indulge in such pursuits. Moreover, stamp collecting's joys could easily be shared with other enthusiasts at a time when people eagerly joined voluntary organizations. (Interestingly, China now has the world's largest number of stamp collectors, who, like the Victorians before them, belong to a growing bourgeoisie whose members can afford to pursue a scholarly interest and enjoy belonging to clubs.)

Stamps generate revenue for a government, of course, but they are also little bits of propaganda that express its values and tell stories about the society that produced them. From the beginning, America's stamps have been carefully designed to deliver such political and social messages. The subjects of the very first ones—the five-cent Franklin and ten-cent Washington—have appeared more frequently than any others over time. (The National Postal Museum owns a cover holding two Washingtons that was postmarked just a day after they were issued, on July 2, 1847, distinguishing the cover as what philatelists call "earliest known use.") They certainly seem like obvious choices, but when the two subjects were initially selected, antebellum tensions between the North and South were high. Washington was a perfect compromise, being both the father of the United States and a proud Virginian. Postmaster General Cave Johnson, a native of Tennessee, had initially preferred Andrew Jackson to Franklin, however, and he ordered the printer Rawdon, Wright, Hatch & Edson to use a portrait of Old Hickory for the five-cent stamp. In the end, however, the fiery southern slaveholder, also only recently deceased, was tactfully superseded by the universally beloved northern postmaster general. As the printer explained in a letter to an assistant postmaster general, "In accordance with your suggestion, we have substituted the Head of Franklin for that of Gen. Jackson, which our Mr. Rawdon was requested to use by the Post Master General." In 1851, Thomas Jefferson entered the philatelic pantheon simultaneously with the American eagle.

Philately is pursued for profit as well as pleasure, and nearly all collectors covet America's rarest and most valuable stamp, which wasn't even produced by the federal government. The "Hawaiian missionaries" stamps were first issued in 1851, when the islands were still more than a century away from statehood, and were locally printed for the use of preachers and planters, who had no other access to postage. The beautiful Hawaiians, which are emblazoned with "H.I. & U.S. Postage" to establish their validity in both places, have that charm peculiar to many small blue and white objects and have inspired many forgeries. (The National Postal Museum owns a Hawaiian whose backstory adds to its appeal: the treasure, also known as the Dawson cover, was discovered in the furnace of an abandoned tannery.)

THE BALLOONING VOLUME OF letters in the mid-nineteenth century had a profound impact on America's antiquated postal facilities, many of which had changed little since Franklin's day. Back then, post offices weren't separate buildings, much less specially designed for their function. In 1642, Great Britain had established New York City's first one in a coffeehouse, and long after independence, the new republic's post offices conformed to that tradition of doubling up in an existing business. Mail handling was problematic in these informal quarters. Letters could be lost or stolen, and, as discussed, recipients could simply refuse to collect them because they didn't want to pay the postage.

Dedicated, or stand-alone, post offices gradually became more common in large cities by the 1820s and '30s, when increased mail volume began to require one or more clerks in addition to the postmaster. These facilities were usually located in commercial districts that were convenient for the merchants and businessmen who could afford the high cost of sending letters. In the early 1850s, the explosion of correspondence transformed the urban post office from a men's club into a tumultuous civic circus crammed with male and female citizens of high and low degree—including notorious pickpockets—who waited in long, clamorous lines to retrieve their mail. These large operations were generally housed in buildings that had been built for different purposes and were ill-suited to their new postal function; in New York City, mailbags nestled among the crypts in a former Dutch Reformed church. Worst of all, these improvised post offices hadn't been designed to hold massive amounts of paper safely, which contributed fuel to devastating fires in Chicago and Boston as well as New York City's Wall Street district.

The great postal reforms of the mid-nineteenth century, especially cheap postage, called for a new type of public architecture. The Treasury Department, which was in charge of constructing and operating all major federal buildings, had previously been cautious about undertaking grand projects outside Washington, D.C., particularly in the South, where they could be seen as federal incursions. As hostility between the North and South steadily mounted in the 1850s, however, the department's new Office of Construction manifested the Union's power and grandeur by creating the first of many of the long Victorian era's greatest public works.

The office's "supervising architects," first led by chief designer Ammi Young and Army engineer Alexander Bowman, took on the ambitious task of designing and building forty-six grand new "customs houses." These facilities had traditionally handled matters pertaining to the shipping trade, such as the payment of duties and the logging of vessels. The new, far more ambitious structures also housed other federal services, including courts and post offices. Moreover, unlike the capital's sober neoclassical government buildings, these customs houses were designed in the far more opulent, fashionable Renaissance Revival, French Second Empire, and Victorian Gothic styles that were popular in Europe. This spectacular architecture was meant to give proud Americans a new kind of grand public space that reflected the federal government's achievements and their own aspirations as a great people, second to none.

A jewel in the crown of public architecture, the stupendous granite U.S. Custom House in New Orleans occupies an entire city block. It served as the town's main post office as well as housing the department that dealt with the Mississippi River port's business and other federal offices. The central Marble Hall, lit by a vast skylight and bounded by giant Corinthian columns, is one of America's finest Greek Revival interiors, albeit with some Egyptian Revival overtones. The building's elaborate, eclectic ornamentation includes sculptures of Mercury, the god of communications and commerce; the moon goddess Luna, whose crescent crown symbolizes the city's location on the river bend; Sieur de Bienville, its founding father; Andrew Jackson, its hero; and the pelican, the state symbol. Construction was begun in 1848, but during the Civil War, the Confederates manufactured gun carriages in the glorious public palace, then the Yankees made it a military headquarters and prison. In the end, it took eight architects working more than thirty-three years to complete the vast project. Not everyone was impressed, notably Mark Twain, who thought it resembled a state prison.

. . .

BETWEEN 1790 AND 1860, America's population had soared from 3.9 million to 31.4 million. Its post offices had increased from 75 to 28,498, and its post roads from 1,875 miles to 240,594. After the War of 1812, settlers had begun the accelerating westward migration that would eventually end only at the Pacific. Establishing the communications link between the country's two great oceans would be an epic enterprise of song and story. Yet the post's steady if less dramatic expansion into the regions in between was no less important: Little Rock, Arkansas, and Green Bay, Wisconsin, in 1821; Rock Island, Illinois, and Hannibal, Missouri, in 1826; Dubuque, Iowa, in 1836.

7

GROWING THE COMMUNICATIONS CULTURE

 AS AMERICA'S FRONTIER continually expanded, mail service played a major role in organizing the physical and social landscape, just as it had since colonial days back East. Washington, D.C., was a vague concept for pioneers, farmers, and settlers of small towns and villages, but the local post office, like the church, school, and general store, was a vital part of life. As Postmaster General John Wanamaker said, whether great or small, a post office was "the visible form of the Federal Government to every community and to every citizen. Its hand is the only one that touches the local life, the social interests, and business concerns of every neighborhood."

Just as postal routes were often the only spatial coordinates in frontier America, post offices were often its only addresses. To start the petitioning process for mail service, local people had to form a community, then name it. This posed a challenge at a time when many places were merely identified by a physical feature, such as a river bend, a rocky promontory, or a business. "Bird-in-Hand, Pennsylvania" took its poetic name from an early inn, and "Carson's Tavern, Ohio" is self-explanatory (perhaps as were the small communities in Indiana and Ohio once called "Henpeck"). Some villages adopted the name of a leading citizen, while others, like Ideal, Georgia, and Admire, Kansas, indulged in boosterism. By the 1840s, there were so many post offices that, to avoid confusion, no two in any state could have the same name. One Texas town gave up after six tries and settled for Nameless. Many small rural and frontier settlements came and went, which further complicated the situation, as did the fact that others changed names, as when Dry Diggins, California, became the more dignified Placerville.

Most post offices were in rural areas, and most of those were situated in general stores whose proprietors were often also postmasters. In 1817, the government started publishing the biannual *Official Register of the United States*, which listed all federal employees, most of whom worked for the post, along with their salaries and other accounting data. The books were published five times as frequently as the census records, and they're particularly important in chronicling rural places, which the census tended to slight. Despite their dull appearance, the thick books offer valuable insights into country communities, especially the ebb and flow of their economies and media consumption reflected in the careful records of their postmasters, who were the federal government's local representatives.

To re-create a sense of what rural America's multitasking community hubs were like, the Smithsonian Institution painstakingly restored the general store–cum–post office of Headsville, West Virginia. (The building has been relocated to the American Philatelic Center in Bellefonte, Pennsylvania.) The shutters of the eighteen-by-thirty-foot 1860 structure still bear poems and inscriptions left by the Union soldiers who stopped by during the Civil War to send and receive letters. Country people generally bought only what they couldn't grow, shoot, catch, or make themselves, so the shelves of the Headsville store would have been stocked with coffee, spices, and tobacco, as well as boots, patent medicines, tools, and sewing notions. The smaller the post office, the less federal funding it received, and most country postmasters, unlike their big-city colleagues, had to supply their own "official" furnishings, which might consist of a shelf or two or a small desk with some pigeonholes. (Prosperous general stores might feature a fine oak "window unit," manufactured by the Postmasters Supply Company, which came with a barred service window, a built-in letter slot, and numbered, locked post boxes.) Some were slapdash shanties, and others, spacious "mercantiles," but the Smithsonian curator Carl Scheele grants these public-private community centers equal status: "The Postal Service is the single institution that has been common to virtually every American's experience throughout more than 200 years, and the most representative type in American history—the most numerous and widespread—has been the country store–post office."

RURAL POSTMASTERS WERE OFTEN proverbial pillars of the community. They were nominated by their fellow citizens, including their predecessors and congressmen, then officially appointed by the postmaster general. Some were town elders in more than one sense. Roswell Beardsley, of North Lansing, New York, was born in 1809 and first appointed during the administration of President John Quincy Adams at a starting salary of less than ten dollars per annum. He went on to serve for seventy-four years in his general store, and his customers valued his equanimity: "He is a Democrat in politics," said one, "but is not offensive." Like Beardsley, most postmasters owned property and businesses, such as shops or inns, so they understood something of accounting and had the resources to be bonded. They took an oath to uphold the Constitution and perform their duties diligently, which included keeping regular business hours. If mail was delivered to their offices on Sunday, they had to remain open for an hour afterward; should church services be going on, that time was adjusted to an hour after the end of worship, lest smoking and card-playing at the post office compete with prayerful contemplation.

Country postmasters were paid only a commission based on their mail volume, supplemented with post box rentals and fees from local "drop" mail sent and picked up in the same office; the total often amounted to less than $100 per year. Their real compensation came from the position's perks: prestige, political clout, the franking privilege, free exchange papers—and especially the increased foot traffic that the post attracted to their primary businesses. Though twenty-four-year-old Abraham Lincoln didn't own the general store in New Salem, Illinois, he was appointed its postmaster by Postmaster General William Barry and served from 1833 to 1836. Other than the valued benefit of access to lots of newspapers, his rewards were modest, amounting to $55.70 in 1835, but then, so were his duties, considering that the mail came to town only once a week. Lincoln obligingly delivered any letters not picked up in a timely fashion, carrying them in his hat.

In hardscrabble regions of rural and frontier America, many general store–post offices simply didn't have enough business to survive, and postmasters had a high rate of turnover. Some months after his workplace was closed, the impoverished Lincoln moved to Springfield, Illinois, where a diligent postal agent hunted him down and asked for the final balance of New Salem's revenue. Honest Abe produced some sixteen dollars in coins that he had dutifully stored in an old blue sock. (Harry Truman, who owned a haberdashery before taking up politics, continued this seemingly unlikely presidential association with store-keeping and the post. In 1914, he was named postmaster of Grandview, Missouri, but he promptly gave the job to a widow who was more in need of the income.)

WOMEN'S PROGRESS IN SECURING postal employment was slow and came in fits and starts. They could not vote and had no legal public standing, period, much less the right to hold a federal office. Nevertheless, a small number of capable, sometimes extraordinary, women postmasters, clerks, and mail carriers somehow managed to secure official roles in civic life.

Many colonial women had handled the mail, and some had also been involved in printing and publishing, but with rare exceptions, such as Franklin's wife, Deborah, they did so as their husbands' or fathers' unacknowledged, unpaid help. The rare woman who managed to become a postmaster—"postmistress" was a little-used nineteenth-century variation—usually inherited the position from a male relative. When postmaster-publisher Lewis Timothy died unexpectedly in 1738, Elizabeth Timothy, his widow, supported the family by running both the post office and the *South-Carolina Gazette*. Still, this enterprising woman had to publish her newspaper under the nominal male authority of her little son Peter.

The remarkable career of Mary Katherine Goddard illustrates the obstacles that confronted even the most competent women. Many postmasters came from families that, like the Franklins, also included printers and newspaper publishers in an era when combining the three careers yielded substantial benefits. Giles Goddard, her father, and probably Sarah, her mother, had taught the family trades to Mary Katherine and William, her brother and later founder of the revolutionary Constitutional Post, who learned on the job.

When the Revolution became inevitable, Mary Katherine joined the many women whose contributions to the war effort modestly improved their sex's status. (Among the most celebrated was Temperance "Tempe" Wick, a fearless New Jersey equestrian who unofficially carried communiqués to General George Washington in the winter of 1777.) She freed William for his crucial service to the cause by leaving her native New England to assume his duties as Baltimore's postmaster and publisher of the well-regarded *Maryland Journal and Baltimore Advertiser*. In 1779, Postmaster General Richard Bache made her a U.S. postmaster, and Congress gave her the honor of being the first printer of the Declaration of Independence and the names of its signers.

Goddard's high position in the intertwined worlds of the post, publishing, and politics was short-lived. The jealous, irascible William returned to Baltimore in 1784 and forced her to resign from the *Maryland Journal.* Then, in 1789, Postmaster General Samuel Osgood fired her from the postmaster's job, mostly on the dubious grounds that a woman couldn't handle the requisite travel in the rapidly expanding city. Political patronage is a likelier explanation for the dismissal, as few officials would waste a good federal position on someone who couldn't even vote. Goddard was joined by 230 prominent Baltimore citizens in protesting this injustice and asserting the superiority of her postal operations. As a respected public figure, she also made personal petitions to the Senate and to President Washington himself, but for the second time, she lost a job in which she had excelled. The resilient Goddard next supported herself by running a bookshop, and one of her last acts before dying in 1816 was to free "Belinda," an enslaved woman, to whom she left all her property.

Despite the barriers, a few other women managed to become postmasters during the Early Republic. Feisty Sarah Decrow, who was appointed to serve in Hertford, North Carolina, in 1792, was reprimanded for daring to protest her inadequate salary. As Assistant Postmaster General Charles Burrall put it: "I am sensible that the emolument of the office cannot be much inducement to you to keep it [the postmastership], nor to any Gentleman to accept of it, yet I flatter myself some one may be found willing to do the business, rather than the town and its neighbourhood should be deprived of the business of a Post Office." Decrow's position was soon filled by such a gentleman. Rose Wright succeeded in securing the appointment in Harrisburg, Pennsylvania, in 1814, but not without hand-wringing by Postmaster General Gideon Granger. He wrote to a Pennsylvania official that, due to a revision in postal regulations, "a doubt has been suggested to me from a source that I ought to respect as to the strict legality of appointing a female." His scruples, however, boiled down to the use of masculine pronouns when referring to postmasters. Mary Dickson, who served in Lancaster, Pennsylvania, from 1829 to 1850, was a rarity among women postmasters in that she made the fifth-highest postal salary in her populous state. Moreover, her important office had been previously held by Ann Moore, who was appointed in 1809, and Dickson was eventually succeeded by Ellen H. Hager, who served until 1876.

By the mid-nineteenth century, women's opportunities for postal employment had somewhat increased, particularly in thinly populated areas where the lack of enough men to fill the jobs superseded bias and Victorian proprieties. Their sisters in the cities still faced opposition. Several prominent citizens in Columbus, Ohio, petitioned Postmaster General Cave Johnson to name the widow of General Jacob Medary to her late husband's position as postmaster. He replied that it "has not been the practice of the Department to appoint females . . . at the larger offices; the duties required of them are many and important and often of a character that ladies could not be expected to perform." Johnson took pains to point out that his opposition was by no means personal but extended to all women. Despite the pleas of "many leading members of Congress, of the Legislature of Missouri and many distinguished citizens in different Sections of the Union," he had rejected a similar appeal to appoint the widow of Senator Linn of Missouri as the postmaster of St. Louis: "I felt myself constrained from a sense of duty to the public to advise the President against the appointment." Mrs. Medary's brother-in-law got the job.

Most female postal employees were postmasters, but a handful of women also transported the mail. Because carriers generally worked for the transportation contractors—often family members—rather than directly for the post, their service often went unrecorded. However, in 1794, Ann Blount covered the route between Edenton and Indiantown in North Carolina, then a remote frontier. By the mid-nineteenth century, the new Star Route service produced some more opportunities for doughty women, such as Polly Martin, a Massachusetts teamster who became its first female carrier around 1860. While driving her rounds on a night as "dark as a pocket," she later recalled, a malefactor had tried to climb into her wagon, which had compelled her to horse-whip him "until the blood ran down," causing him to fall beneath her wagon's wheels. As she remarked, "He had tackled the wrong customer that time."

POLITICIANS KNEW THAT creating a postal bridge between the Atlantic and Pacific was crucial to America's continued growth and development for many reasons. Establishing post offices and mail routes was a concrete way for the federal government to stake its claim to barely explored and perhaps still internationally contested territory. As the founders had foreseen, newspaper circulation helped to unite widely dispersed pioneers under one flag. Moreover, decent mail service heartened prospective settlers and their loved ones and provided epistolary accounts of life on the frontier that encouraged westward migration.

8

LINKING EAST AND WEST

AMERICA'S PHENOMENAL westward expansion in the middle third of the nineteenth century was the greatest overland migration in history. Beginning in the 1830s and accelerating during the fifteen years before the Civil War, an estimated four hundred thousand pioneers took to the Oregon Trail. Some were driven by the exigencies imposed by the great financial Panic of 1837, others by the American tradition of moving on if life in one place fails to meet expectations, and still others by the stirring rhetoric of the imprecise, emotionally charged principle of Manifest Destiny. This theory of American exceptionalism proposed that the United States was a unique, divinely favored country that had a moral duty to spread its enlightened values and government from the Atlantic to the Pacific. The concept cleverly blended the era's "postmillennial" Protestant belief that Christ was already building his new kingdom right here in America and the hard-edged Monroe Doctrine of 1823, which declared that North and South America were now off-limits to new European colonization. Manifest Destiny generally played well in the press and with Democrats, including President James Polk, who used the idea to rationalize taking half the Oregon Territory from Britain and seizing a big hunk of the Southwest from Mexico. Many Whigs, however, later including Abraham Lincoln, suspected that the theory was just wolfish imperialism in sheep's clothing.

Divinely inspired or not, large numbers of peripatetic Americans left their homes back East to pursue such goals as homesteading, mining, commerce, and converting the Indians to Christianity. Armed with Yankee pragmatism, ingenuity, and independence, they were prepared to pay steep personal costs for the chance of a better life, starting with traveling for four to six months in the wilderness past St. Louis, the new gateway to the West. Peter Burnett, an early Oregon Territory settler who later became the first governor of California, described their austere existence with a wonderful economy: he and his few neighbors were "all honest, because there was nothing to steal; they were all sober, because there was no liquor to drink; there were no misers, because there was no money to hoard; and they were all industrious, because it was work or starve."

Among the worst hardships of life in the strange, sometimes savage West was the pioneers' almost complete bifurcation from the locus of civilization back East. This "old" America now enjoyed mail carried by railroads, steamboats, and modern stagecoaches on decent roads. The new country had poor if any postal service, no navigable rivers except the limited Missouri, and no roads other than glorified game trails. Everyone, including politicians, recognized the tremendous need for decent coast-to-coast postal service, but until the completion of the transcontinental telegraph and railroad, there simply *was* no good way, either by water or overland, to transport mail or anything else west of Missouri.

At first, very few Americans had followed Lewis and Clark's Corps of Discovery into the vastness of the "Great American Desert," where the lush prairie of the Great Plains gave way to treeless steppes punctuated by the impregnable "Stony Mountains," an early name for the towering Rockies. Lewis and Clark's harrowing Northwest Passage was initially thought to be the only way to cross the forbidding three-thousand-mile-long range, but some so-called mountain men were lured into looking for better options by the prospect of "brown gold." Europe's booming hat trade had turned the beaver, whose fur made the best felt, into a precious natural resource that had been wiped out east of the Rockies. In 1812, some trappers working for John Jacob Astor's Pacific Fur Company had stumbled upon the one gap in the mountains through which a wagon could be driven. News of this "South Pass" in what's now Wyoming was initially slow to circulate, but by the early 1830s, a few hundred men were crossing the "desert" each year to pursue the lucrative fur trade.

The mountain men were not just trappers but also gifted explorers who mapped much of the West. Jedediah Smith had already become the proverbial "first white man" to travel, mostly on foot, across what's now Nevada and Utah and climb the High Sierras when, in 1831, some Comanches killed him at the age of thirty-two. Kit Carson served as a guide to John Charles Frémont, the Army topographer known as the "Pathfinder," who charted much of the Great Desert in the 1840s. (In 1848, while employed by the Army, Carson also became the first person to carry mail sent overland from one side of the country to the other.) Paradoxically, these adventurers who had fled farming and civilization for a wild life in an unspoiled natural world were crucial to opening it to the military, followed by the waves of settlers who clamored for development and postal service.

Both of the major routes to the West Coast started in western Missouri. The 800-mile Santa Fe Trail dipped southwest to that city. The more northerly, 2,200-mile-long Oregon Trail had begun as a series of game trails—the best ones trampled by buffalo—that were adopted by mountain men, on foot or horseback. From the later 1830s, the rough thoroughfare was gradually improved to accommodate wagons and eventually extended from Missouri through parts of what are now Kansas, Nebraska, Wyoming, Idaho, and Oregon. At the South Pass, settlers heading to what would become California and Utah branched off onto the California and Mormon trails, and those destined for the Pacific Northwest continued on the Oregon Trail. With the help of

Native American friends, Jim Bridger, a particularly gifted mountain man who had a photographic recall of geography, later identified Bridger's Pass, an alternative to the South Pass that shortened the trip by sixty-one grueling miles.

The vast Oregon Territory sprawled from the Pacific to the Rockies across what are now the states of Oregon, Washington, Idaho, and parts of Wyoming and Montana as well as British Columbia. Its rich natural resources and coastal ports had first attracted Russia, Spain, Great Britain, and France, whose colonial forays had created a live-and-let–live, polyglot culture that mostly revolved around commerce. ("Oregon" comes from *fleuve d'ouragan*, or "hurricane river," as the French called the great Columbia.) The other imperial powers eventually relinquished their claims, leaving the United States and Britain to an uneasy joint occupancy. England initially had the upper hand. Its explorers had claimed the region for Great Britain in the late eighteenth century, and its chartered Hudson's Bay Company, based at Fort Vancouver, provided what passed for government and postal service for Europeans, Indians, and Americans alike. Mail delivery elsewhere in the territory depended on accommodating travelers by water, horse, or foot. By the 1830s, however, the Oregon Territory began to exert a powerful pull on swelling numbers of variously motivated American expansionists, from farmers to missionaries.

Narcissa Prentiss Whitman, who was among the very earliest and most famous of the Northwest's pioneers, merits special attention, because this prodigious correspondent's story illustrates the mail's importance both to pioneers and to propagandizing Manifest Destiny. Her much-publicized epistolary accounts of her adventures as one of the first two white women to cross the Rockies helped to popularize Far West settlement—then nearly unthinkable for women and families—and made her one of nineteenth-century America's heroines.

Whitman was a pious, well-educated young teacher from upstate New York's "Burned-Over District," which was known for its fiery fervor during the Second Great Awakening. (The term derives from the assumption that all its residents had been converted, or "burned," so there were none left to evangelize.) She and Marcus Whitman, her husband, were determined to devote their lives to missionary work among the Pacific Northwest's "heathen," of whom they knew very little. To symbolize her death to mere worldly ambition, Narcissa had dressed in funereal black for her marriage in 1836. The next day, the couple set out on the bone-rattling six-month journey to establish a mission in the wild Oregon Territory at what's now Walla Walla, Washington.

The Whitmans took a steamboat to St. Louis, where white civilization and postal service stopped, then traveled overland by wagon and on horseback on the Oregon Trail in the company of trappers, traders, and Henry and Eliza Spalding, another clerical couple. They reached the South Pass on July 4, 1836, in a mile-long pack train led by the legendary mountain man Tom Fitzpatrick and Sir William Drummond Stewart, a Scottish laird and intrepid adventurer. The Indians who had gathered there for a raucous rendezvous with their rugged white peers were amazed by the sight of the blue-eyed, fair-haired bride, who thoroughly enjoyed her unusual honeymoon. "I never was so contented and happy before," Narcissa wrote to her sister and brother. "Neither have I enjoyed such health for years."

That such a fine young lady could and would make the grueling trip, sometimes even astride a horse like an Amazon, was a powerful advertisement for western settlement. Solitary men could explore, trap, and mine, but farmers needed families to work the land if they were to prosper. Writing good-naturedly about the rigors of fording streams, Narcissa confessed, "There is one manner of crossing which husband has tried but I have not, neither do I wish to. Take an elk skin and stretch it over you, spreading yourself out as much as possible. Then let the Indian women carefully put you on the water and with a cord in the mouth they will swim and draw you over."

The Whitmans set about establishing their mission among the Cayuse Indians as soon as they arrived in the Walla Walla Valley.

Marcus had medical training, and along with conducting religious services, he treated the sick and delivered babies. The pregnant Narcissa ran their home and taught in their school, but whatever romantic ideas they had cherished regarding the "noble savages" they had hoped to evangelize were short-lived. The couple couldn't adjust to the Indians' seminomadic, communal way of life, and Narcissa also struggled with their Nez Perce language. For their part, the Cayuse weren't particularly interested in being saved, at least by the Whitmans, whose complex dogma and obsessions with privacy, ablutions, and the extermination of the ubiquitous lice and fleas they found puzzling. This culture clash often surfaces in priggish comments in Narcissa's letters: "We must clean after them, for we have come to elevate them and not to suffer ourselves to sink down to their standard." (Not all missionaries shared this unchristian view. Samuel Parker, a Congregationalist minister who lived with the more congenial Nez Perce nearby, thought that the effort to uplift the Indians would be "fraught with as much promise and encouragement as it was in earlier days to elevate our ancestors.")

Narcissa's poignant letters home bespeak the pioneer's pain of being cut off from all that was familiar: "My dear Mother, I have been thinking of my beloved parents this evening; of the parting scene, and of the probability that I shall never see those dear faces again while I live." It would be more than a decade before the West's first post offices were established, and transporting mail past Missouri was an informal business that depended on kindly travelers and private couriers. The resulting delays and uncertainties of correspondence caused her much anxiety: "I do not know how many of my letters reach home or whether any of them. . . . I hope all who write will be careful to mention the reception of all our letters, so then we shall know what ones fail and what reach you." After Alice, her two-year-old daughter and only biological child, drowned in 1839, Narcissa fell into a depression, which was increased by her isolation: "My Dear Mother, I cannot describe how much I have longed to see you of late. . . . One reason doubtless is it has been so long since I have received a single letter from any one of the dear friends at home. Could they know how I feel and how much good their letters do me, they would all of them write a great deal and write often, too, at least every month or two."

The Whitmans were more successful in ministering to fellow pioneers and in encouraging more to follow; indeed, Marcus even helped to lead a wagon train of a thousand settlers up the Oregon Trail. Narcissa got some solace from caring for the couple's adopted children, including seven white orphans and three of mixed Indian blood, and despite her travails, she, too, continued to encourage migration: "This country is destined to be filled, and we desire greatly to have good people come, and ministers and Christians, that it may be saved from being a sink of wickedness and prostitution." If her own dear mother would but make the trip, she wrote, "once here I think there would be no cause of regret. Families can come quite comfortable and easy in wagons all the way."

In 1847, Henry Spalding, the Whitmans' longtime colleague, had the dismal duty of writing the saddest kind of pioneer letter to Narcissa's family in New York. Measles brought by the settlers had killed about half of the Cayuse, and some survivors had reacted by murdering the couple and twelve others at the mission and burning it down. "Can the aged mother read and live?" Spalding wrote. "I thought to withhold the worst facts, but then they would go to you from other sources, and the uncertainty would be worse than the reality. Pardon me if I have erred." Following what was hailed as her martyrdom, Narcissa's story, gleaned from her letters, many of which were published, made her a posthumous celebrity and role model for the girls and women who followed her hard road west.

THREE MOMENTOUS EVENTS in the 1840s spiked both migration to the Far West and the pressure to link the country from the Atlantic to the Pacific. After the easier route over the Rockies through Wyoming's

South Pass became common knowledge, the surge of pioneers into the Oregon Territory lent ballast to America's claim to all the land up to the latitude line of 54 degrees, 40 minutes north. The United States also won the Mexican-American War and, with it, a vast territory stretching from Texas to California and parts of Wyoming and Colorado. Finally, gold was discovered in California. Opportunities abounded, and many Americans heeded the advice, later popularized by Horace Greeley but purportedly first given by John Babson Lane Soule, an Indiana journalist, in an 1851 editorial in the *Terre Haute Express:* "Go west young man, and grow up with the country."

The Gold Rush of 1848 to 1856 was one of the nineteenth century's most important events, and it enthralled the public with California, which came under U.S. control after the war with Mexico ended in 1848. (Ten years later, the discovery of major silver deposits in the part of the Utah Territory that's now Nevada would send another surge of miners to the West.) The prospect of getting rich quick caused thousands of Americans to mortgage their homes or spend their life savings to try their luck in the Sacramento Valley's streams. California's white population climbed from about 2,000 in 1848 to 100,000 by 1858. The tiny village of San Francisco, which had 200 residents in 1846, became the official port of entry, and by 1852, it was a boomtown of 36,000.

California was desperate for fast, efficient mail. Miners wanted to correspond with the folks back home, perhaps on the new illustrated stationery that predated picture postcards. Businessmen needed to transfer bank drafts and contracts. In 1848, Postmaster General Cave Johnson authorized its first post offices, in San Francisco and Sacramento, but service remained so poor that, in 1850, irate residents didn't get the news that they had achieved statehood until six weeks after the fact.

There was still no reliable overland way to get people or the mail from coast to coast, and even after the advent of oceangoing steamships in the 1840s, the trip by sea was extraordinarily onerous. The worst of the two bad options was a thirteen-thousand-mile, six-month trip around the tip of South America. The shorter, costlier alternative consisted of two voyages broken by a tedious stop at the Isthmus of Panama, a fifty-mile-wide strip of land separating the Atlantic and Pacific oceans; there, the mail was unloaded from one ship and hauled to the opposite coast, where another waited to transport it eastward or westward. This risky, expensive, semimonthly service supposedly took about a month but often dragged on much longer. Nor did the postal problems stop once the mail finally arrived in California. Miners had to leave their digs prey to claim jumpers and spend weeks traveling to and from a chaotic, overwhelmed post office, where they waited in line for hours to pick up their letters or paid a bribe to get a better spot. In short, mail service didn't remotely meet the booming state's urgent economic, political, and social needs, and in 1856, seventy-five thousand fed-up residents signed a petition of protest to the federal government.

Private carriers known as "expressmen," who began to haul freight, people, and mail across the West before the transcontinental railroad's completion, quickly stepped in to fill the communications and transportation void. In 1849, Alexander Todd, a bookkeeper turned failed miner, sensed an opportunity and began to carry letters by horse and boat between San Francisco and the prospectors' camps for an ounce of gold dust per delivery—an impressive measure of mail's value. He soon expanded his business to include bringing the isolated miners' hoards back to the safety of the city's vaults and even selling them necessarily outdated New York newspapers. On one occasion, Todd carried $150,000 worth of gold dust disguised in a butter keg for seventy miles without a gun or a bodyguard.

Much like the East's James Hale and Lysander Spooner, Henry L. Goodwin, a public-spirited, Connecticut-born '49er, disliked monopolies, especially the post's. In 1855, he established the California Penny Post Company, which offered low-priced services such as carrying letters to and from the post office and making after-hours express deliveries in several towns. (Outraged by San Francisco's poor supply of drinking water and the exorbitant prices it commanded, he also dug a deep well in his own lot, installed a free drinking fountain for the public, and charged low prices for commercial use of the well, such as watering stock.) However, his antimonopolist postal system—to say nothing of the post box rental fees his service's boxes siphoned from the city's irate postmaster—attracted the attention of the government's lawyers, who pummeled Goodwin, as they had Hale and Spooner, with lengthy litigation.

IF CALIFORNIA'S MAIL SERVICE remained poor, the more remote Oregon Territory's was worse. As conflict increased between the North and the South, its settlers' rallying cry of "Fifty-Four Forty or Fight"—a reference to Oregon's contested northern boundary—resonated with the northeastern proponents of Manifest Destiny, who were eager to claim Oregon as an antislavery "free state." Their southern counterparts instead wanted to annex Texas as a slave state. President Polk was more inclined to grab Texas from the Mexicans than to risk a third war with England, but Oregon's champions won the day. In 1846, the United States and Great Britain compromised, making the forty-ninth parallel the border between British Columbia and America, and two years later, the wild Oregon Territory officially became part of the United States.

The federal government had been quick to use the post to strengthen its new stake in the Pacific Northwest, at least in theory, by authorizing the first post offices west of the Rockies in 1847: one at Astoria, a deepwater port on the Columbia River, and the other at Oregon City, on the outskirts of today's Portland. By 1851, the region also had eighteen postal routes. However, mail from the outside world still had to reach San Francisco first, then travel north by bimonthly steamers to Astoria, where the portion destined for Oregon City was dispatched. Hopeful recipients had to travel to an often distant post office to fetch their letters in person or wait for an obliging traveler to bring them into the outback.

In 1853, the northern section of the Oregon Territory split off to become the Washington Territory. The tiny village of Seattle, founded in what's now the Elliott Bay neighborhood, boasted a log post office as well as a church, a brothel, and two blockhouses used for protection during Indian attacks. Nevertheless, one of the few things on which its fifty or so white, Indian, Hawaiian, and Cape Verdean residents could agree was that postal service was worse on their side of the Columbia River.

THE WEST'S SETTLERS WERE desperate to maintain their links to what they called "the States" and could be counted on to badger Congress for postal service regardless of the huge effort and cost. Those near the Pacific coast could receive mail by sea, albeit slowly and infrequently. Transporting it overland past Missouri through wild territory still mostly known only to Native Americans and the military was much more difficult. Some mail was carried by wagon trains under postal inspectors' supervision, but most other attempts had been highly unsatisfactory. One wagon operation run by Samuel Woodson and Feramorz Little was so unreliable that the Mormon leader Brigham Young complained to the Utah Territory's official delegate: "So little confidence have we in the present mail arrangement that we feel considerable dubiety of your receiving this or any other communication from us." The inadequate service became even more critical when developing the fertile Great Plains became a national priority, later encouraged by the Homestead Act of 1862, which gave 160 acres of land to any farmer willing to relocate there.

Increasingly powerful and vocal Californians demanded a communications upgrade: a reputable, regularly scheduled, twice-weekly stagecoach service that would carry both mail and travelers. Skeptics ridiculed the idea of a route that proceeded from no place through nothing to nowhere, but in 1857, Congress bowed to pressure and authorized an overland mail coach service from a point to be determined on the Mississippi River to San Francisco that would take no more than twenty-five days. To encourage the spirit of enterprise, the government offered an eye-popping $600,000 annual contract to the transportation company that would take on the daunting challenge. This impressive subsidy wasn't just an investment in better short-term postal service; it was a down payment on the expansionist dream. As Congress correctly bet, the costly mail route would also become the developmental spine from which would spring settlements, industries, and the future transcontinental telegraph and railroad.

For enterprising private carriers, the prospect of the lucrative federal contract turned what would otherwise be a quixotic public service into an attractive business proposition, particularly because, like their eastern predecessors, they would also pocket the revenue from the mail coaches' passengers. However, antebellum politics immediately complicated the overland mail service's birth. The northerners who controlled the House wanted a northerly route from the railroad's Missouri terminus. The southerners who ruled the Senate favored a more circuitous southerly path down through Texas—a much easier trip in terms of terrain, weather, and avoiding hostile Indians but also 900 miles longer, thus slower. As regional hostilities worsened, the prospect of a southerly route heartened nascent Confederates and worried Yankees for the same reason. If war broke out, rebel troops in slaveholding Texas could easily cut off communications between the Union and rich, powerful California.

Despite outraged protests from the eastern and Californian press, in 1857, Postmaster General Aaron Brown, not coincidentally a Tennessean, awarded the stagecoach contract to the Butterfield Overland Mail Company, which would operate on the southerly route. The firm's stagecoaches, each bearing up to 1,200 letters, would travel twice weekly on the so-called Oxbow Route (named for its swooping curves). The vehicles would depart from Tipton, Missouri, and Memphis, Tennessee, dip south and southwest across Texas and parts of New Mexico and Arizona, then head north to end in San Francisco, all in twenty-five days or less. President James Buchanan hailed the new transcontinental mail service as "a glorious triumph for civilization and the Union."

John Butterfield was just the fellow to take on a project of such staggering complexity and scale. He was one of the resourceful western and midwestern expressmen who saw transportation's potential in a rapidly expanding nation that had far too little of it. They grasped that every bucket and axe, boot and sewing needle that the settlers needed would have to be hauled to them over vast, forbidding terrain from a depot town on the Missouri River, and they created an industry to meet the need. Observing expressmen at work in Leavenworth, Kansas, the greenhorn Horace Greeley exclaimed over their huge wagon trains powered by horses, mules, or oxen—the preferred beasts—the pyramids of supplies, and the regiments of drivers: "No one who has not seen can realize how vast a business this is, nor how immense are its outlays as well as its income."

Born into a blue-collar family in rugged upstate New York, Butterfield had had little formal schooling, but he was a natural businessman. As a teenaged stagecoach driver, he had developed a firsthand understanding of the transportation industry, then went on to establish coach, steamer, and rail lines, as well as telegraph services. (He and his wife, Malinda, had nine children, including Daniel Butterfield, who became a celebrated Union general in the Civil War.) By 1850, he was the head of the American Express Company, then the nation's largest private carrier, which was formed when his Butterfield, Wasson & Company merged with Livingston, Fargo & Company and Wells & Company. In addition to transporting passengers and freight, this ambitious new enterprise also offered the financial services, from delivering payrolls to collecting bills, that the expanding economy also desperately needed.

Butterfield had his faults, but the failure to think big was not one of them. His Overland Mail Company's state-of-the-art operation called for relay stations spaced every ten to fifteen miles across a vast area, herds of horses and mules, and a fleet of stagecoaches, the best of which were the "Concords." These BMWs of their day were manufactured by the Abbot-Downing company in Concord, New Hampshire, and were so well built that it was said they didn't break down but just wore out. In his 1872 travel book *Roughing It,* Mark Twain called the Concord "an imposing cradle on wheels."

Twain's encomium notwithstanding, the experience of most of the settlers, businessmen, miners, and other passengers who paid the hefty $200 one-way coach fare to California left much to be desired. As Tocqueville had discovered to his chagrin, the post subsidized stagecoach service but not the roads on which it operated. The comfortable Concords were mostly used early and late in the journey, in more settled areas that had better roads. Elsewhere, conditions often called for rugged, rough-riding "celerity wagons" designed to withstand travel over rocks, ruts, and rivers. (The San Antonio–San Diego Mail Line, which followed part of Butterfield's route, was better known as the "Jackass Mail," because its brutal final stretch had to be covered by mule.)

Inside the coaches, men and women were crammed together amid big mailbags and their own valises, bulging with items hard to find in remote places. They jounced and banged against one another and their seats, the walls, even the roof, and the sheer discomfort, combined with sleeplessness, crowding, and constant risk, caused some to succumb to "stage-craziness." The harsh conditions made it all the more essential to observe the courtesies, albeit of a rough-hewn sort. Rules of etiquette, often traced back to Wells Fargo, included the following:

> Abstinence from liquor is requested, but if you must
> drink, share the bottle.

> Buffalo robes are provided for your comfort in cold
> weather. Hogging robes will not be tolerated and the
> offender will be made to ride with the driver.

Gents guilty of un-chivalrous behavior toward lady
passengers will be put off the stage. It's a long walk back.

The only respites from the misery of traveling with the overland
mail were brief stops at the relay stations. While the horse teams were
changed, passengers stretched their legs, relieved themselves, splashed
their hands and faces, and had a bite to eat. However, even Captain Sir
Richard Francis Burton, the indefatigable English explorer of Asia and
Africa, was appalled by the food and lack of amenities on his stagecoach journey through the West. The *New York Herald* journalist Waterman Ormsby summed up the experience of traveling with the post
this way: "I now know what Hell is like. I've just had 24 days of it."

By 1860, overland stagecoaches carried more mail across America's
sea of grass than steamships on the rivers and oceans, but not even the
postal subsidy and passenger revenue combined could sustain Butterfield's stupendously costly enterprise. In March of that year, he was
forced out of his own firm for failing to cover large debts to Wells
Fargo, its major creditor, which took over his entire operation. A year
later, just days before the Civil War began, the government awarded
the postal contract to the renamed Overland Mail Company, which
operated on the more northerly, soon-to-be-safer "Central" route, from
St. Joseph, Missouri, to Placerville, California.

Traveling with the cross-country mail continued to entail problems
more serious than physical discomfort, notably attacks by bandits or
hostile Indians. Cochise's Apaches alone killed the passengers and
crews of six coaches and destroyed many relay stations. Legendary robbers such as Rattlesnake Dick, who once stole $80,000 from a Wells
Fargo coach, paid informants for tips about shipments of gold, payrolls, and even rich passengers. Arguably the most colorful of these
celebrated criminals was "Black Bart," who committed twenty-seven
stagecoach robberies in California that involved the U.S. mail. After
serving in the Union Army and growing bored with farming and min-

ing, he became a shotgun-toting highwayman who was known for fine manners and a cultivated voice that bespoke his English birth. He sometimes left poems at his crime scenes:

> *Here I lay me down to sleep*
> *To wait the coming morrow,*
> *Perhaps success, perhaps defeat,*
> *And everlasting sorrow.*
> *Let come what will, I'll try it on,*
> *My condition can't be worse;*
> *And if there's money in that box*
> *'Tis munny in my purse.*

The last stagecoach robbery in America was solved by post office inspectors in 1916.

9

THE MAIL MUST GO THROUGH

THE PONY EXPRESS is so closely linked with the U.S. Post Office that the mounted courier who was the post's insignia from 1837 until 1970 is mistakenly assumed to be a Pony Express rider, just as "The mail must go through" is thought to be the post's motto. The private service never belonged to the government and only carried mail for the post during the last few months of its short life, from April 3, 1860, to October 24, 1861. Nevertheless, the dashing endeavor contributed to the evolution of the United States and its communications network in important ways.

The idea behind the Pony Express, soon affectionately abbreviated to "the Pony," was not new, even in America. Postmasters general John McLean and Amos Kendall had sent horsemen racing day and night to speed market information between certain cities for several times the price of normal postage. These express services had indeed cut delivery times—between New York City and New Orleans, say, to half the fourteen days required by stagecoaches—but they were soon replaced in the East by the faster, cheaper railroads.

The state of transportation and communications was very different in the West, where horses and boats were still the only means of getting around. The new settlers had roots and relatives back in Georgia and New York, Virginia and Massachusetts, and they were desperate for news about the looming Civil War, which would test their own loyalties. California was nominally a free state, but many residents were southerners by ancestry, sympathy, or both and eager to secede. Moreover, they were separated by some two thousand miles from the nearest other free states, which aggravated the sense of isolation caused by their still slow, inadequate stagecoach mail service.

The federal government was desperate to keep the huge, resource-laden Golden State in the Union. William Russell, the fast-talking money man at Russell, Majors and Waddell, one of America's major freight and passenger carriers, saw an opportunity. A self-made mogul in America's burgeoning transportation industry, the dapper, handsome "Napoleon of the West" was a gambler. He bet that if his firm could get the mail to California much faster than the Butterfield Overland Mail Company, it could snatch the post's huge transportation contract from its rival.

Russell and his partners knew firsthand that taking on a big federal contract was a risky business. In 1855, he and the sober, businesslike William Waddell had joined forces with the formidable Alexander Majors, a rival expressman, to snag a huge government deal to haul supplies to Army posts in parts of the West and Southwest that had just been won in the Mexican-American War. During the first two years, the ambitious, capable midwesterners made a handsome $300,000 profit. Then, in 1857, when the Mormon War erupted, they went into debt trying to meet the Army's stepped-up demands while simultaneously contending with the hostile Mormons who burned their wagon trains.

Roller-coaster finances notwithstanding, Russell talked his partners, and John Jones, another businessman, into mounting a flashy campaign to secure the postal subsidy. They created a new firm, called the Central Overland California and Pike's Peak Express Company, which would operate a stagecoach line from Leavenworth, Kansas, where Russell, Majors and Waddell was based, through Denver to

California. To convince Congress of the superiority of their company and its northerly "Central" path to the Golden State, Russell proposed a flashy mail service that was partly a publicity stunt. The mounted couriers of this Pony Express would streak across the Great Plains, Rockies, and High Sierras carrying urgent letters and press dispatches to California in just ten days, which cut the stagecoach time by an astounding two-thirds.

Wells Fargo and some other carriers already offered limited local post-rider services in the rugged West, but Russell's proposal for the 1,966-mile, high-speed Pony was breathtaking in its audacity. The westbound mail would travel by train to St. Joseph, Missouri, where the rail line ended and the new service would be based (just a block from the home of the outlaw Jesse James, who would be shot dead there in 1882). Forty riders would race the mail in relays to Salt Lake City through the wilds of what are now Kansas, Nebraska, Colorado, Wyoming, and Utah, following established trails when possible. Then they would take a perilous route through Nevada over the Sierras to Sacramento, finally reaching San Francisco by steamship.

Californians were elated at the prospect of the Pony. Some experienced western hands, however, insisted that the lone riders would be easy prey for hostile Indians and robbers, and others opined that weather alone would render the route's mountainous stretches impassable in winter. Undaunted, Russell proceeded to purchase four hundred to five hundred fine, high-priced horses, each branded with an XP; buy or build some 165 relay stations made of logs, adobe, or sod; hire about eighty riders and hundreds of support workers; and even commission a special Pony Express stamp depicting a mounted courier. The firm's high rates for carrying a half-ounce letter—initially $5 (perhaps $75 today), later $1—attest to the demand for the service, but its revenues couldn't begin to cover the $700,000 start-up costs. Everything depended on the Pony's success in winning the government's overland mail contract.

While Russell did the wheeling and dealing, Majors supervised the

Pony's logistics. A born-and-bred frontiersman, he had become an expressman after fathering daughters rather than the sons needed to work the family farm. He made a fortune in the freighting business but continued to travel with his wagon trains, which could include 100 vehicles, 1,200 oxen, and 120 men. (The ten-year-old William Cody, later the world-famous showman "Buffalo Bill," was one of his messenger boys.) Under Majors's knowledgeable eye, the Pony's route was divided into five geographical segments; relay stations were carefully spaced within each, according to the terrain's difficulty. Most of these pit stops were between ten and fifteen miles apart, which was about the distance a fast horse could travel before tiring. Their crews provided the riders with food and fresh mounts and attended to the horses kept on reserve.

The Pony's technicians were obsessed with gear. To function at top speed, the horses could carry no more than 165 pounds, counting the courier, his equipment, and up to 20 pounds of mail. (The number of letters carried per trip eventually averaged about 90 westbound and 350 eastbound.) To lighten the load, the service adopted a stripped-down McClellan military saddle fitted with a detachable leather *mochila,* or cover, that held the padlocked mail pouches. Thus, the precious cargo could be handed off from rider to rider inside of the two minutes allowed for a relay stop. The men themselves, usually dressed in a deerskin shirt, pants tucked into high boots, and a slouch hat, traveled light, perhaps carrying only a knife and a revolver.

The Pony's most important tools were its horses. (The equine distinction is fuzzy and often based on height, but larger animals are generally designated as horses and smaller ones ponies.) They had to be able to run at ten to twelve miles per hour over varied terrain to qualify, although their average working speed was about seven to ten miles per hour, and they needed extraordinary endurance as well as speed. Rangy racehorses from Kentucky stock were best suited to flying across the easier terrain east of the Rockies, particularly the flat plains of Nebraska and Kansas; they were expected to cover more miles per day than their cousins in the much rougher terrain of the West. Mountains and deserts called for smart, tough, sure-footed little mustangs that could cling to narrow mountain trails like goats and hustle down slick, steep inclines in a semisquat. The Pony's celebrated ponies attracted their own admirers, who plucked keepsake hairs from their manes and tails.

The standards for riders were no less exacting than those for the mounts. A satirical ad later put the job's requirements this way: "Wanted: Young, skinny fellows not over 18. Must be expert riders willing to risk death daily. Orphans preferred." Hundreds of men and boys responded to such spunky rhetoric and the promise of good pay plus room and board and were soon winnowed down to a select crew of outstanding equestrians, each weighing no more than 125 pounds. Tough as nails and slim as a jockey, the Pony rider was, as Twain put it, "a little bit of a man, brimful of spirit."

The riders certainly needed plenty of mettle. They had to promise to protect the mail with their very lives and to complete their seventy-five-mile legs as fast as possible, day or night and regardless of conditions, stopping only to change horses. They continually monitored their mounts' condition, measuring the heartbeat in the neck and watching for the nervous twitches and rasping breath that preceded fatigue and breakdown. If an exhausted horse collapsed on the trail, the rider had to snatch the *mochila* and hotfoot it to the next relay. Speed was their best defense against bandits or Indians. Some routes and relay stations enjoyed relative peace, but others, farther to the west, were menaced by hostile tribes, particularly the Paiutes of Utah and Nevada. Native Americans robbed the mail several times, but usually the Pony riders on their grain-fed mounts simply crouched low in the saddle to make smaller targets and raced away from the slower grass-fed Indian ponies. On the only occasion when they captured both horse and rider, the Indians killed the man, but his mount managed to escape with the *mochila*. The horse was later caught, and the recipients duly received their letters.

The prairies and mountains abounded with fearless roughnecks who could ride, but the Pony's elite corps was at least officially held to a higher standard by a formidable oath demanded by the Bible-reading, abstemious Majors:

> I . . . do hereby swear, before the Great and Living God, that during my engagement, and while I am an employee of Russell, Majors and Waddell, I will, under no circumstances, use profane language, that I will drink no intoxicating liquors, that I will not quarrel or fight with any other employee of the firm, and that in every respect I will conduct myself honestly, be faithful to my duties, and so direct all my acts as to win the confidence of my employers, so help me God.

Stagecoaches and the Pony sometimes traveled on the same route, and some travelers questioned the oath's efficacy, to say nothing of the riders' quality of life. After closely observing them, Richard Burton wrote that "setting aside the chance of death . . . the work [is] severe; the diet is sometimes reduced to wolf-mutton, or a little boiled wheat and rye, and the drink to brackish water; a pound of tea comes occasionally, but the droughty souls are always out of whisky and tobacco." He acknowledged that Majors forbade his drivers and employees to "drink, gamble, curse, and travel on Sundays" and "desired them to peruse Bibles," but that he personally "scarcely ever saw a sober rider; as for the profanity . . . they are not to be deterred from evil talking even by the dread presence of a 'lady.'"

AN ENORMOUS AMOUNT OF trouble and expense had gone into what was partly a public-relations scheme to snag the overland mail contract, but no one could be sure that the untried Pony would work. On April 3, 1860, big crowds gathered at its eastern and western terminals to watch the debut of what had been promoted as "The Greatest Enterprise of Modern Times." Thousands of spectators in San Francisco thrilled to the sight of Jim Randall, dressed in showy Western regalia, tearing off on a flashy golden palomino. In St. Joseph, Mayor Jeff Thompson sought to calm a rowdy mob of hard-drinking frontiersmen with some purple prose: "The mail must go through! Hurled by flesh and blood across two thousand miles of desolate space . . . neither storms, fatigue, darkness, mountains or Indians, burning sand or snow must stop the precious bags. The mail must go!"

A few highlights from the Pony's more difficult eastbound maiden voyage suggest the challenges. After his elaborate show in San Francisco, Randall boarded the steamer *Antelope* for Sacramento, where the real race would begin. The boat was more than two hours late, and Mother Nature was not cooperating. Two days of hard rain had turned Sacramento's mud roads into glue, and a huge blizzard racked the Sierra Nevada Mountains above. According to Majors's account, despite the terrible conditions, Harry Roff grabbed the *mochila* from Randall, plunged into rainy darkness, and slogged through twenty miles of sludge in a mere fifty-nine minutes. Then, as the trail ascended and the weather worsened, he raced fifty-five miles more, to end his round at the foot of the High Sierras.

Completing the next relay over the icy summit through the accelerating blizzard was a nearly impossible task. Bolivar Roberts, the Pony's clever western superintendent, assigned it to Warren "Boston" Upson, the adventurous twenty-year-old son of a wealthy publisher. Roberts had sent teams of sure-footed pack mules high into the peaks, where they tramped through the deep snow in an effort to keep the sketchy trail open. The muleteers had subdued the worst drifts, but others forced Upson to make treacherous detours from what little trail there was. He sometimes dismounted to walk behind his horse, allowing it to pick their way. His mount collapsed under him just short of the summit, so he staggered to the relay station on foot and took off on his next horse, making the easier descent in better weather conditions. Somehow Upson reached his destination, Friday's Station, near Lake Tahoe, in the eight hours scheduled for the leg in summer. By the time William "Sam" Hamilton completed the next leg, to Fort Churchill, at what's now Silver Springs, Nevada, the riders had covered 185 mountainous miles in a freakish spring blizzard in fifteen hours and twenty minutes—nine hours faster than planned.

The next man to race off with the *mochila* was "Pony Bob" Haslam, a twenty-year-old welterweight who later earned the distinction of completing the service's longest and most dangerous ride. Born in London, he made his way to America, traveled west with the Mormon migration, and arrived in Salt Lake City at the age of fourteen. Roberts first hired the teenager to help build relay stations but soon sensed his spunk and made him a rider. Haslam leapt onto one of the barely broken desert mustangs he preferred—this one had been shod for the first time just the day before—and tore through hostile Indian country in a third of the scheduled time.

The high-spirited eastern and western riders raced against time and also, encouraged by Russell, against one another. The Californians and Mormons even competed among themselves for the title of the West's best horsemen. (One contender was Major Howard Egan, an Irish immigrant, former bodyguard of Joseph Smith, and the superintendent of the Pony's Mormon division, who blazed trails and rode relays while in his forties.) The outcome of the Pony's first intramural contest was clear on the night of April 9, when the resilient little mustangs crossed tracks with the hot-blooded Thoroughbreds. The eastbound mail was fourteen hours ahead of schedule, while the westbound was almost twenty hours late, so the westerners had won.

The Pony Express's real victory came on April 13, when it decisively beat the clock by delivering the mail across nearly two thousand miles even faster, by some hours, than the ten days promised. The service had proved itself and seemed poised for success.

. . .

As AMERICA THRILLED to the exploits of the Pony Express, the wildly overextended firm of Russell, Majors and Waddell was in desperate financial straits. Rumor had it that it lost thirty dollars on every letter, and Congress had still not produced the long-term federal mail contract the partners had banked on. In January 1861, the discovery that the frantic Russell had conspired with a clerk at the Department of the Interior to "borrow" some bonds from the Indian Trust Fund to use as collateral to pay off debts caused a major scandal. Russell was arrested, and although he was not convicted, he and his partners were disgraced and bankrupt.

History intervened to sustain the Pony, now on life support, for ten more crucial months. The secession of Texas in February had disrupted the operations of the southerly stagecoach mail line to California, so the federal government, in an irony surely not lost on Russell and his partners, decided to reroute service to the safer Central route blazed by the Pony. The Overland Mail Company was still the post's official contractor but didn't have the resources to take over the new northerly route. The federal government brokered a compromise in which the Central Overland California and Pike's Peak Express Company, which was a separate entity from Russell, Majors and Waddell, became a subcontractor of the Overland Mail Company and continued semiweekly courier service. Thus, the Pony finally carried some U.S. mail.

Not even the gallant Pony Express could outrace time and technology. The transcontinental telegraph line, proceeding at twenty-five miles per day, was finally finished on October 24, 1861, just in time to provide instant news for the war's duration, and the cross-country railroad's completion was now within sight. The government balked at supporting an expensive mail service that suddenly seemed antiquated. After carrying 35,000 pieces of mail over 650,000 grueling miles—equivalent to twenty-six times around the globe—the Pony was abruptly out of business when many of its riders were barely past adolescence.

After triumphing over their rival expressmen, Henry Wells and William Fargo enjoyed a monopoly on transportation and mail service past the Missouri River. Their reliable, businesslike firm, which soon legitimately claimed to go everywhere and do almost everything for anybody, became the West's biggest, most important institution, public or private. Indeed, for a while, the better-equipped Wells Fargo carried more mail than the U.S. Post Office in the West, even installing its green mailboxes next to the government's red ones. By 1853, however, the post, always jealous of its monopoly, required private carriers to use government-stamped envelopes, to which they added their own franks—a clever scheme that enabled the post to reap revenue without doing the work.

The days of the Pony Express and the Overland Mail's stagecoaches have become so romanticized that fact and fable are not easy to tease apart. Indeed, the reputations of some famous westerners have been burnished with dubious Pony credentials. Scholars debate whether Bill Cody, certainly a remarkable horseman, actually rode for the service. However, he hired many of its former employees to perform in what he called his traveling historical exhibition of the Wild West, inaugurated in 1883, which drew Queen Victoria, the pope, and many thousands of others at home and abroad for nearly forty years. Bronco Charlie Miller, a native New Yorker, improbably claimed to have joined the Pony at the age of eleven, but he certainly became a riding-and-roping star in Cody's circus. James "Wild Bill" Hickok, who had been a stableman for the Pony, only briefly shared the stage with Cody. (Hickok's nom de guerre derives from a taunt from a drunken bully, who imprudently called the bucktoothed youth "Duckbill." Wild Bill shot him dead, then was tried and released by a grateful community.) Seemingly indestructible "Pony Bob" Haslam—who had once completed a relay of 120 miles in eight hours and ten minutes on twelve horses despite bullet wounds to his left arm and a jaw fractured by an

arrow—did work for Cody, whom he had also accompanied on a belated trip to persuade Sitting Bull to surrender in 1890. After stints
as a Wells Fargo courier, an Army scout, and a U.S. marshal, Haslam
eventually settled in Chicago, where he became a hotel porter, entertaining guests with stories of his adventures. He died at the age of
seventy-two, a forgotten, impoverished hero of a bygone era in the new
age of the automobile.

During a crucial period before the completion of the transcontinental telegraph and railroad, the Overland Mail Company and the
Pony Express united the East and West into one America in very real
ways. They improved communications despite daunting circumstances,
laid down important infrastructure for the frontier's development, and
also made vital contributions to preserving the Union. While California agonized over whether to ally itself with the North or the South,
Yankee politicians decided that getting President Abraham Lincoln's
inaugural address to Sacramento as quickly as possible would help to
rally the state. Gearing up for the task, the Pony hired extra men,
added relay stations, and logged its fastest trip ever, and California
remained a free state. Nor was this the only occasion on which the
Pony aided the cause. General Albert Sidney Johnston, who was in
charge of the Union's Army of the Pacific in California, was preparing
to surrender its stores to the Confederacy, to which he would soon
defect. At the last minute, Lincoln got word of the scheme via the
Pony and replaced Johnston with General Edwin Sumner.

At a time when power was still centered in the Northeast, the ambitious Overland Mail and Pony Express highlighted the can-do spirit
and huge potential of the emerging Midwest and West, which changed
the way Americans saw themselves and were seen around the world.
Here is Twain, while traveling west on a stagecoach, on the transporting experience of watching the Pony Express in action:

"HERE HE COMES!" Every neck is stretched further,
and every eye strained wider. Away across the endless

dead level of the prairie a black speck appears against the sky, and it is plain that it moves. . . . In a second or two it becomes a horse and rider, rising and falling, rising and falling— . . . another instant a whoop and a hurrah from our upper deck, a wave of the rider's hand, but no reply, and man and horse burst past our excited faces, and go winging away like a belated fragment of a storm! So sudden is it all, and so like a flash of unreal fancy, that but for the flake of white foam left quivering and perishing on a mail-sack after the vision had flashed by and disappeared, we might have doubted whether we had seen any actual horse and man at all, maybe.

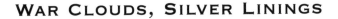

WAR CLOUDS, SILVER LININGS

WARFARE CHANGES through the ages, but the necessity for good communications remains one of its constants. Mail during the War of Independence was largely limited to official correspondence. Average soldiers and their families, like most civilians, depended on verbal or written messages delivered by willing travelers. By the outbreak of the Civil War, nearly a century later, a vastly expanded postal system, increased public education, and cheap stamps and stationery supplies had thoroughly democratized the mail. The Yankees would send more letters than the Confederates, but the two armies were the most literate in history, and these active correspondents imposed tremendous burdens on their posts.

Long before the Civil War, the post had been involved in the great political and moral issue of slavery. In the eighteenth century, enslaved African Americans had routinely delivered letters between southern plantations, and some had even served informally as postal carriers after the Revolution. In 1794, Postmaster General Timothy Pickering, who strongly opposed slavery, wrote that if the citizens on one mail route in Maryland "should deem their letters safe with a faithful black, I should not refuse him." Postmaster General Joseph Habersham felt similarly in 1801, "especially as it came within my knowledge that slaves in general are more trustworthy than that class of white men who will perform such services."

Such relative tolerance was short-lived. Southern politicians increasingly feared that if enslaved people, some of whom were literate, had access to the mail, particularly newspapers, they might learn of the Haitians' successful rebellion against the French in 1791 and follow their example. Gideon Granger, Habersham's successor, shared this anxiety, writing in 1802 that because white masters chose the "most active and intelligent" slaves to handle the mail, "they will learn that a man's rights do not depend on his color. They will, in time, become teachers to their brethren." Congress responded by declaring that "no other than a free white person shall be employed in carrying the mail of the United States"—a prohibition that obtained until 1865.

In the early nineteenth century, white southerners' growing fear of rebellion had made the rules that had previously governed slavery tighter and much harsher, yet the enslaved generated a surprising amount of mail. Despite the constraints and the low literacy rate even among free blacks, some individuals managed to write or dictate letters to friends, family, and the abolitionists and celebrities whose support they sought, and even to masters and former masters. After he escaped from bondage while accompanying his owner to New York, John S. Jacob informed the latter of the fact in a letter wittily signed "no longer yours." Henry "Box" Brown, born enslaved in Virginia, even successfully mailed himself to freedom inside a wooden crate that, with help from a white storekeeper and an unwitting private express company, delivered him to Philadelphia.

By the 1830s, northern abolitionists' mass mailings had helped to thrust slavery into the public arena and frame what had often been regarded as a regional matter as a moral issue for the whole country. From that point, the North and South alike saw the post as both a potent symbol of the federal government and, for better or worse, an active agent in fomenting rebellion. Even after the Confederate states had seceded and formed a government, in February 1861, President

Lincoln and his postmaster general, Montgomery Blair, wanted U.S. post offices in contested territory to remain open as long as possible as a political statement. As the president put it in his inaugural address, "The mails, unless repelled, will continue to be furnished in all parts of the Union." In April, the Confederates fired the first shots at Fort Sumter, outside Charleston, and Lincoln, urged on by the bellicose Blair, finally declared war.

The new Confederate States of America, like the revolutionary United States of America before it, urgently needed an independent, secure communications-and-information network. President Jefferson Davis chose wisely in appointing John Henninger Reagan as postmaster general. The Texan was a former U.S. congressman and a capable, experienced postal administrator who had initially turned down the job out of well-founded fears that the new network couldn't possibly measure up to expectations. Once committed, however, he recruited many former federal postal employees, who brought their equipment as well as their experience to the huge task ahead. After Reagan announced that the South's new network would begin operating on June 1, Blair suspended U.S. mail service to the rebel states as of May 31, and like the country itself, the postal system was sundered.

The Confederacy simply seized the 30 percent of the federal government's post offices and the 40 percent of its routes in rebel territory. Indeed, these resources had only recently been increased by a Congress eager to reinforce the increasingly precarious Union by wooing the testy South with federal handouts. The C.S.A.'s new post was closely modeled on its institutional parent, right down to its procedures and policies, including, much to the dismay of General Robert E. Lee, exempting transportation contractors from military service. Unlike the federal post, however, the Confederacy censored the mail. (That said, Blair authorized the North's generals to declare articles that damaged the war effort to be treasonous and have them pulled from the mail, which set a precedent for the unpopular Palmer Raids designed to arrest political radicals in World War I.) Whether because of the expense or the desire to suppress unfavorable opinions and reports that weakened loyalties, it also didn't subsidize newspaper circulation as robustly. In hindsight, these policies seem either unwise or unnecessary. Excepting border states, such as Missouri, the southern press mostly censored itself to reflect a unified Confederate point of view. Had the South done more to circulate newspapers, it might well have boosted rather than impeded its cause.

The postal network's bifurcation caused enormous private as well as institutional distress. There was now no official mail service between the two warring Americas. Individuals and organizations alike were suddenly unable to reach friends and family, colleagues and customers, across strange new borders. Previously, when Americans thought of themselves as citizens, some thought first of the republic—"nation" was not yet much used—but many others identified most with their states. After refusing to take a major command in the U.S. Army, Lee said to a friend, "If I owned four millions of slaves in the South I would sacrifice them all to the Union; but how can I draw my sword upon Virginia, my native state?" Once war was declared, however, people became Confederates or Unionists, dirty rebels or damn Yankees, and the change was disorienting.

Simply trying to carry on postal business as usual was a trial for both countries. Much of the correspondence addressed to the South after June 1 was hand-stamped MAILS SUSPENDED and forwarded to the post's Dead Letter Office in Washington, which reeled under the added burden. The only letters that passed between the two sides were taken across enemy lines under a flag of truce in a border state, transported covertly by blockade runners, or carried by the likes of Confederate captain Absalom Grimes. Union forces arrested the former Mississippi River boat pilot five times for sneaking substantial quantities of mail across the shifting borders. He always managed to escape until 1864, when he was seriously wounded and finally scheduled for hanging. Union friends interceded with Lincoln, who, late in the conflict, commuted Grimes's sentence to a brief imprisonment.

The war perturbed postal service even far from the battlefield. Good access to transportation turned the quiet county seat of Elmira, New York, into a military depot and arguably the worst of the camps for Confederate prisoners. The town's post office, which already served a sizable community, suddenly had to accommodate the needs of the Union forces now stationed there, plus some ten thousand POWs, whose letters were transported between the North and South on flag-of-truce ships. Elmira's mail volume quadrupled, but the strenuous efforts of postmaster Daniel Pickering and his staff, particularly a teenaged clerk who had a special genius for "throwing the boxes," or sorting mail, enabled the office to process between two thousand and four thousand letters each day.

Writing to the folks back home was a major activity for soldiers, and humble privates as well as officers expected to send and receive mail regularly. (Narrative from their letters accounts for much of the poignancy of Ken Burns's television series *The Civil War.*) They kept close tabs on their correspondence, often numbering as well as dating their letters to keep the chronology straight. Soldiers who lacked mothers, wives, or sweethearts to write to could become pen pals with respectable female volunteers, and those who lacked stationery supplies could receive special gift packs containing paper, pens, and pencils.

Getting the mail to and from the armies in the field, even within the two sides' own borders, took anywhere from a few days to a month or so, depending on the location of a soldier's camp and the duration of his stay there. On the Union side, delivery was a collaborative effort between the post and the military, aided by such private groups as the U.S. Sanitary Commission, a relief organization headed by the civic-minded landscape architect Frederick Law Olmsted. In a typical scenario, the post forwarded a letter to a soldier's brigade or regiment, where its own agents and army quartermasters worked together to send it down the line to the right unit. Then mail orderlies would carry the letter to the soldier's company and, in a same-day turnaround, bring back outgoing mail for delivery. The Confederates' process was similar but beset with the same economic, material, and transportation disadvantages that plagued its government's other functions.

STAMPS WERE A HUGE PROBLEM for both the North and the South, albeit for different reasons. The C.S.A. had none at all and had to start the entire philatelic process from scratch. (In the meantime, its so-called independent states often happily used federal stamps and postal markings.) Any postage still in rebel hands could also be used as money, so the United States had to void its entire existing supply, redeem any old stamps, and print and circulate new ones. (When the Union ran low on coins later in the war, stamps were sometimes enclosed in little discs and called "encased postage," which functioned as currency.) Both governments recognized that soldiers didn't always have access to stamps or money to buy them and forwarded many of their letters—but not those of officers—with a notation of "postage due."

The trouble Civil War stamps caused notwithstanding, they are one of American philately's most popular categories, for several reasons. By that era, the Industrial Revolution had wrought major technological changes in the printing process that delight collectors who focus on production matters. To prevent counterfeiting, for example, so-called security printers, who made stamps as well as banknotes and stock certificates, developed intricate designs and distinctive markings that were very hard to duplicate. (One technique for producing these "printing varieties" soon after the war used a waffle-iron-type tool to make impressions and breaks in the paper, which also discouraged the practice of washing off a stamp's postmark so that it could be reused.) The Confederacy didn't have the same quality of facilities for engraving, so its postage was not as finely crafted as the Union's.

Both the North and South used stamps as political propaganda, starting with classical philatelic portraits of their heroes. The C.S.A.'s first stamp, issued in 1861, rebelled against U.S. tradition by honoring a living subject: Jefferson Davis, its new president, who was portrayed in green ink. Ceding nothing to the enemy, both governments staked philatelic claims to George Washington, Thomas Jefferson, and Andrew Jackson, all southern icons as well as U.S. presidents.

Philatelic imagery was a far more decorous weapon in the antagonists' psychological warfare than their flamboyant, highly emotional "patriotic stationery." These specially designed sheets and envelopes were adorned with colorful partisan iconography meant to stir the sentiments and stiffen the resolve of the military and civilians alike. Some of the images—a lynched Abe Lincoln, an American eagle attacking writhing southern snakes—simply vilified the enemy, but much of it struck an exalted, inspirational tone. Gallant soldiers accomplishing glorious feats and fallen heroes were especially popular. The Union's dashing young Colonel Elmer Ellsworth, the Union's first casualty, met both criteria. When a Confederate flag flying at an inn in Alexandria, Virginia, spoiled President Lincoln's White House view, Ellsworth hastened to remove it, only to be shot by the outraged innkeeper, who in turn was killed by a Union corporal. Both men were quickly declared martyrs and emblazoned on stationery.

Printers and stationers were eager to capitalize on the patriotic vogue, although the South was inclined to regard profiting from the brave fighting men as yet another crude, money-grubbing "Yankeeism." (Merchants also sold other war-related wares, such as special "correspondence packets" that even supplied little charms to send to the girl left behind.) Soldiers paid up to fifteen cents, then a considerable sum, for stationery depicting elaborate regimental scenes or battlefields created by skilled artists. Many chose bucolic scenes of camp life to convey something of their calmer everyday experience to distant loved ones. These elaborate landscapes offered insight and reassurance to those back home, and sometimes a nudge. One illustration showed two soldiers poring over letters outside their tent—a hint of mail's importance to those who serve far away.

Correspondence between the battlefield and the home front did more than sustain relationships. If soldiers' messages reassured those left behind, their replies were reminders of a gentler world and a source of moral uplift for men engaged in a brutal conflict. Especially eloquent letters might be published in newspapers as reportage, widely shared as sources of inspiration, and used to comfort the dying. A slim bundle of carefully saved letters, accompanied by an officer's note of condolence, was often the only relic of a soldier killed and buried far from home.

POLITICIANS OFTEN SPEAK OF turning a crisis into an opportunity, but Montgomery Blair, one of America's most gifted and effective postmasters general, was a master of the art. The haughty scion of a prominent family of slaveholding Southern Democrats, who presided over an estate in Silver Spring, Maryland, and a mansion across the street from the White House (now the residence for the president's state guests), used the Civil War to expand the post's mandate and services in major ways. After graduating West Point, he became a protégé of the powerful Missouri senator Thomas Hart Benton, and then a lawyer, a district attorney, and a judge. Returning to the practice of law, he specialized in Supreme Court cases, notably as counsel for Dred Scott, an enslaved man. (In this famously controversial case, Scott argued that he should be emancipated by virtue of time spent in a territory made free by the Northwest Ordinance; the Court, however, ruled that Congress did not have the power to prohibit slavery in the territories.) By 1860, the powerful Blairs, mostly motivated by the preservation of the Union, decided to break with their family's political tradition. They became major Lincoln supporters, war hawks, and founding members of the Whiggish new Republican Party that would run the federal government for the next twenty-five years.

The influential family had been crucial in keeping both Maryland and Missouri in the Union, and the new president acknowledged the debt by offering Montgomery Blair the expected cabinet position. Given his West Point background and choleric temperament, he might have preferred to be Secretary of War, but he settled for postmaster general. The "Stormy Petrel" was not a beloved figure, yet he had a certain brooding charisma (inherited by his great-grandson the actor Montgomery Clift) that comes across in a description published in the *London Times:* "a tall, lean man, with a hard, Scotch, practical-looking head—an anvil for ideas to be hammered on . . . he speaks with caution, as though he weighed every word before." Blair was the most conservative member of Lincoln's cabinet, and he especially disliked Secretary of State William Seward and Treasury Secretary Salmon Chase, whom he called "radicals." The antipathy was mutual. These abolitionists doubted Blair's commitment to their cause and thought him too soft on the matter of the South's treatment after the war. Nevertheless, for several years, the brilliant, belligerent lawyer had great influence with Lincoln, especially regarding military issues.

Blair quickly mastered his new postal duties, starting with oversight of the spoils system that rewarded his fellow Republicans with postal jobs. Both he and Lincoln were besieged from morning to night by applicants whose only essential qualification was party membership. One appointee was remarkably candid about his lack of credentials: "I knew nothing of the postal service . . . ," he wrote, "and was fortunate to retain an experienced clerk." In a purge that made Andrew Jackson's seem moderate, Lincoln's administration replaced some twenty-one thousand of the post's twenty-eight thousand employees.

Next, Blair focused on using the war to expedite postal improvements that had been in the air but were too costly to implement before secession eliminated the burden of the South's largely unprofitable system. The first of these much-needed advances was Free City Delivery, as bringing their mail to urban residents was called. Like their colonial forebears, mid-nineteenth-century Americans still had to trudge to the local post office to send and receive their mail. The advent of cheap postage had only increased the congestion in big cities' facilities, where the atmosphere was more like that of a circus than that of a government institution. Even the opening of urban branch offices and the installation of mailboxes on streets beginning in the 1850s had done little to reduce the crowding, which consigned many customers to wait in long lines at the General Delivery windows only to be told they had no mail. Pliny Miles and other midcentury reformers had long insisted that Free City Delivery was an idea whose time had come. The service could be arranged in New York and a dozen or so other big cities, but it was not free. Indeed, the term "penny post" originally referred to the private letter carriers, such as Boyd's in New York and Blood's in Philadelphia, that offered services that skirted the postal monopoly, such as bringing a letter from a residence to a post office for a fee of one or two cents.

The war supplied the emotional momentum necessary to make Free City Delivery a reality. No single person can take exclusive credit, but Joseph Briggs, a postal clerk in Cleveland, played a crucial role. Bad news came by letter, and soldiers' families and sweethearts had to wait nervously in long lines to learn whether their loved ones had been wounded or captured or were among the 620,000 men who would die. Briggs's excruciating experience of handing officers' notes of condolence and bundles of returned letters to the suddenly bereaved had convinced him that post offices should not be public stages for personal heartbreak. He persuaded his supervisor to allow an experiment, and during the frigid winter of 1862, the city began to deliver correspondence free of charge—a valiant example that was not lost on his boss in Washington.

Blair knew that the greatest obstacle to adopting Free City Delivery on a large scale was convincing Congress to pay for a new workforce of letter carriers—a huge financial burden for a government already strained by the war's vast expense. However, he had an advantage in that he no longer had to deal with southern lawmakers, whose constituencies were likelier to be rural and who had long opposed the city delivery service favored by their peers from the urbanizing North. The canny postmaster general successfully retrofitted the

ABOVE: Paul Revere, a courier for the revolutionaries' Constitutional Post

LEFT: Mary Katherine Goddard, America's first woman postmaster in her own right

ABOVE: Dr. Benjamin Rush, physician, philosopher, and champion of a distinctively American post

RIGHT: Vexed by the railroads' charges for transporting mail, Postmaster General Amos Kendall chose the old-fashioned post rider, glimpsed here outracing the locomotive, for the Post Office Department's insignia.

ABOVE: Andrew Jackson, here in his general's regalia, satirized as founder of the corrupt "spoils system" by cartoonist Thomas Nast

LEFT: Narcissa Whitman, an early eastern missionary to the Native Americans of the Oregon Territory, whose letters "back home" helped popularize the Northwest's settlement

The mid-nineteenth century's cheap postage turned women into active correspondents, but they were segregated in large, urban, traditionally "male" post offices.

By the mid-nineteenth century, Star Route carriers like this later contractor transported the rural mail by the least expensive, most expeditious means available.

No. 1638. "The Deadwood Coach."
Photo. and copyright by Grabill, '89.

For many decades, the stagecoach ruled America's roads and carried its mail, both in the East and the West.

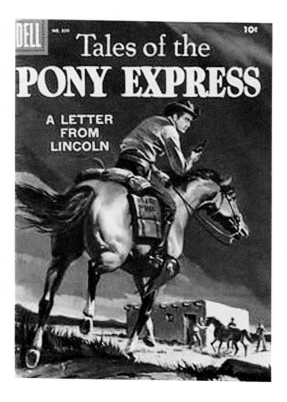

DELL

Tales of the
PONY EXPRESS

A LETTER FROM LINCOLN

10¢

Although short-lived, the Pony Express demonstrated America's can-do spirit and helped keep California in the Union.

Brilliant Postmaster General Montgomery Blair, appointed by President Abraham Lincoln, used the exigencies of war to improve mail service.

Both the Union and the Confederacy used stamps and "patriotic stationery" as political propaganda.

LEFT: The desire to afford privacy to recipients of bad news during the Civil War provided the final impetus for mail delivery to urban homes.

BELOW: The U.S. mail steamboat *Chesapeake*

THE MAIL CARRIER OF 100 YEARS AGO.

The FLIGHT of the FAST MAIL on the
LAKE SHORE MICHIGAN SOUTHERN RY.

RIGHT: By the late nineteenth century, Americans regarded their efficient Railway Mail Service as a "wonder of the age."

BELOW: Owney, the well-traveled, much-beloved mascot of the Railway Mail Service

LEFT: Well into the twentieth century, most of America's intercity mail was efficiently sorted as well as transported aboard rapidly moving trains.

BELOW: In 1900, more than 60 percent of Americans were still served by small rural post offices housed in general stores like this one in Ruidoso, New Mexico.

Born enslaved, "Stagecoach" Mary Fields, a popular figure, drove the mail by wagon in the Montana wilds around the turn of the twentieth century.

Postmaster General John Wanamaker, a brilliant merchant prince, wanted to revolutionize mail service as he had merchandising.

In 1902, Rural Free Delivery finally brought the mail to the homes of delighted agrarian and small-town Americans.

Postal savings banking encouraged thrift, moved cash from under the mattress into the economy, and especially benefited underserved Americans of modest means.

ABOVE: Postal savings customers could open an account with $1 but could not invest more than $500, later raised to $2,500. They received 2 percent interest, which pressured private banks to raise their own rate to 3 percent.

RIGHT: Some RFD carriers began their careers in horse-drawn wagons and ended them in trucks. This carrier weighs a baby as part of a public health program.

During World War I, mail to and from the troops abroad
had to be transported by transatlantic ships.

Through its crucial early support of the infant aviation industry,
the post gave Americans their fast Air Mail Service and a new
means of transportation, eventually even by night.

RIGHT: Iconic airmail pilot "Wild Bill" Hopson died on the dangerous job at the age of thirty-eight.

BELOW: The innovative technology of "Victory Mail" enabled even soldiers in World War II's remote Pacific Theater to receive letters flown from home.

Wars had long provided postal employment opportunities for women, including Jeannette Lee, Chicago's first female carrier, in 1944.

The forward-looking Postmaster General Arthur Summerfield, appointed by President Dwight Eisenhower, tried to modernize an anachronistic post in desperate need of mechanization.

Overwhelmed workers in the antiquated Chicago post office, where operations famously ground to a halt in 1966

America's highly automated twenty-first-century post handles 40 percent of the world's mail and is its most productive and lowest-priced mail service.

argument used by the cheap postage movement to convince a cautious legislature that more convenient delivery would generate more postal business, which in turn would pay for the new corps of letter carriers, as it had in Britain. In 1863, despite some dithering about the propriety of mailmen approaching homes where women might be alone, Congress authorized a new, peaceful army to march through the Union, starting with big northern cities. Blair sweetened the bitter financial pill for the legislators by adopting the popular policy of giving preferential postal employment to veterans and their families. He also recognized Briggs's contribution by bringing him from Ohio to Washington to help administer the program, including the design of the carriers' first uniform.

The post's new letter carriers had to work hard for their salaries, which ranged downward from $800 per annum. They walked an average of twenty miles per day, six days per week, fifty-two weeks per year until the 1880s, when they finally received two weeks of vacation, a shorter (eight-hour) workday, and overtime pay. They were obliged to hand letters directly to their customers, which entailed endless waiting and rapping—some mailmen used wooden knockers to save their knuckles—and often hauling the same letters back on their next round if no one answered. (Despite the obvious inefficiency, home owners were not required to install mail slots or boxes until 1923.)

Free City Delivery was a great success, and as it gradually spread, the service changed America in significant ways. After all, trips to the post office, convenient or not, had been part of life's rhythm and structure since colonial days. Home delivery also altered and reclassified the country's physical and social landscape. Communities that sought it had to demonstrate that they were populous enough to pay for the necessary carriers and amenities, such as decent sidewalks. Delivery required that streets be named and marked, and houses and buildings be numbered. Many Americans got their first formal addresses, which added a new dimension to their identity and sense of how the world was organized. The wealth of addresses also encouraged the new industry of large-scale commercial mailers, as well as the perpetrators of fraud and get-rich-quick swindles, which swelled the volume of junk mail.

In 1864, Blair used the post to help democratize America's financial services by introducing the department's money order system. For most of history, only the wealthy had enjoyed banking privileges in the modern sense. Even registered mail, which since 1855 had provided a safer way to deliver currency, important documents, and small valuables, had primarily benefited the businesses that could pay a premium for the service. The popularity of unguarded urban mailboxes had proved Americans' trust in the post's security, and Union soldiers' pressing need to send their salaries home without the risks of mailing cash provided the final impetus for postal money orders; the first averaged about five dollars delivered for ten cents. The program soon proved to be a huge boon for the population at large, and by 1880, the orders' total amounted to several times the postal budget.

The indefatigable Blair even tried to impose some order on the byzantine postage-rate system. In 1863, dismayed by his department's hundreds of fees, he oversaw the categorization of mail into three groups. The most expensive "first class" letters, weighing a half ounce or less, could travel any distance for three cents. "Second class" newspapers, periodicals, magazines, and pamphlets, which continued to make up the bulk of the mail, still paid just a fraction of their delivery cost. Advertisements and other printed materials that constituted the "third class" paid a higher rate. These numerical classifications also caught on with other organizations and became part of American speech.

That same year, Blair tapped his skills as a statesman and initiated the heroic effort to standardize the chaotic international mail service and postage rates by proposing a conference on the subject. Since 1844, Congress had tried to help by authorizing postal "conventions," or bilateral agreements, with England, France, and Germany; the first was with the city of Bremen, then the locus of much trade and emigration between central Europe and the United States. The International Postal Congress, held in Paris in 1863, was more ambitious. The U.S. delegate was the impressive Congressman John Kasson, a former assistant postmaster general and future diplomat, who advocated that international postal policy should be based on the American precedent. This important meeting laid the foundation for the formation, in 1874, of the General Postal Union, one of the world's first multinational organizations, which initially set standardized postage and reconciled accounting among Western nations; four years later, as more countries joined, it became the global Universal Postal Union.

Despite Blair's many achievements, his influence with Lincoln was waning. He was already greatly disliked by the cabinet's abolitionists. Then, in 1864, General Henry Halleck, the president's military adviser, demanded that the postmaster general be fired for accusing Union officers of cowardice after they failed to stop rebels from burning Blair's family seat at Silver Spring. Lincoln finally asked Blair to resign, which he did in that year, then gamely proceeded to campaign for the president's second election.

Mail service during the war had significantly improved in the North even as it had deteriorated in the South. After the war, strained postal finances as well as lingering political resentments kept the region from regaining its full complement of post offices until 1878. (Indeed, Blair himself rejoined the Democratic Party to protest the Republicans' policies during Reconstruction.) Over time, however, the resumption of good federal mail service helped draw the South back into the United States and its economy. Former Confederate postmaster general Reagan, who had been arrested after the surrender, was not only pardoned but also returned to Congress, where he became chairman of the Committee on Post Offices and Post Roads.

THE POST OF THE turbulent Civil War era underwent important internal as well as external changes, particularly regarding the employment of women and African Americans. Like the Revolution before it, the war had of necessity provided opportunities for women to show what they could do outside the home, which affected their standing in society. Blair even took the extraordinary step of allowing female clerks to work in the august postal headquarters in Washington, although they had to use a segregated entry and work space. By 1865, the women employed in the high-profile Dead Letter Office, a popular destination for tourists, outnumbered their male colleagues thirty-eight to seven.

Americans were fascinated with the Dead Letter Office for several reasons. In an era when money and valuables routinely traveled by mail, they imagined a kind of federal Aladdin's cave filled with cash, jewelry, banknotes, wills, deeds, and other treasures gleaned from undeliverable letters. The office was presided over by a highly professional staff that unusually included many clergymen as well as women, because both groups were considered more honest and diligent than the average man. These skilled detective-clerks did not read the letters but strove earnestly to get their contents, which amounted to millions of dollars per year, to the rightful recipients. They successfully redirected a letter addressed only to "Dr. Washburn, Roberts College," and an accompanying $1,000 check, to him at an institution not in the United States but in Constantinople (today, Istanbul), Turkey. They forwarded another letter, sent to "Mr. James Gunn, Power-Loom Shuttle Maker, Mass., America," to the addressee in Lowell, Massachusetts, a center of the textile industry. At a time when many people were phonetic spellers, one clerk was even able to translate "Reikzhieer, Stiejt Kanedeka" as Roxbury, State of Connecticut. Some curiosities that remained in limbo ended up in the Dead Letter Office's museum, a major attraction that suggested the startling range of arcana that circulated in the mail, from loaded pistols to butterfly cocoons. While examining its vitrines, one visitor discovered two valuable miniatures that had been stolen from her family home six years before.

Blair praised the female Dead Letter clerks as "more faithful in the performance of their duties than the men," yet they earned just $400 to

$700 per year, about 35 percent less than their male colleagues. The men opened the dead letters to see if they contained valuables, while the women researched the addressees' whereabouts, which would cause a droll reader writing in to the *New York Times* to attribute the former's higher wages to the fact that "immoral things are sometimes found in [the mail, and] to see these things would, it is supposed, corrupt the morals of women."

Vinnie Ream, a Dead Letter clerk who became a world-famous artist, is among American history's least heralded, most fascinating heroines. In 1862, the bright fifteen-year-old girl took the job to help support her family in the wake of their recent move from Wisconsin to the capital. During her wanderings in the city, she came upon a sculptor, picked up some of his clay, and modeled an Indian chief's head with preternatural skill. Soon Ream was making widely admired busts of some of the government's most powerful figures, including President Lincoln, who was charmed by her and her story. After much debate, Congress gave the obscure teenaged postal clerk a $10,000 commission for a full-size statue of Lincoln to stand in the Capitol Building, which made her the youngest artist and first woman to receive such an honor. Ream went to Europe to supervise the process of translating her clay model into marble and was feted by famous figures from Franz Liszt to the pope. She described the unveiling of her sculpture, completed in 1871, as her life's supreme moment thus far and seemed destined for many more. She went on to produce highly regarded works until her marriage at the age of thirty, when her husband insisted that she give up art.

The end of the Civil War also created a modest increase in employment opportunities for women postmasters, both on the expanding western frontier and in the historically Democratic stronghold of the South. Prospective postmasters had to take an oath affirming that they hadn't aided the Confederacy, which eliminated men who had served in its army but not most of their wives and daughters. However, the case of Mary Sumner Long, who aspired to become the postmaster of Charlottesville, Virginia, was particularly complicated. Powerful friends in Washington pleaded her case to President Ulysses S. Grant, stressing that she was the daughter of the Union's own General Edwin V. Sumner. The president tartly observed that as much as he respected her father, her spouse was no mere soldier but Confederate general Armistead L. Long, who had been one of Lee's closest aides and friends. Nevertheless, shortly before leaving the White House, Grant appointed Long as postmaster of Charlottesville, where she served until her death, in 1900.

THE CIVIL WAR FINALLY enabled African Americans to join the ranks of postal employees—a truly momentous development that had been a long time coming. The victorious Republican Party, which dominated the Reconstruction era (roughly from 1865 to 1877), used postal patronage jobs both to reward its supporters and reinforce its political values. Thus, Andrew Jackson's spoils system now rewarded some of the four million formerly enslaved, particularly the men enfranchised by the Fifteenth Amendment—a group who now not coincidentally comprised the electorate's majority in parts of the South.

The 142 new African American postmasters faced formidable challenges. For many, these included producing considerable sums in order to be bonded, but James Mason, also known as James Mason Worthington, the first known black postmaster, had no such financial problems. He and his sister, Martha, were the privileged only children of an enslaved woman and Elisha Worthington, a rich Arkansas planter, whose legal wife had had their marriage annulled on the grounds of adultery. The young Masons studied at Oberlin Academy and later ran Sunnyside, their father's biggest plantation. James became the local postmaster in 1867 and also served as a county judge and sheriff before his death in 1875.

Most of the early black postmasters worked in small offices in rural districts, but not all. In 1881, the obituary of Benjamin A. Boseman, a black physician in Charleston, South Carolina, appointed to head the important city's bustling post office, stated that he had been "civil and accommodating" and that "he enjoyed, deservedly, the reputation of being thoroughly honest"—strong praise for officials of any race at the time. Anna Dumas, the first known black woman postmaster, served in Covington, Louisiana, from 1872 to 1885. African Americans were also employed by the post in other white-collar capacities. John P. Green, who received a prestigious appointment as a postage stamp agent, oversaw a staff of eight white men charged with inspecting each issue of stamps for quality and uniformity. Isaac Myers, the first known black postal inspector, helped solve several notorious crimes, including thefts by Baltimore postal clerk George W. Claypole, which, according to *The New York Times*, had "puzzled the efforts of the shrewdest detectives in the Post Office Department." George B. Hamlet, the only known African American chief postal inspector, proved to be more resilient than principled. He was demoted for abusing the privileges of his office, allowed to resign, and then, thanks to powerful political connections, reinstated and transferred to the Treasury Department.

A position as a clerk at a major post office was very well paid and much sought-after, and William Cooper Nell, who served in Boston from 1863 to 1874, was one of the most accomplished. He was a civil rights pioneer who worked tirelessly to counter racial stereotypes and discrimination in Boston's public schools, as well as the first published African American historian. Harriet Beecher Stowe, whose *Uncle Tom's Cabin* had made her a celebrity, wrote the introduction to his *Colored Patriots of the American Revolution*, which appeared in 1855. Its heroes were all the more remarkable, she observed, because they fought for a freedom that most of their people were denied. In 1863, John Palfrey, Boston's white postmaster, appointed Nell to the clerk's position he had long aspired to, giving this scholarly man another historical distinction as the federal government's first known black civilian employee.

The several hundred African American letter carriers who were hired around the time of Reconstruction were not as well paid as clerks, but they also experienced less friction in a culture that regarded them as less threatening blue-collar workers. William Carney, a Civil War hero, was born enslaved in Virginia, but his family later managed to migrate to New Bedford, Massachusetts, where the Underground Railroad and jobs in the whaling and shipping industries had created a prosperous black community. When Lincoln welcomed African Americans to the Union Army, Carney gave up his dream of entering the ministry and enlisted in the all-black 54th Regiment of Massachusetts. During heavy fire at the battle of Fort Wagner, which protected the harbor at Charleston, South Carolina, he grabbed the flag from its wounded bearer before it fell to the ground and, though shot in the leg, carried it to the ramparts. After the Union's defeat was clear, he was shot three more times while returning it safely to his regiment, crying out, "Boys, the old flag never touched the ground!" He was promoted to sergeant and eventually returned to New Bedford, where he worked as a letter carrier. In 1900, Carney became the first African American to earn a Congressional Medal of Honor, and he and his regiment were celebrated a century later in the movie *Glory*.

Full Steam Ahead

THE POST IMPROVED IN major ways during the Civil War, but its Railway Mail Service was an innovation of a different order, which changed Americans' concepts of distance and time, national and local, modern and old-fashioned. The completion of the five transcontinental railroads, starting with the Union Pacific and Central Pacific in Promontory, Utah, in 1869 and ending with the Great Northern in Seattle in 1893, was one of nineteenth-century America's signature achievements. The advance opened both its own West to development and the Far East to commerce. At the same time, the vast rail networks allowed most of the nation's intercity mail to be sorted as well as transported aboard moving trains—a tremendous boost to the country's booming industrial economy and its population of passionate correspondents alike.

Trains had improved considerably since their early days in the 1830s, and locomotives equipped with headlights now chugged down tracks of a standardized gauge even by night. By the 1850s, more mail traveled by rail than by stagecoach and steamship combined. Aside from a few experiments, however, trains initially carried bags of mail from place to place in the right general direction, just as post riders and stagecoaches had done. Then, the increase in letter volume generated by cheap postage, combined with the demands posed by the Civil War, required an American version of the "railway post office" (RPO).

England and Canada had already experimented with these specially equipped train cars that enabled clerks to sort mail while moving between cities and drop it off at various destinations en route. In 1862, General William A. Davis, who before the Civil War had been employed at the post office in St. Joseph, Missouri, where the railroad ended, decided to follow their lead. Standard operating procedure called for the enormous volume of the East's westbound mail to be unloaded from the trains, processed in the post office, and then transferred to the overland stage. However, Davis had been struck by the short-lived Pony Express's efficiency in presorting its mail aboard trains before handing it over to the riders. He outfitted a baggage car that enabled a clerk to perform the same task on the Hannibal and St. Joseph Railroad, and the acceleration in service had attracted postal management's attention.

Two years later, a crisis brought on by the exigencies of war finally pushed the post to inaugurate the official Railway Mail Service (RMS). General U. S. Grant had made Cairo, Illinois, the headquarters for his western campaign because of its proximity to the railroad and the Mississippi and Ohio rivers. The backlog of mail to and from the huge Union force stationed there forced Congress to allow the post to try something new. Always quick to seize an opportunity, Postmaster General Montgomery Blair authorized George Armstrong, an inventive assistant postmaster at Chicago's huge distributing post office, to run America's first official railway postal route, which operated on the Chicago & North Western line. The experiment was such a success that customized RPO cars were deployed on many routes between big cities. The service was well established nationwide by the 1880s, and sending a letter from New York City to Raleigh, South Carolina, which had taken ninety-four hours in 1835, took just nineteen hours in 1885. By 1910, the RMS would handle an astonishing 98 percent of America's intercity mail.

The RMS increased the post's speed and efficiency not just by combining the mail's processing and transportation but also by decentralizing certain costly, time-consuming operations. Previously, a letter from the East that was destined for Michigan, say, or Wisconsin had to pass through Chicago's big regional distributing post office, which would then forward it to the right local office. The RMS skipped the bottleneck of Chicago and got the letter right to Ann Arbor or Milwaukee in record time—an advance that also required fewer general clerks and distributing post offices. By the 1870s, the post collaborated with several large railroads to offer special express service between certain big cities on "Fast Mail" trains, equipped with four RPO cars, that were the locomotive equivalent of the Pony Express. One such train, traveling from New York City to Chicago with thirty-three tons of mail to be sorted and delivered en route, completed the nine-hundred-mile trip in twenty-six hours, but at the end, "the exhausted engineer fainted."

Fast Mail trains were especially important for businesses, but average Americans were also well served by regular RMS lines. Most correspondence traveled within a radius of fifty miles, and given good rail access and the multiple daily mail deliveries that many homes enjoyed, it was possible to send a postcard at 8:00 or 9:00 a.m. that invited a friend who lived thirty or forty miles away for dinner and receive a reply by 4:00 or 5:00 p.m. By the turn of the century, some big cities even had RPOs on streetcars.

THE EIGHTEENTH-CENTURY PHILOSOPHER Edmund Burke's notion of the unfathomable "sublime" was customarily applied to breathtaking, even frightening, natural phenomena, such as a lion attacking its prey or a gale at sea. Their technological and bureaucratic equivalents included the nineteenth century's great industrial looms, which transformed textile production and changed society (wonderfully chronicled in Elizabeth Gaskell's *North and South*), and the RMS, a proverbial "wonder of the age." Like the crouching tigers that fascinated the painter Eugène Delacroix, the almost inconceivable power of the huge black, smoking locomotives that sped the nation's mail inspired the awe of average Americans as well as their artists. (They would later include the Futurists and musicians such as Hank Williams: "The midnight train is whining low / I'm so lonesome I could cry.")

The RMS was also sublime in the sense of its enormous complexity, which exceeded the comprehension of any single individual. Average folk puzzled over the new railway timetables, and even postal employees were hard-pressed to stay abreast of the continual changes in service. The department published a daily newspaper to update its workers and employed a topographer to adjust its twenty-six maps, which showed the great steel rivers of the populous East dividing into smaller streams as they flowed westward.

Each state had hundreds of railway mail routes, which had to intersect at scheduled times both within and outside its borders. Pennsylvania, aptly named the "Keystone State," had industrialized early and had both the most post offices and the largest RMS network. A letter sent from Philadelphia to a small town in, say, Illinois, traveled west on the mighty Pennsylvania Railroad, known as the "Pennsy," which had quickly become one of the nation's largest companies and employers. Passing through Harrisburg and Altoona, it reached the major junction at Pittsburgh, then the great hub of Chicago, and finally its destination via one or more small regional railroads.

Not even Theodore N. Vail, its gifted superintendent during the 1870s, could grasp the organization of the whole RMS. (Not coincidentally, he later became the president of American Telephone & Telegraph [AT&T], another extensive communications network, whose organization he based on the post.) Nevertheless, RPO clerks, who were known to have the hardest job in the entire department, were expected to master their pieces of the national puzzle. Only two-fifths of the applicants who passed the test for general postal clerk made the cut for this elite corps. They had to be much faster and more accurate sorters than average, and to prove it by earning at least 97 percent on a test of their home state's hundreds of routes; many did better. Elijah Fraser, a musician and former soldier who rose from letter carrier to RPO clerk on the line connecting Detroit and Chicago, once "threw" 2,444 cards with only four errors, setting a record of 99.49 percent accuracy. Most of these clerks had better-than-average educations, but P. J. McDonnell, an unschooled Irish immigrant, scored 99.31 percent on a test involving 11,743 cards and also won a gold medal for outstanding service.

Much was expected of an RPO clerk, because, as Postmaster General John Wanamaker said, "On his memory, accuracy, and integrity hang the engagements of the business and social world. An idle minute on the railway post car may be felt across the continent." Clerks trained for the Herculean feats of memorization that their job required by continually drilling with flash cards. (One side was printed with a location—say, "Hoboken, N.J."—and the other with pertinent railroad information, such as "Jersey City Direct.") However, their work called for quick thinking and dealing with complexity as well as rote learning. If a train missed a connection, the clerk had to choose the best alternative route for the mail while continuing to rocket down the tracks. Letters that were headed north didn't necessarily have to wait for a northbound train, because a southbound one might be able to speed a "turn-back pouch" to a quicker northbound connection farther down the line.

Functioning as a human computer was essential but not sufficient for success as an RMS clerk. Candidates also had to be physically hardy enough to handle two-hundred-pound mailbags and work shoulder to shoulder for hours on end while traveling at high speed without succumbing to seasickness, a common problem. (Suggested questions for an applicant's mandatory physical included "Any indications of derangement of abdominal viscera?") The "pouch clerk," who had to drop off and pick up the leaden mailbags at train stations, was often a muscular ex-farmer. If no stop was scheduled at a particular station, he had to toss or kick the station's incoming mailbag onto the platform from the streaking train, then wield a heavy hooked metal arm to snag the outgoing bag suspended from a crane. A miss cost him five demerits.

RPO clerks were charged with keeping the mail secure, so they were expected to be trustworthy and temperate enough to forswear drinking on duty. They also needed to be flexible. Many clerks worked for a week straight on the railroad, putting in thirteen-hour days, followed by nights passed in dormitories or rooming houses. Then they spent a relaxed week or two at home with their families, during which they also caught up on paperwork and mastered the constantly updated routes and schedules. Those able to adjust to the job's demands enjoyed some real rewards, starting with good wages. (During the twentieth century's Great Depression, unemployed teachers and other professionals were among those to take refuge in the job's security and benefits.) Clerks had to reside within five miles of their assigned rail line, so that they could "deadhead," or ride free, from their local station to the larger hubs where they caught their "head-outs." Thus, workers who lived in small towns enjoyed what struck many as the best of both worlds: experiencing the big cities' excitement without leaving comfortable homes in bucolic communities where comparable salaries were hard to come by.

Some of an RPO clerk's perquisites defy categorization. The late-twentieth-century singer Andy Williams recalled that one of the greatest pleasures of his Depression-era boyhood in Wall Lake, Iowa, was to hop a train with his father, who was an RPO clerk. As they approached their hometown, his dad would pop him into a big canvas mailbag and "deliver" him to the train station, where his mother waited to feign astonishment at finding her child in the sack.

SORTING THE MAIL on the go called for a new workplace as well as a new workforce. The custom-designed interior of a long, narrow RPO car was lined with shelves with pigeonholes for sorting letters, sliding racks for holding heavy mailbags, and locked drawers, cupboards, or even a small safe or cage to secure registered mail, which often contained money or other valuables. Just supplying and maintaining all this special equipment was a huge undertaking that was handled by regional repair facilities and the post's huge Mail Equipment Shop in Washington, D.C. (Hattie Maddux, a blind expert in crochet who worked there in the late nineteenth century, was paid forty dollars per month for fixing damaged cords.)

Not even the gaily painted exterior of the cheap wooden RPO car could disguise the fact that it was a very dangerous working environment. Fire was a constant threat. The cars were lit by oil or gas lamps, heated by burning stoves, full of tinder-like mail, and located right behind the locomotive, which threw off sparks. If a train was derailed by an open switch or errant livestock, a flimsy RPO could be crushed between the heavier engine and the passenger cars. Between 1890 and 1905 alone, 143 RMS employees were killed and 3,887 were injured in wrecks and other mishaps.

Some understandably anxious clerks turned to superstition to ward off the danger of fires, crashes, robberies, and other disasters, and a classic shaggy dog called Owney (1888–97) became their legendary talisman. He had strayed into the post office in Albany, New York, one day and soon began riding mail wagons to the train station. Before long, he was traveling by rail to New York City and beyond, wearing a metal baggage tag that gave his name and address for the return trip. The clerks he encountered on the journeys began to add their own lines' tags for good luck, until the smallish dog was so heavily decorated that the postmaster general gave him a special fabric vest that allowed him to wear his ornaments in comfort. When Owney died, RMS clerks hired a taxidermist to preserve him, and he was eventually enshrined at the National Postal Museum, in Washington, where he's among the most popular attractions. (Nero, a collie at the post office in Germantown, Pennsylvania, never enjoyed Owney's celebrity, but he reported to the railroad tracks six times a day just as a train was due, jumped up and down at its approach, and caught the mail pouch.)

In the early twentieth century, the RMS switched from the hazardous wooden RPO cars to much safer steel ones, which increased the competition for the clerks' well-paid positions. These modern cars came in three standardized sizes: the sixty-footer, which could carry between nine and twelve clerks; the thirty-footer, which could hold five; and the fifteen-footer, just one or two. A train moving between major cities might pull two or more of the largest RPO cars, as well as other cars filled with presorted mail and packages.

THE VAST POST-RAIL NETWORK quickly became a cornerstone of America's thriving industrial economy, which depended on a fast, secure means of transporting money and valuables as well as communications and information. Indeed, one major reason why the RMS has remained so little remarked upon is that its managers deliberately shrouded its details in secrecy in order to thwart robbery at a time when millions of dollars, including huge payrolls locked in safes as registered mail, routinely traveled around the country by rail. In his wonderful postal history, published in 1892, Marshall Cushing, who also served as Postmaster General John Wanamaker's private secretary, mentions one train that carried $20 million in gold as registered mail packed in five hundred boxes; it traveled from Santa Fe, New Mexico, to the subtreasury in New York City for a cost of $3,500—a bargain compared to the cheapest private express carrier's estimate of $60,000. (Even more impressively, starting in 1934, postal inspectors supervised the safe transfer of America's $15.5 billion in gold reserves from New York to Fort Knox as registered mail in five hundred railcars.)

Not all RMS trains that transported treasure were so fortunate. That *Butch Cassidy and the Sundance Kid* and other crime sagas of the late nineteenth and early twentieth centuries often feature exciting railroad holdups is no accident. The post's policy of vigorously pursuing thieves and offering big rewards for their capture inspired the saying that if you stole ten cents from the post, it would spend a million dollars hunting you down. Many train robbers wouldn't touch the mail car out of fear of reprisal. Those who were bold enough to do so often robbed the independent express carriers' railcars, too, which gave postal inspectors the additional help of Pinkerton's National Detective Agency, the private security force that famously pursued Butch and Sundance.

Robberies of post offices and mail trains peaked in the 1920s, when the department even armed some of its clerks and carriers. The most notorious of the crooks were the D'Autremont brothers, who made the serious mistake of killing an RMS clerk and three other men when blowing up an RPO car at Tunnel 13 in Oregon in 1923. The postal inspectors' only clue was a charred logger's coat that the culprits had left behind, which led to the identification of three men who had recently worked in the area's timber industry. The worldwide manhunt took three and a half years and included sending the brothers' medical records to every dentist and optician in the United States. One man was finally found in Manila, in the Philippines, and the others in Ohio, and all were sentenced to life imprisonment.

The mobile nature of the RMS helped to curb postal crime of a tamer, bureaucratic sort. Previously, managers at the big distributing offices had received a commission on the postage for any mail handled in their facilities, and some were said to run up those numbers by routing mail through several offices, which delayed service. Their resistance to any change that would cut into their own compensation, along with Congress's initial reluctance to pay for its expansion, helps explain why the RMS developed slowly at first.

JUST AS THE POST had always been about much more than the mail, the railroad was about much more than transportation, and their collaboration in the RMS accelerated the nation's development to a degree sometimes hard to believe. In the summer of 1867, the Union Pacific Railroad's chief engineer established Cheyenne, in what's now Wyoming, as a supply depot for the company's workforce and "Hell on Wheels" camp followers, and a tent served as the tiny settlement's first post office. By year's end, daily mail and train service had turned Cheyenne into a boomtown of some four thousand citizens.

When the railroad finally reached a miners' camp known as Creede, Colorado, its mail volume jumped from a small bundle of letters per week to many thousands, to say nothing of newspapers. Hundreds of fuming customers lined up all day long outside the twelve-by-fourteen-foot shanty that was the post office. Postmaster C. C. Meister had originally agreed to serve his colleagues purely out of good nature, and he was overwhelmed. He finally got some help in the form of a female clerk, who boldly posted a sign saying that all mail not retrieved within thirty days would be burned. (Miners tired of waiting in line bribed her small son to sneak in and get their letters.) Meister was greatly relieved when the post finally accepted his resignation.

Although an important regional distributing point for mail and goods delivered by the Atchison, Topeka & Santa Fe railroad, the first post office at Oklahoma City was also a makeshift affair, established in 1888 in a stockade that was one of the raw settlement's nine buildings. Mail volume was initially light, consisting of about one hundred letters and one hundred newspapers per day, yet its first two postmasters were apparently not up to the task and were fired. G. A. Beidler, their successor, was already apprehensive when he arrived at the desolate outpost late at night, accompanied by his young son, and instead of being welcomed, he was sharply questioned by the military, then told to sleep on some mailbags. Nevertheless, the diligent postmaster soon established a regular, orderly operation, dignified by the Stars and Stripes floating proudly above, just in time for the great land rush of "Boomers" and "Sooners" eager to settle the territory and their floods of mail. By 1890, the erstwhile wilderness outpost was a town of nearly ten thousand people that boasted a gasworks, municipal water, and a post office situated in its own building, albeit a former chicken coop.

. . .

THE POST AND THE RAILROAD were the nineteenth century's two great monopolies—one public, one private—and their partnership was tetchy. As in many marriages of convenience, money played an important role. The tone was already set in the 1840s, when the combination of the railroads' heavy charges and competition from the private mail carriers had helped to plunge the post into its worst crisis. Some social critics had urged the government to force the railroads to reduce their exorbitant fees. In 1845, Congress settled for a new merit-based classification system that paid more money to companies that transported important mail faster. Those assigned to the first class received up to $300 per mile per year; those in the second class, $100; and those in the third class, $50. Nevertheless, American railroads continued to receive much higher compensation than those of other nations. Between 1870 and 1912, Congress conducted five major investigations of suspiciously high costs, which revealed some bureaucratic corruption on one side and some seamy pork-barrel politics concerning rail expansion on the other. The government kept on complaining about the railroads' poor, overpriced service, and the latter about the former's inconvenient schedules and underpayment.

One typical contretemps began in 1873, when Congress authorized a new weight-based sliding scale that appeased the railroads at great cost to the post. By 1876, the national slump following the financial crash of 1873 forced the government to cut this inflated compensation by 10 percent, to be followed by a further 5 percent reduction in 1878; payments to railroads that had received land grants for carrying mail were also reduced to 80 percent of what the others got. The four major eastern companies retaliated by slashing their employees' salaries by 10 percent, which set off a major rail strike in 1877. The public was infuriated by the disruption, and the post once again tried to mollify the railroads with more money.

The post may have overpaid the railroads, but its transportation costs, compared to its soaring administrative expenses, remained relatively stable as the Post Office Department and its network continued to expand. Moreover, by the later nineteenth century, Americans generally agreed with Massachusetts senator Charles Sumner that "of all existing departments, the post office is most entitled to consideration for it is the most universal in its beneficence. . . . There is nothing which is not helped by the post office." On the other hand, the railroads had earned the dubious distinction of becoming the first industry to be put under federal regulation and the monopoly that the people loved to hate. A famous vignette from 1883 that featured William Vanderbilt, owner of the New York Central Railroad, suggests that the feeling was mutual. While traveling west in his private railroad car, the tycoon was questioned by a Chicago journalist about his company's cancellation of an express mail train that the public had valued but that Congress had refused to pay extra for. Vanderbilt replied, "The public be damned."

Theirs was a complicated relationship, but it's no accident that, driven by the same political, social, and economic forces, the long golden ages of the great postal and railroad monopolies overlapped. The Interstate Commerce Commission, which was established in 1887, regularly reviewed the post's transportation compensation, and its records show that into the 1950s, both partners felt they were mistreated and misunderstood—one measure of a kind of fairness.

BY THE MID-NINETEENTH CENTURY, steam power dramatically improved America's international as well as domestic communications. Just as it had been quick to subsidize the railroads to carry domestic mail, the post gave early, crucial support to the young oceangoing steamship industry that sped up service to the West Coast and Europe. In the process, the post amplified its role in spurring the nation's industrial development and promoting its economic and political interests abroad.

Well into the nineteenth century, the world's posts operated independently, each with its own elaborate rate structures, accounting procedures, and regulations. Americans who wanted to send letters abroad faced an ordeal that included getting them to a domestic port, across the ocean, and to their addressees in foreign countries. The process took anywhere from one to three months and involved at least three separate costs; the complicated postage was hard to calculate in advance, so the recipient was stuck with paying it. For a long time, British packets had dominated transatlantic mail, but in 1818, the American Black Ball Line's fast, regularly scheduled ships began to sail from New York to Liverpool in a mere twenty-three days. By the 1830s, many other U.S. shipping firms carried foreign correspondence as well.

By the 1840s, it was clear that the government had to do something about the maddening state of international mail. Floods of European immigrants had swelled the volume of transatlantic letters, and merchants eager to increase foreign trade clamored for better communications. Moreover, the military was greatly concerned by the advent of new oceangoing steamships and America's lack of them. Britain had already built up its industry by subsidizing Cunard and other shipping firms, which gave it the edge in dominating both international mail service and trade; should the need arise, the government could even commandeer the steamships for its Navy. America had plenty of fine sailing ships but no private steamship industry. Worse, the U.S. Navy had only 77 vessels, just 3 of which were steamers; for England, those numbers were 636 and 199. This imbalance, at a time when many Americans were enamored with Manifest Destiny and competing with the former mother country over trade and the ownership of the Oregon Territory, finally pushed the government to take action.

In 1845, a Congress determined to improve international communications, trump Britain, and develop America's merchant marine authorized the postmaster general to contract with ship owners to carry the mail abroad. By the next year, new oceangoing routes connected New York to Southampton, England, and Bremen, Germany. To help jumpstart what was a brand-new, very costly industry, priority was given to firms that built steamships for the purpose; these vessels also had to be suitable for military duty. As was the case with the railroads, the government ensured that America would get the steamers it sorely needed not by incurring the huge expense of building them but only by assuring payment for carrying the mail—another vital postal-private collaboration that improved transportation and communications alike.

In 1847, Congress authorized the secretary of the Navy to contract for additional steamship mail service. One route ran from New York to Charleston, Savannah, New Orleans, and Havana; another from Havana to the Isthmus of Panama, then up the Pacific coast to California and Oregon; and still another—the most important—between New York and Liverpool. By 1853, Congress tried to soothe a South disgruntled by the stimulus to the North's shipping industry and trade with a steamship line from New Orleans to Tampico and Veracruz in Mexico.

The effort to produce the great steamships drove the development of more sophisticated industry, technology, and engineering in an America poised to become a world power. The new ships were soon big and fast enough to compete with Cunard over passengers and light freight as well as mail. The *Pacific,* one of the ambitious, enormously expensive vessels built by the entrepreneurial E. K. Collins, crossed the Atlantic in a mere ten days, about five days faster than the British record. This progress, however, came at a high cost that transcended mere money. Two of his experimental ships sank at sea: the *Arctic,* lost in 1854 with his wife and two of his three children aboard, followed by the *Pacific* in 1856. That same year, much like his fellow transportation moguls John Butterfield of the Overland Mail and William Russell of the Pony Express, Collins went bankrupt and later died with his once golden reputation tarnished.

By the 1850s, American opinion had become more divided over using the postal subsidization of the steamship industry as an economic as well as military weapon. As tensions eased with Britain, some politicians argued that investing in a big fleet of potential warships was an unnecessary extravagance and that the money would be better spent on improving mail service at home. The huge subsidies also invited the usual complaints about favoritism and corruption in the department's transportation contracts—particularly in the Democratic South, which still lacked the much-desired steamship line from New Orleans to Europe and the economic boost from the shipping industry that the North enjoyed.

These dissenters aside, the post's steamship policy resonated with Americans who still favored expansion and competition with Britain, as well as immigrants, shipbuilders, publishers and merchants eager to flood Europe with their products, and the military. By the time the initial subsidies were halted, in 1859, America's international mail service was much faster, and its foreign trade had also greatly increased. This growth resumed just after the Civil War, when Congress authorized the postmaster general to contract with steamship owners to transport the mail from the East Coast through various ports to Brazil, and from San Francisco to Japan, China, and Hawaii.

By the 1870s, the political parties had divided over the post's support of the international shipping industry. Among Democrats, expansionist sentiment focused on improving transportation in America's own West rather than foreign parts; they also argued that low tariffs alone would stimulate trade without the costly subsidies. Republicans advanced the viewpoint of the nation's increasingly powerful and productive manufacturers, which were eager to reach new foreign markets; they wanted expansion overseas, high tariffs, and postal subsidization of a robust merchant marine. In 1891, the Republicans assumed control of the government just as nationalism and expansionism surged again, and Postmaster General John Wanamaker was authorized to contract with ship owners to improve both international mail service and commerce still more. (That entrepreneurial official went further, even installing post offices on some vessels.) By the turn of the century,

America had expanded its global influence with floods of newspapers, books, and consumer products as well as correspondence circulated by the ocean-going post.

International mail's transportation had advanced in tandem with its processing, which had greatly benefited from the establishment of the General Postal Union in 1874. By 1875, an American could send a letter to Europe for five cents that arrived in a week; postcards and newspapers cost just two cents.

STEAM POWER HAD IMPROVED postal service for most Americans by the late nineteenth century, but others, particularly in the western outback, remained beyond the pale. Letters that arrived at the nearest regional postal hub or train station in these remote places still had to be transported, usually on a weekly basis, to small rural post offices to await retrieval by recipients on foot or horseback. The need for Star Route carriers who could get this tough job done as cheaply as possible by whatever means necessary had increased with the nation's rapid western expansion following the Civil War.

Star Route contractors usually took on the difficult work to help cover the costs of their main businesses. They were obliged to function regardless of conditions that often ranged from inclement to hazardous. A carrier recorded only as "Stringer" set out on horseback one spring day to carry the mail from Buffalo, Wyoming, to the hamlet of Ten Sleep. When the snow became too deep, he switched to snowshoes and a toboggan. After one of his snowshoes broke, he staggered and fell for twelve miles back to his ranch, made a new snowshoe, and finally got the mail delivered in a week. Something of what even much later Star Route contractors experienced comes across in recollections from the 1930s by Harry Elfers, who transported the mail by boat from Sandusky, Ohio, to Kelleys Island in Lake Erie, some ten miles away. He wrote that just sailing one four-mile leg of the trip could take twenty minutes or eight hours, depending on the weather, particularly in winter:

> As soon as the ice begins to form, I feel eager to get out
> one of the "ironclads" and fight my way across. An
> "ironclad" is a flat-bottomed skiff. There's a sail in the
> bow to carry us through the water or over the ice when
> conditions are right. There are two iron-shod runners on
> the bottom so the boat may be used as a sled. The sides
> are sheathed with galvanized iron. This is very important,
> because thin ice will cut a boat like a knife.

The Star Route system was plagued with the problems endemic to transportation contracts, starting with the objective measurement of actual mail-related costs, especially in rural regions. The post tried to exert some control over the process with very detailed contracts, which in turn generated Talmudic arguments over interpretation. (In 1900, the economist H. T. Newcomb estimated that the cost of sending a letter bearing a two-cent stamp from New York City to Circle City, Alaska, was $450.) In the 1880s, the "Star Route Scandal" focused the nation on a florid example of collusion between corrupt officials and contractors. Assistant Postmaster General Thomas J. Brady and other department bureaucrats conspired with equally venal carriers and politicians, including former Arkansas senator Stephen Dorsey, to get rich by exploiting the difficulty of monitoring transportation costs in remote areas. The contractors falsely claimed the need for faster or more frequent mail service in their regions and, in exchange for kickbacks, were awarded exorbitantly inflated sums. A route that had previously cost about $1,200 per year, for example, might suddenly command $11,200. Congress had periodically investigated such overt fraud since Grant's administration, and Brady and many others were tried, but few were convicted. However, public outrage over the scandal that had bilked taxpayers of millions fueled the passage of the Pendleton Civil Service Reform Act in 1883, which helped to reduce internal corruption and incompetence throughout the federal government.

Despite its flaws, the Star Route system remained a vital part of postal service and the development of America's rural and wild places into the twentieth century. The history of communications in Yellowstone National Park, in what was still vaguely called the Montana Territory or the Upper Yellowstone when President Grant established the park in 1872, suggests the challenges. For some time after its founding, a kind of chaos reigned in the park, which is the size of Rhode Island and Delaware combined. Poachers hunted the protected animals, tourists brought by the new railroad helped themselves to geological souvenirs, and guides set up impromptu camps where their clients bathed and washed laundry in the pristine hot springs.

America's postal and transportation networks had always been linked, and the Yellowstone region had precious little of either. Communicating with the outside world and obtaining goods of any kind were formidable challenges. Letters for the park initially went to Bozeman, in the Montana Territory, where they waited for a rancher, tourist, boatman, or stagecoach driver willing to carry them closer to their destination. In 1880, a post office was established at "Mammoth Hot Springs, National Park County," and a Star Route contractor began to circulate mail to various stations within the park. Nevertheless, service remained erratic. A carrier based in tiny Cooke City, just outside the park's remote northeast corner, quit after the postmaster rebuked him for warning some locals that they were about to be arrested for illegally fishing in the sanctuary. Then, in 1882, the railroad reached the new town of Livingston in Montana—still seven years away from statehood—and daily mail service to Mammoth began a year later. In 1884, Clarence Stephens, the park's first postmaster, was succeeded by Jennie Henderson Dewing Ash, who held the position under three names during her three marriages.

The park's civilian superintendents proved unequal to the task of imposing order in their portion of the Wild West, and in 1886, General Philip Sheridan sent in the U.S. cavalry. The soldiers established Fort Yellowstone at what's now the trim, pleasantly martial village of Mammoth Hot Springs, and within the year, the rule of law was restored. A "snowshoe cavalry" patrolled the park during its brutally hard winters, and even the soldiers' wives and children had to get about on skis.

Young private Edwin Kelsey, a future editor of the *San Francisco Chronicle,* sent a charming holiday letter to his niece that suggests the difficulty of communications in the region. He explains that he had ridden a horse forty-six miles through deep snow in temperatures that sank to -22 degrees F. in order to reach the fort a few days before Thanksgiving. Then he rhapsodizes over a feast that was "a beaut. . . . Turkey, roast pork, sweet spuds, cranberry sauce, oyster stew, chocolate, three kinds of cake, pie, pickles, nuts and apples—how's that for soldiers?" He allows that "there's something about life in the wilderness that fascinates me," but he doesn't sugarcoat the privations of being off the grid: "Don't suppose you will hear from me before Xmas, so I'll wish you all a Merry one. . . . One can buy nothing here and as the troop has not been paid for two months I have no money or I would send it to you to spend with my compliments."

The Star Route system that served such wild places had many colorful contractors, but "Stagecoach" Mary Fields remains one of the most remarkable. The sturdy, six-foot-tall African American woman had been born into slavery in Tennessee, then was taken in by Ursuline nuns after the Civil War. The sisters chose wisely when they brought her to Montana to help them establish St. Peter's mission and school for Native Americans. Fields was a capable, well-respected jack-of-all-trades and a crack shot who, like teamster Polly Martin before her, was not one to be trifled with. When her propensity for fisticuffs earned the local bishop's ire, the nuns helped her relocate to nearby Cascade and get the job of driving the mail between there and St. Peter's, which she did from 1895 until 1903; the sisters even supplied the necessary wagon and horses. Fields was a popular figure, known for cigar smoking, sharpshooting, and buying candy for children, and her obituary in 1914 was front-page news in both of the area's papers.

Fields relished her work as a Star Route contractor, but young N. C. Wyeth, later a famous painter, illustrator, and father of artist Andrew, had a far briefer and less enjoyable career as a postal carrier. The easterner was fascinated by the West's vistas and iconography and traveled there several times just after the turn of the century. On one excursion, Mexican bandits robbed the trading post where he had secured his money, leaving him penniless. His only recourse was to sign on to carry the mail between Fort Defiance, Arizona, and Two Gray Hills, New Mexico. His diary records that he received "$1.25 a day above horsefeed" for making this eighty-five-mile trek through a barren, sandy waste on horseback. The entry on his final day of service reads: "My last trip! Thank God."

BY THE LATE NINETEENTH CENTURY, the inescapable fact that urban and rural Americans now lived in different worlds had become an issue of great domestic importance. Residents of cities and towns increasingly enjoyed the world's most modern homes, equipped with clean water, indoor plumbing, and central heat and light. They had good roads, rail service, municipal utilities, and libraries, as well as access to mass entertainment and the latest consumer goods. The post brought the latest news and information to their doorsteps and enabled many to carry on same-day correspondence.

The lives of many of the farmers and settlers who still made up 65 percent of the population were nearly medieval in comparison. Maintaining a home equipped with a hand-cranked cold-water pump, a woodstove, and an outhouse was backbreaking labor for women, who fled in droves to find work in the industrial cities. The awful roads and distance from the railroad kept country folk immured in tiny hamlets that offered few choices of things to do or buy. Their postal service differed little from that of the founders a century before, yet these

Americans paid the same postage as town folk, which added injustice to the hardships of being cut off from the rapidly modernizing mainstream culture.

America needed its farm families to provide food, so stopping their flight from unrelieved isolation and drudgery became a national concern. Powerful new agricultural organizations, such as the Grange and the Farmers' Alliance, joined high-minded East Coast social reformers and the leaders of the new home economics movement in an effort to improve the quality of rural life. Using the post to reconnect these overlooked Americans to the society that had left them behind became one of the great achievements of the liberal-minded "Progressive Era," which lasted roughly from 1890 to World War I.

THE GOLDEN AGE

Messenger of Sympathy and Love
Servant of Parted Friends
Consoler of the Lonely
Bond of the Scattered Family
Enlarger of the Common Life
Carrier of News and Knowledge
Instrument of Trade and Industry
Promoter of Mutual Acquaintance
Of Peace and of Goodwill Among Men and Nations

—"The Letter," by Charles William Eliot, as revised by President
Woodrow Wilson. Inscription from the façade of the Smithsonian
National Postal Museum, in Washington, D.C., formerly
the city's main post office and the companion
building to Union Station.

THE POST'S DYNAMISM and centrality to America's public and private life were most fully realized between 1880 and 1920. During these glory days, the institution's success in bringing more public services to many more people both supported and reflected an America that was tapping the riches of its vast West, moving to the center of the international stage, and exulting in its position as the world's leading industrial powerhouse—all achieved in little more than a generation. Yale University's president Arthur Hadley had to agree with the sentiments his institutional rival Charles William Eliot, president of Harvard, expressed in "The Letter," his paean to the post. In Hadley's opinion, "our whole economic, social and political system has become so dependent upon free and secure postal communication, that the attempt to measure its specific effects can be little else than a waste of words." Cushing went further and used the language associated with Burke's notion of the sublime to describe the post's annual growth as "enormous, resistless, inconceivable," proudly adding that "we beat the world."

A few numbers suggest the turn-of-the-century post's growth and scope. Between the Civil War era and circa 1890, the number of post offices doubled to 62,401. In 1860, the Railway Mail Service had operated on 27,000 miles of track, employed 600 workers, and cost $3 million per year; in 1891, it used 160,000 miles of track, had 6,000 employees, and cost $21 million per year. Between 1866 and 1891, registered letters increased in number from 275,103 to 15 million (with only 1 in 12,227 lost); the number of post offices that handled money orders rose from 766, producing $4 million in business, to 30,000, generating $140 million. Just between 1889 and 1892, the network added 8,120 new offices and 2,480 new routes and increased its revenue by 26 percent.

The postmaster general officially controlled this enormous business, but since Andrew Jackson's day, he had also been much concerned with political matters. Four assistant postmasters general, who were in charge of post offices, transportation, finance, buildings, and other affairs, actually ran things on a day-to-day basis. Each of the Post Office Department's many divisions, including money orders, dead letters, contracts, inspection, and foreign mail, was a major enterprise in itself. The Division of Supplies, for example, handled the entire department's printed forms, stationery, ink, stamp pads, twine, scales, and so forth. (In 1890, this complex operation was under the command of the formidable Major E. H. Shook, a former "printer's boy" who during the Civil War had fought in thirty-one battles, been taken prisoner, and escaped.) The fabled Dead Letter Office alone required the services of more than a hundred of the five hundred clerks employed at postal headquarters. Many of the others bent over the ledgers of what was one of the world's largest accounting offices, keeping track of the quarterly statements of all the nation's post offices, which in 1891 did $450 million in business; money orders just from New York City numbered 80,000 per week.

The post's ascent began during the Civil War. Despite its terrible toll, the conflict had temporarily relieved the department of its costly responsibilities in the rural South and enabled the launching of expensive new programs, such as Free City Delivery and the Railway Mail Service. The huge simultaneous demands of the South's repatriation and the West's development caused a brief retrenchment, but by the 1880s, the department was ready for more major advances. The railroad system, too, had greatly expanded and, despite the chronic complaints of overcharging on one side and underpayment on the other, had become the post's functional linchpin. In addition to its sheer efficiency, the RMS enabled the post to exploit the modern bureaucracy's economies of scale. Back in 1830, Andrew Jackson's often-vilified postmaster general William Barry had recognized that once the post had established its centralized national network, it could increase its revenue simply by adding more local offices and mail routes. As the frontier pushed westward, the railroads greatly accelerated this cookie-cutter growth by helping the post to mechanize its development in more and more places.

The long joint apogee of the post and the railroads not coincidentally overlapped with the expansive, open-minded Progressive Era and its broad-based, largely bipartisan effort to rethink democracy's meaning and goals for a rapidly industrializing and urbanizing America. Between 1860 and 1900, the country's total and urban populations would both double, and its young people were primed to embrace new, modern ideas and ways of doing things.

If the raw young republic had initially been intent on maximizing development, America was now increasingly focused on the problem of how to continue growth without succumbing to slums, sweatshops, and the powerful new businesses that economist Henry C. Adams described in 1887 as "natural monopolies." Jay Gould of Western Union, Andrew Carnegie of U.S. Steel, William Vanderbilt of the Pennsylvania Railroad, and other titans of what Mark Twain called the Gilded Age bought up thousands of small companies and consolidated them into a few hundred corporations; they gleaned enormous profits largely because their costs declined as their scale increased, which enabled them to knock out smaller competitors and dominate the market. These huge nationwide enterprises soon virtually controlled the economy, threatening the order of what had long been a country of farms and small businesses. That both the railroads and Western Union were involved with the all-important dissemination of information only heightened the public's anxiety.

The severe depression of 1893, which caused high unemployment, violent strikes, farm foreclosures, and generally hard times, further increased the people's concern over the consequences of industrialization and urbanization and drew supporters to the Progressive movement. This unusual affiliation of very different social, economic, and political groups recoiled alike from the prospect of becoming cogs in the Industrial Revolution's monstrous wheel. Members of the new urban workforce employed in factories and offices; the growing professional class of businessmen, doctors, lawyers, and teachers; the isolated, underserved agrarian population; and the reform-minded Protestant churches—all looked to government to protect them from vast new forces beyond their control, especially corrupt political machines and the greedy monopolies that posed a threat to affordable utilities and public services. As a result of this widespread concern, the Progressive Era saw some of American history's liveliest policy debates, many of which concerned the proper spheres of government and private enterprise.

Where the post was concerned, the stage for the latest installment in the perennial government-versus-business drama had been set by earlier spirited exchanges over control of the telegraph. Even after Congress had initially declined to buy his invention, Samuel F. B. Morse, President U. S. Grant, and many other prominent citizens continued to assert that the telegraph was a natural extension of the post's mandate and that the government should redeem it from private hands. After all, such a step would conform to the often-invoked "post office principle" of serving all the people at a uniform rate, including those in less populous regions. Illinois senator Stephen Douglas had put forward the basic argument in 1857: the telegraph "is for the transmission of intelligence, and that is what I understand to be the function of the Post-Office Department."

In 1866, Congress responded to the surge of antimonopoly sentiment by passing the National Telegraph Act, which was meant to curb Western Union's hegemony by sparking competition from its much smaller rivals. The bill authorized the postmaster general to set telegraph rates for government agencies, but, more important, it gave companies that agreed to let Congress buy them out after five years the right-of-way to string their wire along post roads. This policy made the post's acquisition of the telegraph seem almost inevitable; indeed, Great Britain would take the step in 1868. Grant himself stressed that the telegraph circulated information as well as communications, and that the federal government had an obligation to foster public education. Other advocates emphasized that a postal telegraph would improve the free flow of news, which was obstructed by private deals between the telegraph companies and the New York Associated Press, an agency that restricted its reportage to select member papers.

Two Republican postmasters general, both appointed by Grant, expressed opposing views on the postal telegraph. John Angel Creswell agreed with his boss. Creswell might have been a highly partisan wielder of patronage, but he was a creative executive who even briefly succeeded in abolishing the wasteful franking privilege that allowed congressmen to generate tons of self-serving mail at the department's expense. He also believed that the post should offer more public services, including a savings bank that would help to fund a postal telegraph. Creswell's view reflected his larger conviction that certain resources belonged to the people and should not be privatized. In one memorable example, he described electricity as "that most subtle and universal of God's mysterious agents"; as to using it to generate private profit, he said, "As well might a charter be granted for the exclusive use of air, light, or water."

Postmaster General Marshall Jewell argued against a postal telegraph by falling back on the traditional argument against increasing federal power, especially at the expense of corporate profits. "There must be a limit to government interference with private enterprise," he said, "and happily it better suits the genius of the American people to help themselves than to depend upon the state." Leonidas Trousdale, a prominent Tennessee journalist, enthusiastically agreed: "Let us adhere, as closely as changing events and shifting scenes may permit, to the wise maxim of our patriot fathers, that 'that government is best which governs least.'"

Soon to become Alexander Graham Bell's father-in-law and the first president of both the Bell Telephone Company and the National Geographic Society, Gardiner Greene Hubbard took a measured stance on the telegraph's ownership. He argued that the system should become what would later be called a public utility, an enterprise that's regulated but not owned by the government. In defense of federal supervision, he wrote: "It is not contended that the postal system is free from defects, but that it removes many of the grave evils of the present [telegraphic] system, without the introduction of new ones; and that the balance of benefits greatly preponderates in favor of the cheap rates, increased facilities, limited and divided powers of the postal system."

These early debates over control of the telegraph had failed to settle the question, but after 1881, when Jay Gould, the Gilded Age's deeply unpopular robber baron par excellence, took control of Western Union, the public's mounting antipathy to monopolies and their scandalous profits thrust the issue back onto the national stage. Western Union's supporters countered with the familiar argument that it was both unfair and impractical for the government to compete with business. However, social critics stunned by such huge corporations' growing might increasingly disagree. To them, the natural monopolies, much like government itself, had the power to transform society, and therefore should be either owned or regulated by the government for the public's good. The Populist Party, which advocated public ownership of utilities, was defeated in elections during the 1890s, but its pro-government sentiments endured well into the next century among a huge, diverse swath of Americans, including Republican presidents Theodore Roosevelt and William Howard Taft as well as the Democrat Woodrow Wilson.

TURN-OF-THE-CENTURY Postmaster General Charles Emory Smith called the post at its zenith "the greatest business organization in the world," but unlike a private company, its aim was expanded public service, not profitability. The long-neglected majority of Americans who lived in rural areas were the first to benefit, thanks largely to Postmaster General John Wanamaker, the self-made, fabulously rich Republican founder of the namesake Philadelphia department store. A pioneer of modern marketing and advertising as well as one-stop shopping ("Everything from Everywhere to Everybody!"), he had made a fortune from inventive strategies, such as charging low prices to generate a huge volume of sales, and catchy innovations, such as the price tag, the money-back guarantee, the in-store restaurant, and even the annual "white sale." Wanamaker was the very personification of industrious, upwardly mobile, business-oriented, forward-looking, turn-of-the-century America, and he was determined to modernize the post, now more than a century old, just as he had revolutionized merchandising.

After making his own fortune, Wanamaker had deployed his skills on behalf of the Republican Party's finance committee, which for the first time was dominated by businessmen. In 1889, President Benjamin

Harrison duly rewarded him with a cabinet position, but instead of the Department of State, as had been rumored, Wanamaker got the Post Office Department. The merchant prince proceeded to become one of the nation's most gifted postmasters general, but he had timing as well as talent on his side during the Progressive Era, when the public was more receptive to ambitious plans for improving the commonweal than at any time before or since.

Like all postmasters general, Wanamaker wanted the mails to go faster—so much so that he ordered that if no mailman were available to attend immediately to a letter sent via special delivery, a service added in 1885, the postmaster himself must deliver it. (When he heard that one such letter had taken ten hours to travel from Philadelphia to its destination in New York City, he ordered an investigation.) Wanamaker was also a business genius, however, who had become rich by anticipating what the public most wanted and needed next. He was determined to use his combination of acumen and chutzpah to update the post with the telegraph that his predecessors Blair and Creswell had coveted and more, including telephone service, parcel delivery, savings banking, and especially the free delivery of letters and newspapers to long-neglected rural homes.

Most politicians interested in the idea of Rural Free Delivery (RFD) had been Democrats, but the new Republican postmaster general became its doughtiest champion. His passion for such public services had complicated roots. On one hand, Wanamaker was a businessman who had made a fortune through private enterprise and a tough politician who vigorously exploited the spoils system on his party's behalf. On the other, he was the son of a religious family of hardworking brickmakers, who had had just three years of schooling before starting to work at fifteen for $1.50 per week. He was also a fervent, activist Presbyterian and patron of the Young Men's Christian Association, who attributed his fund-raising success for the Republican Party to the same techniques he employed on behalf of Protestant missions.

Wanamaker's cultural and religious roots inspired his unshakeable belief that all people were equal before God and deserved the same fair treatment, whether from government or from business. This powerful conviction fed the hatred of monopolies that he shared with many contemporaries—in his case, particularly the railroads and private express carriers that had troubled the post he now ran. He regarded such huge companies as robbers who had carved the nation into sections under their control, then amassed fortunes by depriving average folk of competitively priced goods and services. Thus, the hardheaded merchant whose government office had a direct telegraph line to his business headquarters nevertheless insisted that the post office had a higher purpose than merely making money: "I do not think it essential, and do not know why we should be self-supporting any more than the Interior and other Departments."

Wanamaker believed that establishing RFD to connect more than half of the American people with modern mainstream society was first and foremost the right thing to do, but it also made good political and business sense. Home delivery would help keep country folk on their vitally important farms. Employing one carrier to bring the mail to fifty customers was far more efficient than requiring all of them to drop everything and walk or ride a horse to fetch it, and would also allow thousands of small, unprofitable fourth-class post offices to be closed. Finally, RFD would be a tremendous stimulus to the economy. Simply by delivering a newspaper to every home, it would draw new customers into the national market and benefit businesses from publishers to the fledgling mail-order merchants and advertising agencies. As one of the nation's foremost entrepreneurs, Wanamaker could defend RFD and his other progressive goals with a hard-nosed challenge: "See if each one does not commend itself to your business judgment. See if you don't even feel sorry that politics and private interest stand in the way of these improvements."

The arguments for establishing RFD were as fair and commonsensical then as now, but Wanamaker failed to close the deal with Congress. Reflexively oppositional Democrats were part of the problem, but so was the postmaster general himself. He had a judgmental, puritanical streak—vividly expressed in his vigorous opposition to labor unions and the use of the mail by state lotteries—that rubbed some people the wrong way and even led to death threats. Many others were simply jealous of the rich, powerful man who was used to getting his way. They sniped that he had bought his way into the cabinet, that he ran his department too much like his department store, and even that he wanted to use the post to increase his own company's mail-order business and ruin the competition. Not surprisingly, third- and fourth-class postmasters, Star Route contractors, and general store proprietors also vehemently opposed a service that would jeopardize their livelihoods, and they lobbied Congress against it.

His opponents' small-mindedness sorely vexed Wanamaker, and the capital's corridors of power frequently echoed with rumors that he was fed up and about to resign. Petty concerns aside, however, there were also serious practical obstacles to initiating a huge program like RFD, starting with the huge expense. Like Free City Delivery, the service would require a new workforce of tens of thousands of mail carriers and incur other costs that no one knew exactly how to calculate, which gave squeamish legislators an excuse to equivocate. Wanamaker secured $10,000 to run a small test program in a few districts in 1891, then proposed nationwide RFD the following year, but Congress continued to dither and stall.

Wanamaker left office in 1893 without the satisfaction of seeing his democratic dreams fulfilled on his watch, but he had planted the idea that the post could and should provide Americans with new services in the national consciousness. Congress was besieged by thousands and thousands of petitions for RFD and was forced to weigh the estimated costs against its benefits. In 1896, legislators authorized enough funding for a larger experiment on five routes in West Virginia, which just happened to be the home state of Postmaster General William Wilson. Within a year, there were forty-four routes in twenty-nine states. In 1902, RFD finally became a permanent postal service, which expanded over time.

RFD was a wildly successful if initially costly boost to both rural America and postal efficiency. In 1901, the country had 76,945 post offices—the highest number ever—most of which belonged to the smallest fourth class; by 1920, RFD had cut the total to some 52,000. (Covers stamped in decommissioned "dead post offices" are prized by philatelists, especially those who specialize in particular geographic areas.) Just as the founders had foreseen, better postal service once again promoted local development. Citizens of rural communities first had to band together to petition for RFD routes, then provide carriers with the decent roads and bridges that had hitherto been few and far between. The improved transportation network changed agrarian America's social and economic as well as physical landscape. Terrible roads no longer restricted people to their tiny villages. They could venture to towns that offered new experiences, more choices, and competitive prices, and their children could travel to larger, consolidated schools that offered better facilities and instruction.

Like their urban peers, the new RFD carriers, whose numbers climbed from fewer than 500 in 1899 to more than 32,000 in 1905, worked hard—until 1923, even on Christmas Day. At first, they were paid only about $200 per year, on the assumption that theirs was primarily a part-time job for farmers. Most drove their own horse-drawn wagons over rugged terrain, stopping to deposit letters in the pails and cigar boxes that predated the familiar rounded rural mailboxes. The carriers also collected outgoing mail and postmarked it with a special RFD "cancel"—handwritten and hand-stamped markings that are another philatelic specialty—which meant that many local letters could be delivered without processing at the post office. The carriers' job called for special inventiveness and fortitude during hard northern winters, when horse-drawn buggies might sport sled runners in front instead of wheels and drivers fended off frostbite with bearskin coats and brass foot warmers filled with hot coals. After 1908, carriers who began their careers behind a horse could end them in Model Ts, sometimes also fitted for winter with front skis.

RFD changed the quality of life for many Americans more profoundly than mere facts and statistics can convey. Some of the most poignant tributes to the service concerned its impact on long-isolated rural people's mental health. In addition to information from the outside world, the carriers brought friendly faces and news of recent events, from fires and floods to epidemics, as well as the latest gossip. As Postmaster General George Meyer observed in 1907, "medical men" declared that because of RFD, "insanity is on the decrease." In the latest evolution in the founders' vision of what the post was for, people who had felt cut off from the national and even local community suddenly had, right at their doorsteps, a bridge that united them with a larger America.

THE POST AT ITS ACME was generally regarded as an exemplary institution, public or private, and mostly enjoyed the support of the people as well as both political parties, some predictable partisan carping notwithstanding. During the presidential electioneering of 1880, Abraham Hazen, a postal official, tried to drum up support for the Republicans by contrasting the department's affairs during the Democrats' tenure between 1853 and 1861—"financial ruin, general demoralization of the service, and popular discontent"—with those of his party's years between 1861 and 1880—"filled with great questions successfully grappled with . . . with immense strides in all avenues of human thought and action."

Despite the post's high repute, a few problems drew disapproval from the citizenry and journalists alike, especially the continuing scandal of the spoils system. By 1880, most of the nation's one hundred thousand federal workers were employed by the post and thus subject to partisan firings. In 1881, President James Garfield's assassination by a disgruntled office seeker amplified the demand for reform, and in 1883, Congress passed the Pendleton Act, which created a bipartisan

Civil Service Commission to ensure that federal jobs would be awarded on the basis of merit. The law turned out to have some conspicuous holes, however, particularly regarding the post. Its provisions applied to clerks and letter carriers in twenty-three big post offices, including New York City and Washington, D.C., but not to the rest of the department's employees, including tens of thousands of postmasters and rural carriers. As Theodore Roosevelt, the commission's director in 1890, rightly observed, apart from its gross unfairness, the spoils system also exacted an enormous toll on congressmen's time and efficiency, as they were expected to recommend appointments for all of the postmasters in their districts, which could be a full-time job in itself. (Commissioner Roosevelt had been particularly infuriated by Postmaster General Wanamaker's disregard of the new civil service rules, but in 1903, President Roosevelt would be embarrassed by a major scandal over postal corruption during his administration that resulted in much-publicized firings and indictments.)

The welfare of the nation's tens of thousands of postal clerks and carriers, who still worked long hours for low wages, was also a turn-of-the-century public concern. In 1902, President Roosevelt issued his infamous "gag order," which prohibited postal workers from lobbying Congress for better pay and conditions. Nevertheless, in 1907, the department's high turnover rate and slumping quality of service forced the government to give the clerks and carriers a raise. Much to management's dismay, postal workers had also begun to organize labor unions in what was now an industrial nation. In 1913, about sixty black RMS workers founded the National Alliance of Postal Employees, which would become the broader National Alliance of Postal and Federal Employees in 1965.

Not all of the era's postal workers were discontented. Postmasters who had begun their careers on the frontier wondered over the changes they'd seen and the pace of their institution's progress. When Joel Newson was appointed to serve in Azalia, Indiana, in 1862, the mail arrived just once a week and a letter took five days to reach Washington, D.C. Just thirty years later, the mail came twice daily, and a letter could reach the capital in twenty-seven hours. Even post offices in remote regions could attract talented personnel. D. S. Richardson, a Massachusetts native who served as an assistant postmaster in Santa Fe, became a correspondent for the *San Francisco Chronicle* in Mexico in 1874, then America's minister to Mexico between 1875 and 1876. He resumed working for the post, this time in San Francisco, interrupted by a stint as secretary to the city's Japanese consul. In his leisure time, Richardson wrote for many western periodicals. When a yellow fever epidemic broke out in the bustling postal-rail hub of Jacksonville, Florida, in 1888, Postmaster Harrison W. Clark was determined to maintain service despite the quarantine. It was thought at the time that contagion could be inhibited by dipping letters in vinegar, which incidentally turned black ink rosy, then slitting and fumigating them. Clark set up a station where the mail was perforated and smoked with sulfur for six hours and even sprinkled his post office floor with carbolic acid. Only one of his twenty-six clerks quit, though many got sick and two died.

The ranks of rural postmasters, which have included both northern abolitionist John Brown and southern writer William Faulkner, continued to harbor some eccentrics. E. P. Page, of Ingersol, Texas, precipitately left his position after his wife gave birth to quadruplets, then wanted his job back. He appealed to higher-ups in the post, then controlled by the Republican Party, on the grounds that although he was a Democrat, his four little girls might one day marry Republicans; he was reappointed. The editor of the local paper in one southern town caused a fracas when he criticized the postmaster in print for burying his dog in the family plot at the cemetery. An outraged citizen then dug up the pet on the grounds of sacrilege. The angry postmaster retaliated by calling the editor names, refusing to sell him enough stamps, and threatening to kick him out of the post office.

. . .

ONE INESCAPABLE ASPECT OF the post's history casts a dark shadow on its long golden age. The department had hired women and ethnic minorities, particularly African Americans, well before most other institutions, but the groups' jagged progress toward equal employment opportunity continued to reflect the larger culture's norms.

Women had made modest advances in securing postal jobs by the later nineteenth century, particularly in rural areas. Flora Hawes, of Hot Springs, Arkansas, a city of fifteen thousand, was one of the few allowed to run larger post offices, at least in less populous areas. Cushing describes her as an iron butterfly: "Though modest in manner, she is as determined as a queen. With her, to determine is to execute, and to plan is to accomplish." Of the country's some 67,000 postmasters around 1892, more than 6,000 were women, most of whom served in small country post offices. Cushing observes that some were "the most important persons in their towns" and commends their characteristic way of combining efficiency with "trying to please their patrons and the Department alike, and pleasing both because they try." Hattie Connors, postmaster of Sorrento, Maine, made that extra effort by sharing her musical talents, especially whistling with her fingers "unlike any other feminine artist." In the early 1890s, sixty-one female postmasters participated in conducting a massive survey of post offices ordered by Postmaster General Wanamaker. They included an Idahoan who did her three-hundred-mile inspection tour on horseback and a Mississippian who traveled mostly by sailboat.

By the early twentieth century, Postmaster General George Cortelyou could celebrate the pioneer "lady postmaster" who featured in the lore of the Wild West: "And yet while there are no monuments to her and while she has not been eulogized in Congress, she is very close to popular affections. The writers of romance weave their spells around her, and she figures in many American novels that have to do with real life." He took pains to point out that women were well suited for postal jobs, because "no part of the Government's work comes more in contact with the home and family than the postal service," and stressed that the department was exceeded only by the public schools as women's largest and best employer.

By that time, the ranks of postal employees also included 105 redoubtable female RFD carriers. Determined to help her parents raise a large family of girls, Viola Bennett, of Suwanee, Georgia, made headlines when she beat seven better-educated male applicants for the job in 1904; she was in the news again in 1906, when she narrowly escaped death on the job after her frightened horse overturned her buggy. Etta E. Bolton, an RFD carrier from Mobile, Alabama, won special praise for repeatedly wading to the rescue of her mailbags after a bridge collapsed, causing her carriage to fall into a river. On one occasion, a certain Miss Westman, the twenty-two-year-old daughter of the local stagecoach proprietor, encountered three bears on the trail while carrying the mail in the vicinity of Eugene, Oregon. She was thrown by her startled horse but remounted and completed her route without recourse to her revolver.

Despite their gains, particularly as rural postmasters, women still faced plenty of discrimination in the post. Federal law specifically authorized the heads of government departments to appoint female clerks in 1870, but only about a sixth as many women as men were called for interviews from the Civil Service Commission's list of candidates. Those who were chosen had limited opportunities for advancement and were routinely paid less. As Cushing put it, they "fill places where skill, diligence and tact are required . . . but they have not been put in places of command much yet, and many appointing officers who want clerks and especially stenographers and typewriters prefer men." Pittsburgh's fine new distributing post office, which handled sixty-five million pieces of mail in 1891 alone, appears to have been an exception in this regard. Its departments of registered letters and money orders were among its most efficient and were run and staffed by women, yet Cushing fails to name even their chief clerks. The omission is the more notable when contrasted with the detail lavished on Postmaster James

McKean by an unnamed journalist, whom Cushing quotes at length: "a Scotchman, a bachelor, fat, pleasant, rosy-cheeked, and . . . 'as sweet as a woman.'"

Married women confronted particular obstacles. In 1902, the *New York Times* reported many civil service employers, including the post, requested only male names from the registers of qualified applicants. By way of explanation, one official said, "Every time a woman is appointed to a clerkship in one of the departments she lessens the chances of marriage for herself and deprives some worthy man of the chance to take unto himself and raise a family." Postmaster General Henry Payne, who served in President Theodore Roosevelt's administration between 1902 and 1904, ordered that women employees who change their names by marriage would not be reappointed, adding that wives should "stay at home and attend to their household duties." This official bias against married women extended to 1921, when it was lifted by Postmaster General Will Hays, and was especially strong in cities, where large male workforces made women's services less essential.

The exigencies of frontier life that created opportunities for women, if only by default, also admitted some ethnic minorities into postal service. Francisco Perea, who served as the postmaster of Jemez Springs, New Mexico, between 1893 and 1904, belonged to a wealthy Hispanic family who had sent him to be educated by Jesuits in St. Louis. As a young man, he had been the bilingual interpreter in negotiations between local leaders and General Stephen Kearny, who led the Army into Santa Fe and seized New Mexico for the United States in 1846. Perea later became a successful merchant, served as a lieutenant colonel in the Union forces, and in 1863 became one of the first Latinos to be elected to Congress, where he fought for improvements to New Mexico's transportation and postal systems.

CONVENTIONAL WISDOM HAS IT that racism slowly but steadily declined after the end of slavery. In reality, following some progress during the Reconstruction era, prejudice surged again, peaking around 1900. The Republicans who dominated the White House after the Civil War had tried to use the spoils system to advance social justice as well as their own clout by giving postal jobs to their party's new African American members. In 1876, however, a very close, contentious election led Rutherford B. Hayes, the new Republican president, to placate the South's angry white Democrats by withdrawing the federal troops who had kept order after the war. This retreat ended the progress made during Reconstruction and emboldened racists to threaten and even assault African Americans who held enviable federal postal positions.

The sad coda to the exemplary career of Minnie Cox, the postmaster of Indianola, Mississippi, illustrates this dismal political and racial dynamic. The black graduate of Fisk University and fervent Republican was first appointed by Postmaster General Wanamaker in 1891. She and her husband, Wayne, a school principal and later an RMS clerk, were respected figures in the community, and the new postmaster was accepted at first. She was known to be kind as well as competent, even to the point of spending her own money to pay late post office box rental fees to install a phone for her three thousand customers' convenience.

Despite her ability and standing, white aspirants to her good federal job threatened Cox's life. The danger was real. In 1898, a mob had murdered Frazier Baker, the postmaster of Lake City, South Carolina, and his baby daughter. (Postal inspectors closed that town's post office and investigated the crime, but the accused killers were released after a jury failed to reach a unanimous verdict.) President Theodore Roosevelt, who wanted to use the post to combat racism, first refused to let Cox resign, but fearing for her safety, she left Indianola in 1903. Her story made national headlines along the lines of the *Cleveland Gazette*'s: "Mrs. Minnie Cox, Postmistress of Indianola—A Faithful and Efficient Official Driven from Office by Southern White Brutes."

African Americans' plight grew still worse during President Woodrow Wilson's administration (1913–1921). The Democratic champion of

Progressivism was also the first southern president since the Civil War. He feared jeopardizing the support of his party's regional base, but he also personally supported the Jim Crow laws that limited African Americans' rights as citizens, just as he opposed women's suffrage, Native American assimilation, and Asian immigration. In a shocking reversal of justice, his postmaster general Albert Burleson—a pompous, overdressed Texas politician known as "the Cardinal"—set about re-segregating the federal government. Beginning in 1914, applicants for civil service exams had to supply a photograph, supposedly for identification purposes, that made discrimination easier. Burleson not only tried to prevent the post from hiring African Americans in the first place but also fired and demoted many of those already employed. Black workers in the department's headquarters in Washington were hidden behind screens and forced to use separate dining rooms and bathrooms.

Because they shared the cars' close quarters with white coworkers, the black clerks in the Railway Mail Service were Burleson's particular obsession. Their situation had already worsened after the service switched to safer steel cars in 1913, which increased competition for the well-paid jobs. They were subjected to indignities and physical assault, and one man was even pulled off his train and killed. (Nevertheless, James Julian, whose parents had been born into slavery, held his hard-won RMS job for twenty-five difficult, dangerous years, and he and his wife, a teacher, were able to send their six children to college. Percy Julian, their firstborn, became a world-famous scientist who held some 130 chemical patents, and with a certain poetic justice, he was honored with his own stamp in 1993.)

In the end, the racist treatment of African American postal workers backfired. They continued to be highly respected within the black community; indeed, in 1895, ten of Frederick Douglass's pallbearers in Washington, D.C., were mail carriers. Moreover, the gross injustices they faced led black RMS clerks to form the powerful National

Alliance of Postal Employees, a labor union that would vigorously protest discrimination for decades. The Republican administrations that followed Wilson's ended the disgraceful effort to resegregate the government, and the post went on to add significant numbers of black employees.

BY THE HEADY YEAR OF 1913, the triumphant post and its civic mandate had reached their fullest expressions. Some of its greatest achievements during its zenith were particular boons for the long-underserved agrarian population, but other important advances benefited rural and urban Americans alike.

REDEFINING "POSTAL"

JUST AS THE POST in its golden age did much to develop rural America's physical and social landscape, it also contributed to the progressive City Beautiful movement, which flourished between 1890 and 1920. Its sponsors attempted to counter urban ugliness and squalor with grand architecture that glorified the public commons and fostered civic pride. The palatial new post offices designed for big cities combined beauty, utility, and grandeur to celebrate both the government's commitment to the people's good and the Post Office Department's importance to civic life. No less than Egyptian pyramids or French cathedrals, these heroic American buildings illustrate an institution's peak and a culture's moment in time.

Like the new national parks, the buildings of the City Beautiful movement were aesthetic antidotes to the Industrial Revolution's environmental toxins. Rapid, unplanned urban growth had produced densely populated slums crammed with smoky factories and pestilent tenements, which cast a pall on the quality of life for rich and poor alike. With a largeness of spirit and purpose now almost unimaginable, an idealistic group of civic leaders, philanthropists, and architects, including Daniel Burnham and Frederick Law Olmsted, decided to combat this blight with an "American Renaissance." No less than Boston's Copley Square library, New York City's Metropolitan Museum, and San Francisco's Civic Center, the magnificent new post offices that became the vibrant cores of many cities and towns were among the movement's most impressive achievements.

The precedent for grand post offices had been set much earlier by the department's own stately headquarters in the General Post Office building in Washington, D.C., which Andrew Jackson had commissioned from architect Robert Mills. The elegant Palladian structure, which was expanded between 1855 and 1866, had become a major attraction for proud American tourists. As *Harper's New Monthly Magazine* put it, "We doubt if there is a building in the world more chaste and architecturally perfect than the General Post-Office as now completed." Nevertheless, by 1890, the department had outgrown Mills's masterpiece and overflowed into five rented buildings. In 1899, it moved to much larger quarters in what's now called the Old Post Office building. The huge pile designed in the Romanesque Revival style was no match for its predecessor in aesthetic terms, but its size and soaring clock tower, second in height only to the Washington Monument, proudly proclaimed the post's status.

After the war, Americans were more comfortable with heroic federal structures outside of Washington. The Treasury's Office of Construction, esteemed for its custom houses, began a major building binge. By the later nineteenth century, the post had established major regional headquarters throughout the nation that were housed in grand buildings of their own. Large "first class" postal palaces sprang up in Albany, Little Rock, St. Louis, and other regional centers to serve as vital communications and information hubs in America's booming, business-oriented economy. Politicians in both parties supported the splurge on these opulent buildings, which enabled them to brag about the fancy facilities they had secured for their constituents.

As the department increased the number and range of its services, postal architecture became a form unto itself. These huge, lavishly embellished, government-owned buildings resembled chateaus or citadels and were located in the best part of town. They had to be easily identifiable, as were Ammi Young's similar designs for Galveston, Richmond, and Cleveland, but they also had to have the distinguishing characteristics that local pride demanded. The dormers, rounded arches, heavy masonry, and square tower of architect Mifflin Bell's vast General Post Office and Federal Building in Brooklyn, New York—then a prosperous independent city—say "castle." The interior of this gem of the Richardsonian Romanesque Revival style, built between 1885 and 1892, is embellished with luxurious details, including carved fireplaces, marble floors, and wainscoting; the beautiful atrium is surrounded by a three-level loggia whose cast-iron columns are decorated with classical acanthus leaves and anthemion palmettes. Around the same time, Bell also designed a Romanesque Revival post office for remote Carson City, Nevada. Then the state's second federal building, this frontier post office is more modest than its regal Brooklyn relative, yet it was à la mode, took up an entire city block, and featured the town's first clock tower, which soared 106 feet above the ground.

THE PROGRESSIVE ERA'S postal architecture also had to accommodate new functions that stretched the traditional meaning of "postal" itself. Since the days of Thomas Jefferson and Andrew Jackson, many Americans had been suspicious of banks, and at the turn of the twentieth century, millions of rural people and urban immigrants alike still stowed their money under a mattress or a loose brick. The big banks were just as uninterested in these humble depositors, and many smaller ones were either uninsured or unreliable to the point of failure. Philadelphia and a few other cities had philanthropic "savings banks," and ever since Postmaster General Creswell's efforts in 1873, Congress had received periodic proposals to expand such services. Postmaster General Wanamaker had more recently used the financial precedent of the widely trusted postal money order service to argue for providing average folk with safe, government-backed postal banking. However, legislators had continued to respond to pressure from a banking lobby wary of any government competition by consigning the idea to death by committee.

As happened with RFD, public pressure fueled by Progressive ideology finally forced the government to authorize postal savings banking. Both political parties supported the policy at their conventions in 1908, and a year later, President William Howard Taft advanced a good Republican argument: the service would not just encourage thrift and otherwise benefit the people but also get more cash into circulation—particularly the many millions of dollars that immigrants sent back to their banks in "the old country" each year. The big banks still huffed that the very idea was unconstitutional, but in 1910, Congress authorized certain post offices outside the big cities to serve as savings depositories.

Partly to appease the banking industry, the Postal Savings System was designed for Americans of modest means, particularly those in areas that were underserved by banks. Customers could start an account with $1 but could not invest more than $500, later raised to $2,500. They received 2 percent interest, which not coincidentally pressured private banks to raise their own rate to 3 percent. (Even children could have accounts, and married women could open accounts under their own names that were not subject to their husbands' control.) The program also benefited the government, which invested the deposits in local banks at 2.5 percent and used the profit to cover related costs. The service was slow to catch on at first, but by the early days of the Great Depression, more than $300 million had been deposited in postal savings, which, unlike deposits in private banks, was backed by the full faith and credit of the United States. The program service had an educational benefit as well, because it helped to familiarize average Americans with finance and ultimately made them savvier consumers of commercial banking services.

In 1913, the government authorized another radical extension of "postal" to include binding the nation with things as well as information. RFD had established the precedent for providing rural folk—still the majority of the population—with better connections to mainstream society, and they soon wanted more. First on their list of demands was better access to the national market and the consumer goods churned out by the nation's new mass manufacturers, which their small general stores either didn't carry or overcharged for. England had inaugurated its Parcel Post service in 1883, and the U.S. post had begun to transport large packages across international borders in 1887. Much to Americans' dismay, however, domestic parcels that weighed more than four pounds still had to be carried by private express companies, such as Wells Fargo and American Express. They established regional monopolies able to command steep fees and opposed competition from a postal parcel service. (Like the post riders before them, many RFD carriers earned extra income by unofficially toting packages to the homes on their routes.)

Americans' voluble demand for modern merchandise delivered for fair prices was amplified by an explosive business phenomenon. The mail-order catalog per se wasn't entirely new—Benjamin Franklin printed one to sell academic books back in 1744—but Aaron Montgomery Ward took the concept to hitherto unimaginable heights. The midwestern blue-collar boy and former traveling salesman understood firsthand how the monopolies enjoyed by the private carriers and the general stores affected rural people. In 1872, he offered them the convenience of both ordering and receiving goods at home and the lower prices made possible by eliminating the middlemen between him and his customers. By the 1890s, his revolutionary "Monkey Ward" catalogs ran to more than five hundred pages and offered some twenty thousand items, from mirrors to dolls, sewing machines to kit houses. In 1893, his competitors Richard Warren Sears and Alvah Roebuck, who shared a similarly down-to-earth, midwestern perspective, put out their own ambitious catalog, soon known as "the consumer's bible."

Industrial America's new material culture lacked only one element to become nationwide: the cheap delivery of goods. The debate over

Parcel Post, like many during the Progressive Era, cast into high relief the dual and often dueling ethics of business and government, of doing well and doing good. As *Harper's Weekly* pointed out, "Express companies extend their business wherever it promises to pay. The Post-office extends its operations wherever there are settlers." The express carriers, railroads, and country shopkeepers vehemently disagreed with this Progressive attitude and sicced their lobbyists on Congress to fight against Parcel Post. C. A. Hutsinpillar, an Ohio merchant, spoke for those interests: "The effect of such a law is beyond the calculation of man, and almost beyond his contemplation. It would certainly revolutionize the whole system of business, and would be the death knell of retail houses generally, and in a measure the depopulating of towns and villages, the natural effect of destroying the retail business." Many Americans, however, especially in rural regions, agreed with James L. Cowles, a social reformer and founder of the Postal Progress League, who declared the post to be the sine qua non of American liberty and "our great cooperative express company, our only possible agency for the cheapest, most prompt, and most efficient collection, transportation, and delivery of the products of industry."

Just as it had with RFD and postal savings banking, Congress stalled on authorizing Parcel Post—and antagonizing the corporate donors that lobbied against it—by conducting endless debates. Finally, the public's ire over reports of the huge dividends reaped by the express companies' stockholders—as much as 300 percent from Wells Fargo—seemingly at the public's expense forced the government to authorize the service. In 1913, Parcel Post began delivering packages weighing up to eleven pounds for low rates nationwide. More than two decades after John Wanamaker had advanced the cause, he was given the honor of mailing one of the first packages.

Parcel Post was a phenomenal success and remains a powerful counter to the argument that private industry always serves Americans better than the government. Almost overnight, the high-priced express companies were consigned to carrying heavy freight and providing financial services. Parcel Post delivered more than 300 million packages in its first six months, causing some post offices to rent extra space, and Sears's orders quintupled during the first year. Suddenly, rural Americans who needed a new bed or table, dress or shirt, didn't have to overpay or make it themselves; moreover, they could have the same model as residents of Boston or Chicago. Participants in the Farm-to-Table program, which lasted from 1914 until the end of World War I, "mailed" their fresh vegetables, eggs, cheeses, and other products to urban customers by rail. (Cartoons showed post offices equipped with holding pens for pigs and sheep.) College students used specially designed cases to mail their dirty shirts back home to Mother for laundering. A bank in Vernal, Utah, even constructed the façade of its new two-story building from pressed bricks sent via Parcel Post in batches from Salt Lake City, some 150 miles away. As Clyde Kelly later put it, the post had become the greatest distributing organization on earth.

THE POWERFUL POST INAUGURATED innovative services, such as RFD, Parcel Post, and the Postal Savings System, but it also continued to update and enlarge upon its original mission of circulating news and information for a now better educated, more sophisticated people. This amplification had begun back in 1851 and '52, when daily as well as weekly papers could circulate within their counties of origin for free, postage for periodicals was lowered to the same rate as newspapers, and hardcover books were finally admitted to the mail. Then, in 1863, Postmaster General Montgomery Blair had simplified the pricing system by categorizing the mail into first-class letters, second-class publications such as newspapers and magazines, and third-class advertisements, hardcover books, and other miscellaneous printed matter. By 1870, Ralph Waldo Emerson could laud the post for its "educating energy augmented by cheapness, and guarded by a certain religious sentiment in mankind, so that the power of a wafer or a drop of wax or gluten to guard a letter, as it flies over sea, over land, and comes to its address as if a battalion of artillery brought it, I look upon as a fine meter of civilization."

As the nineteenth century progressed, Americans especially wanted more magazines, whose format was better able to satisfy their thirst for different kinds of knowledge. Members of the prosperous new bourgeoisie were curious about the great world beyond provincial borders. Rural people were eager to stay abreast of the latest trends. The swelling ranks of immigrants wanted to master the rudiments of their adopted culture. These groups still needed newspapers, but they also wanted more comprehensive coverage of subjects from the distant realms explored by the new *National Geographic* to the new science of home economics to the proper observance of national holidays.

An indulgent Congress responded by subsidizing what amounted to an informal nationwide educational system based on second-class mail. A series of laws passed between 1874 and 1885 made the already inexpensive delivery of newspapers and magazines even cheaper by calculating postage on weight rather than on a per-piece basis; the very low initial charge of two cents per pound was soon dropped to one cent. The circulation of second-class materials quadrupled, from almost 70 million pounds in 1881 to some 312 million pounds in 1895. In exchange for this bonanza, publishers had to prepay postage at the post office where their materials were mailed, rather than shifting the burden to customers at the receiving end—an obligation often previously ignored.

The post's subsidization of second-class publications fueled the growth of magazine publishing, which surged from six hundred titles in 1850 to more than five thousand in 1900, which in turn helped support the new advertising industry. The manufacturers of popular new brands, such as Campbell's Soup and Lipton Tea, were no longer satisfied with amateurish promotions placed in local newspapers. By the 1870s, they were paying for truly professional, nationwide ad campaigns in magazines.

Americans were captivated by advertising's catchy slogans, such as "You Press the Button, We Do the Rest" for Kodak's camera and

"99 and 44/100% Pure" for Ivory soap. Women made 80 percent of household purchases, and the male editors of the new *Ladies Home Journal* and *Good Housekeeping*, as well as the venerable *Godey's Lady's Book*, eagerly sold ad space to manufacturers that wanted to target these major consumers. By the 1890s, aided by the post, the publishing and advertising industries were vigorously stimulating each other's growth, and by 1910, magazines were almost as likely to be found in middle-class homes as newspapers.

To qualify for the favorable second-class postage rate, publications had to meet certain criteria. They had to balance commercial content with worthy information and maintain a list of legitimate subscribers, a headquarters, and a regular publishing schedule; material in cloth or board bindings was unacceptable. Previously, determining what was or was not a legitimate type of mail had mostly been left to the discretion of individual postmasters. Now, however, these new rules obliged the department to undertake the task of inspection, which was complicated by the efforts of wily publishers. Hardcover books were consigned to the more expensive third class, so some companies churned out softbacked pulp thrillers and weepers that could qualify for the cheaper rate. Others produced "magazines" that were little more than advertorials.

Some Americans questioned whether the government should be subsidizing what amounted to sleazy advertising supplements and serialized sagas, such as *The Wolves of New York* and *Wild West Weekly*, which had flooded the mail as an unanticipated result of the second-classpostage reforms. James Britt, an assistant postmaster general and lawyer, even argued that periodicals should pay *higher* rather than lower postage, maintaining that the rate of 1 cent per pound introduced in 1885 led to a flood of materials "so trashy and wishy-washy . . . that they scarcely deserve to be mentioned in connection with respectable literature."

Publishers feared that Congress would raise their second-class rate and vigorously defended their right to low postage by maintaining that their publications contributed to the market's growth and, in some cases, to the Progressive Era's reform-minded culture. The windfall of ad revenue helped to pay for more elaborate articles, including the new in-depth, investigative reporting that appeared in *McClure's* and other journals that specialized in what President Theodore Roosevelt called muckraking: exposés of political and corporate corruption, from the dismal conditions in urban ghettoes to the abuses of Standard Oil and U.S. Steel. Wilmer Atkinson, the founder of the *Farm Journal*, cast the industry's self-interested concerns in high-minded terms: "As long as the people get the benefit of the low rate, as they are doing now . . . it matters not much what the rate is except that it should be kept at the very bottom notch."

By 1891, the popular essayist Edward Everett Hale felt justified in declaring that the post was the "most majestic system of public education which was ever set on foot anywhere." All Americans benefited from the increased access to information, but once again, particularly those in rural regions. As Congressman A. F. Lever of South Carolina put it, postal service had become "a great university in which 36 million of our people receive their daily lessons from the newspapers and magazines of the country. It is the schoolhouse of the American farmers, and is without a doubt one of the most potent educational factors of the time."

THE POST'S INFORMAL educational system was a great public service, but the huge increase in second-class mail also had a dark side. The department staggered under the torrent of printed matter that Congress had obliged it to deliver regardless of cost and ran big deficits. Moreover, the same laws that protected the security and privacy of America's mail also shielded criminals who used second-class material to perpetrate fraud and extortion. (The expression "sold me the goods" refers to "green goods," or counterfeit money, which con artists often sent via the post.) Theft continued to be the most common crime, but with the passage of the Mail Fraud Act in 1872, postal inspectors also increasingly pursued vendors of quack remedies and perpetrators of lonely-hearts schemes, real estate scams, and other dubious solicitations for payment, including chain letters, which count as lotteries and are thus illegal to mail.

It took more than offers of shares in phantom gold mines or tonics for bad nerves, however, to ignite the nation's second major controversy over postal content and censorship. Congress passed a law in 1842 that prohibited importing obscene materials from abroad and another, in 1865, that banned the mailing of such things. Following the Civil War and the popularization of photography, the second-class mail included an increasing amount of pornography—a notable Victorian enthusiasm. Anthony Comstock, a governessy former dry-goods clerk who became a postal special agent and founder of the New York Society for the Suppression of Vice, convinced Congress that the post was being used to promote degeneracy. The evidence ranged from racy books and pictures delivered to boarding schools to surprisingly available "feminine hygiene aids," such as condoms, pessaries, and abortifacients, that had been mail-ordered even by seemingly respectable women.

The Postal Obscenity Statute that Congress passed in 1873 made it a crime to use the post to transport "Obscene Literature and Articles of Immoral Use." This so-called Comstock Law had the support of evangelicals, the YMCA, and Americans who clung to the old-fashioned, agrarian values that they perceived to be endangered by industrialization and urbanization. Antagonists included the members of the Free Love Movement and advocates of birth control. (The law ultimately helped to cast the hush-hush subject of contraception as a legitimate medical and social issue.) Comstock's personal critics included George Bernard Shaw, whose play *Mrs. Warren's Profession* had been deemed obscene. The author responded by declaring that "Comstockery is the world's standing joke at the expense of the United States. . . . It confirms the deep-seated conviction of the Old World that America is a provincial place, a second-rate country-town civilization after all." Comstock's riposte was to call the distinguished playwright and cofounder of the London School of Economics an "Irish smut dealer."

The Comstock Law notwithstanding, Congress had always been wary of interfering with freedom of speech and the mail, and it mostly resisted further efforts to strengthen anti-obscenity laws. In 1892, the Supreme Court ruled that banning certain printed matter, such as lottery materials, from the post did not prevent its publication and thus was not censorship. Yet Congress remained sympathetic to the sentiments expressed in an essay called "Our Despotic Postal Censorship" by social reformer Louis Post: "Shall the right to mail service in the United States, now become a necessity of the common life, depend upon the caprice, the bigotry or the corruptibility of one man at the head of a Washington department or his subordinate at the head of a bureau? . . . What has Congress to say?" Their relative silence suggests that the legislators agreed with Emerson: "Good men must not obey the laws too well."

As with any enterprise, the post's status reflects its customers' satisfaction, and in bustling late-nineteenth-century America, the department strove to please with new products. Correspondents who hadn't mastered the formal letter as well as businessmen who wanted a quick, cheap way to communicate with customers had welcomed the pre-franked penny postcards that the forward-looking Creswell had introduced in 1873, twenty years after prefranked envelopes. Some thirty-one million of the cards—the stationery equivalent of the new shorthand writing—were sold in the first seven weeks. Then, around the turn of the century, independently produced picture postcards took the simple form to another level and generated a new mainstream hobby as well as postal revenue from stamps.

If their plain predecessors were about efficiency, the colorful new postcards were about the pleasures of preserving a memory and sharing it with others. Iconic scenes of Old Faithful and Niagara Falls celebrated the wonders of long-distance travel, which, though not easy, was easier than it had been before the transcontinental railroad.

Humbler cards documented small-town Americans' pride in their new hotels, fairgrounds, and paved, electric-lit main streets. Still others, such as drawings of Victorian ladies careering about in hot-air balloons, were meant to amuse, as were those that stooped to crude ethnic caricature. That the postcard craze peaked in the first decade of the twentieth century helped the department recover from the deficits produced by RFD and other new services.

American stamps had previously been "regular" or "definitive," meaning that they were intended for ongoing use, and they accordingly depicted timeless subjects, notably portraits of presidents and other great national figures. The innovative Postmaster General Wanamaker dramatically changed this staid tradition in 1893 with the debut of "commemorative" stamps, which were meant for short-term use and designed to tell patriotic stories or mark important recent events. (A year later, the U.S. Treasury's Bureau of Engraving and Printing took over the production of stamps from private contractors.) The first commemorative celebrated the "World's Fair: Columbian Exposition," which was held in Chicago in 1893 to mark the four-hundredth anniversary of Columbus's arrival in the New World.

The handsome commemoratives were an immediate sensation in an America just coming into its own as a global power. Politicians liked the idea of using postage to communicate the country's history and values, especially to new immigrants who couldn't read English. Postal executives were pleased that some of the appealing stamps were kept rather than used, which generated revenue at little or no cost. Philatelists were especially delighted with the affordable little works of art, which attracted new enthusiasts and made narrative a compelling principle for organizing a collection.

Many experts consider "Western Cattle in Storm," the crown jewel of the early commemoratives, to be the most beautiful engraved stamp ever made. The image of a great black bull leading his herd through a snowstorm's near-whiteout, dramatically framed by intricate filigree, was issued in 1898 to honor the Midwest's ascendancy in general and the Trans-Mississippi & International Exposition in Omaha, Nebraska, in particular. The ranchers of the Great Plains surely related to the depiction of livestock coping with ferocious weather, but they would have been surprised to learn that the seemingly local scene was based on a similarly rugged part of Scotland.

IF THERE'S A PHYSICAL SYMBOL of what the combination of the post at its peak, the mighty railroad, and the Progressive Era's politics had achieved by the early twentieth century, it must be the James A. Farley Post Office, in New York City. (First known as the Pennsylvania Terminal, then the General Post Office Building, it was later renamed for President Franklin Roosevelt's powerful postmaster general.) This treasure of the City Beautiful movement, built in 1912 by the prestigious architectural firm of McKim, Mead, and White, proclaims itself to be the epicenter of the busiest, most important city in the United States—perhaps the world. The building sprawls across two full blocks of prime Manhattan real estate, on Eighth Avenue between 31st and 33rd Streets; its five stories wrap around a great central courtyard that flooded its work spaces with glorious natural light. The unbroken front stairs run the entire length of the façade and lead up to a spectacular gold-embellished lobby that would have gratified Louis XIV.

The Farley is one of America's most beautiful post offices and also its most famous. The grand façade is engraved with what's often mistakenly assumed to be the post's motto: "Neither snow nor rain nor heat nor gloom of night stays these couriers from the swift completion of their appointed rounds." (The quotation, paraphrased from Herodotus, is appropriate enough, but the post has no official maxim, and the "couriers" referred to in the original text were the Persian empire's.) The building was also the architectural costar, along with the nearby Macy's department store, in the classic 1947 holiday film *Miracle on 34th Street*, which was based on the thesis that the Santa Claus on trial must be real because New York City's august post office—and thus the federal government—delivered children's letters to him. (The labyrinthine building is also said to have been an inspiration for Terry Pratchett's noir novel *Going Postal*.) Until 2009, the Farley had the distinction of being the only post office in the nation that was open twenty-four hours a day, every day of the week.

Like some other great post offices of the era, the Farley was built as the companion of an equally magnificent railroad terminal across the street. (The original Pennsylvania Station building was tragically demolished in 1963 to create the ugly, dysfunctional Madison Square Garden.) Locating major mail facilities next to, or on top of, the new "union" stations that merged the tracks of a city's various rail lines increased postal efficiency by enabling Railway Post Office cars to be loaded and unloaded without delay. The grand post office that Daniel Burnham designed for Washington, D.C., which is now the home of the National Postal Museum, is similarly located just across the street from his Union Station. Although Chicago handled about a sixth of the nation's mail and was a major rail hub—and therefore an airline hub later—its Old Main Post Office lacked this vital connection with a train terminal, which compromised its efficiency long before its famous crisis in the 1960s.

The Farley was a world unto itself, complete with its own carpenters, electricians, nurses, and cooks. The city's mail volume required at least two thousand employees to be on the job at any one time. The vast work area behind the elegant lobby hummed with hundreds of clerks sorting the mail sent up from the rail tracks below; to get the job in such a big city, they had to be able to process at least a hundred addresses in five to six minutes with very few errors. The building provided them, the big corps of letter carriers, and other employees with lockers, lunchrooms, and amenities including an elaborate ventilation system that rid the air of dust, horse manure, and detritus that clung to mailbags. Postal crime was a major concern in the nation's financial capital, and the building was equipped with safes, a barred, room-size vault, and even a jail; inspectors on the lookout for theft prowled unseen on windowed walkways concealed in ceilings.

The Farley's executive suite, illuminated by floor-to-ceiling windows running along the great eastern façade, was as grand as the headquarters of the era's richest robber baron. The gorgeous reception room opened onto a conference room to the right and a secretary's office to the left, which in turn led to the postmaster's inner sanctum, complete with a white marble fireplace, four huge chandeliers, and a full bath. These swanky rooms were linked by interior doors that protected top postal executives from mingling with the rank and file, but in keeping with the era's Progressive politics, the Farley's utilitarian spaces were dignified by high-quality materials, custom hardware, and beautifully designed staircases.

Even the most junior of the Farley's hundreds of clerks or thousands of daily visitors could not have missed the architectural message sent by the post at its peak: being an American is a very fine thing, and so too is this great public institution. As Clyde Kelly, one of its powerful members, wrote, "Congress was building on the policy that the paramount duty of the Post Office Establishment is to furnish the most useful facilities that the mind of man can provide, at charges which will lead to the widest possible use, through workers who are assured fair play and working conditions."

14

STARVING THE POST

 LIKE INDIVIDUALS, societies respond to changes in the environment with changes in behavior. By 1920, powerful political, social, and economic forces had shifted mainstream America's mood from the Progressive Era's expansive extroversion and idealistic view of government toward a fractious introversion and skepticism of President Woodrow Wilson's reforms and exalted rhetoric. In 1917, he had drawn the United States into World War I in order to make the world "safe for democracy," but that bloodbath had produced little but barbarism abroad and disillusionment at home. His oracular pronouncements—"You are not here to make a living. . . . You are here to enrich the world"—no longer resonated with working people after his economic policies contributed to high inflation and violent strikes in 1919 and a recession in 1920. During this time of heightened tensions, millions of European immigrants and rural blacks flocked to the big industrial cities in search of employment, which increased competition for jobs. The "Red Scare" set off by the Russian Revolution of 1917 fueled suspicion of alleged socialists and anarchists. This tumult in urban America added to the general sense that the federal government, so recently widely admired, could no longer seem to control events at home, much less abroad.

The antigovernment sentiment even extended to the post, long its most popular enterprise. The department offered a stunning array of cheap, excellent services, now including Rural Free Delivery, Parcel Post, and Postal Savings, and during the war, it had made heroic efforts to get the troops' mail overseas by ship. The post had lost personnel to the military, however, and suffered from war-related problems with the railroads that compromised domestic mail service. Periodic congressional investigations of its finances had also drawn attention to its high transportation expenses. As usual, no one could figure out the exact cost of moving the mail, but there was general agreement that the railroads' compensation was suspiciously high; one report showed that the companies charged the post five times what they charged other freight customers.

In 1916, a Congress now fixated on the department's costs authorized like-minded Postmaster General Albert Burleson to pay the railroads on the basis of the space the mail required rather than on its weight. This change, along with his decision to reduce rail-mail mileage, significantly cut the post's costs, and the next year, Burleson went further. Taking on the powerful publishing lobby, he orchestrated the first true increase on postage for periodicals since the 1790s. The Democrats' strenuous efforts to report a surplus also worsened postal service, however, which further soured public opinion and gave Republicans a potent campaign issue.

America's shift toward favoring business over government was writ large in an important legislative decision that ended a policy debate that had bridged two centuries. In 1918, Wilson and Burleson had taken control of the telegraph and the telephone, along with the railroads, as a wartime measure, in hopes that this step would lead to securing the communications services permanently for the post. The war had temporarily increased the two systems' volume, operating expenses, and charges, however, which cast an unflattering if unfair light on the government's management abilities. Private enterprise, which had opposed the postal telegraph since the 1840s, now had the advantage over the equally enduring forces asserting that Americans were better served when the government ran the nation's communications. In 1919, Congress reflected the national mood by finally settling the question and returning the telegraph, along with the telephone, to private control.

If the post sometimes suffered unjustly from the antigovernment backlash, it was also tarnished by its involvement in the wave of xenophobia sweeping the nation. The Espionage Act of 1917, passed during World War I, made it a crime to "willfully utter, print, write, or publish any disloyal, profane, scurrilous, or abusive language about the form of the Government of the United States." To the dismay of the First Amendment's defenders, Burleson ordered local postmasters to hand over any suspicious pamphlets, magazines, or antiwar materials they encountered; he also used the law to try to put dissident publications out of business by refusing to circulate them in the mail. Authorized to censor foreign communications as well, the postmaster general set 1,600 monitors to opening some 125,000 pieces of mail from abroad each day in search of "socialistic," antiwar, and pro-union matter. In 1917, even Christmas gifts to American troops abroad were opened, inspected, and repacked before shipment. (The postal censorship imposed during the war was discontinued soon after the armistice in 1918.)

The fear of danger lurking in the mail, though disproportional, was not entirely unfounded. In April 1919, thirty-six bombs designed to explode on the Communist holiday of May Day had been mailed to prominent American politicians and business titans. The Department of Justice responded to these grave crimes with the so-called Palmer Raids, named for their leader, U.S. Attorney General A. Mitchell Palmer, a presidential contender and mentor of the young J. Edgar Hoover. Agents conducted warrantless searches, tampered with mail, and arrested thousands of people on the mere suspicion of treason. Hundreds of citizens were convicted, and hundreds of foreigners were deported. The Palmer Raids proved to be unpopular, however, and were ended in 1920 by strong opposition from political liberals, the press, and the Department of Labor, which was in charge of deportations.

The war had been a tremendous stimulus to American industry, and pro-business sentiment swept Republican Warren G. Harding into the White House in 1921. The new president was a folksy Ohioan whose "front porch" campaign had promised to put an end to federal controls, public unrest, and Wilsonian philosophizing. He guaranteed a return to "normalcy," based not on "heroics, but healing . . . not revolution, but restoration; not agitation, but adjustment . . . not experiment, but equipoise; not submergence in internationality, but sustainment in triumphant nationality." This new credo asserted that America's future lay with the private sector and an enthusiastic embrace of mechanization, technology, and efficiency. The Progressive politics of social reform gave way to the "business progressivism" personified by Thomas Edison and by Henry Ford, the father of the industrial assembly line. Government's role was no longer to lead but to cooperate with private enterprise or get out of the way.

In a momentous if little remarked upon change, some legislators and even some of the department's own managers began to drift away from the broad historical understanding of the post as an almost open-ended public service and began to recast it as a business. Instead of thinking in terms of what the post could next do for the people, officials grew preoccupied with increasing its revenue and reducing its deficits. In 1929, Postmaster General Walter Brown, appointed by Republican president Herbert Hoover, reflected this change by flatly stating that the post was simply a business whose narrow purpose was the profitable transmission of first-class letters. (When the press gleefully discovered that the postmaster general had ordered a special government limousine that enabled him to get in and out without removing his top hat, "High Hat" Brown soon became a symbol of Republican elitism amid the Depression.)

Some in government did not accede to this diminution of the postal mandate, notably Republican congressman Clyde Kelly, a force on the Committee on Post Offices and Post Roads, and a progressive defender of public service and postal innovation. To him, the department's deficit was an investment in the nation's future prosperity: "The great postal highway of the United States is the people's thoroughfare, the main artery of the nation's life. It was not built in a day or a generation, nor is its task finished today, but its record in the past is the inspiring promise of its betterment in the future." Kelly took particular exception to Brown's attempt to redefine the post as a mere business for transporting letters, calling it instead a "great adventure in human service." He reminded Americans that historically, whether Republicans or Democrats controlled the White House or Congress, "the Post Office has been used in new ways for the promotion of the general welfare. . . . When new conditions arose where additional benefits could be extended through this nationwide enterprise, there was no hesitation in following the path of national progress." Nothing illustrated Kelly's assertion more vividly than the post's new Air/Mail Service, which he championed.

LONG BEFORE THE TERM "business progressivism" was coined, the post's subsidies had supported independent carriers from stagecoach proprietors to railroad moguls, but of all these contributions, its often single-handed support of the aviation industry from 1918 into the 1940s stands out as the most remarkable. As Kelly observed, "The greatest single difference between America and other countries is that America has discovered the importance of saving time." Postal executives since Benjamin Franklin had been obsessed with speeding up the mail and were quick to seize on flight's potential in that regard; in 1856, the American balloonist John Wise had carried the first official U.S. mail by air across thirty miles of Indiana.

When Orville and Wilbur Wright made history at Kitty Hawk, North Carolina, in 1903, even the fastest train still took four and a half days to travel coast to coast. Postal management saw that the new aeroplane was the ultimate mail carrier, but to put it mildly, there were major obstacles to realizing that dream. America had no aviation industry to fulfill transportation contracts and none of the infrastructure, from airports to runways to searchlights, that would allow for flight on a large scale. Other than entertaining the crowds at air shows, planes themselves didn't seem to have much utility, much less airmail.

Postmaster General Frank Harris Hitchcock, an energetic, progressive Republican politician and aviation enthusiast who served from 1909 to 1913, was nevertheless eager to run the experiment. In 1911, he appointed Earle Ovington to be the post's first official "aeroplane mail carrier" and paid the pilot a dollar from his own wallet to seal the deal. During a weeklong aviation meet, Ovington boarded the *Dragonfly*, his monoplane, settled the mailbag on his lap, and did daily six-mile round-trips from Garden City, on New York's Long Island, to nearby Mineola. On the first day, he tossed the bag to the ground from an altitude of five hundred feet, whereupon it broke and spewed the contents. In the best postal tradition, the letters and postcards were quickly retrieved and delivered to the recipients.

World War I provided a showcase for demonstrating the new airplane's potential, at least for military purposes. Congress remained skeptical but nevertheless authorized an airmail trial, conducted by the post and the Army, between New York City and Washington, D.C. The plane selected to launch what was first called the U.S. Aerial Mail Service in 1918 was the Curtiss JN-4 single-engine biplane. The light, fragile "Jenny," constructed largely of wood and cloth, had been designed to train pilots for warfare, not to transport cargo; its interior was tiny, and its small 150-horsepower engine could only travel at 66 miles per hour for 175 miles before refueling. Damning the Jenny with faint praise, Army pilot Ernest M. Allison said that it was "a very safe airplane, because the carburetor would vibrate the airplane so badly that it would shake the ice off the wings."

Something of the sheer zaniness of aviation's early days, when daredevil barnstormers and their stunts drew crowds to fairgrounds across the nation, comes across in accounts of the Aerial Mail Service's northbound kickoff on May 15. President Wilson, Postmaster General Burleson, Assistant Secretary of the Navy Franklin D. Roosevelt, Admiral Robert Peary, Alexander Graham Bell, and many other dignitaries gathered to watch Lieutenant George L. Boyle, a socially well-connected if newly fledged Army pilot, take off with the mail. After a twenty-minute delay, someone realized that the Jenny had no gas. After it finally departed, the unfortunate Boyle got lost, heading south instead of north because he had followed the wrong set of train tracks out of Washington. In hopes of getting his bearings, he landed the plane in a field, breaking the propeller in the process. When his second attempt the next day ended with a crash on a Philadelphia golf course, he was sent back to flight school. The service's southbound flight from New York City, however, was a success.

The hapless young aviator's northbound debacle was partly excused by the early planes' technology or, rather, the lack of it. Pilots flew in open, deafeningly noisy cockpits in all weather, protected only by a pair of goggles and clothing made of wind-resistant leather and warm fur. Their compasses were unreliable, and they had no other navigational instruments, much less radios, airports, or control towers. They mostly relied on "dead reckoning," gauging their position by estimating the direction and distance they'd traveled, and on "contact flying"— looking down at the terrain below for landmarks, such as towns, rivers, or the "iron compass" of railroad tracks—which in bad weather might require a descent to a mere forty feet above the ground.

To pilot Slim Lewis, the instrument panel was "just something to clutter up the cockpit and distract your attention from the railroad or riverbed you're following." Some aviators developed their own eccentric technology, such as using a lit cigar to time a route or a half-empty whiskey bottle as a flight level indicator. Coping with the aircrafts' frequent mechanical glitches and crashes also required ingenuity. When a major hailstorm that pierced his flimsy plane with some three hundred holes forced Clifton P. "Ole" Oleson to land in a field, he patched the rips with dish towels soaked in egg whites donated by a farmer's wife, then took off for his destination.

In August 1918, the post took over airmail operations from the military, and the department's own civilian pilots began to fly its own biplanes, which were either custom-built or remodeled for postal service. (De Havilland's DH-4, which had a more powerful 400-horsepower engine, superseded the Jenny as the fleet's workhorse.) Much like Pony riders, the aviators were expected to satisfy their employer's obsessions with speed and sticking to the schedule regardless of conditions. They raced their finicky, flimsy, unreliable aircraft through dense fogs, blizzards, and towering mountain ranges, protected mostly by the small planes' responsiveness and slow speeds. Of the two hundred pilots who belonged to the service's "suicide club" between 1918 and 1926, thirty-five died on duty, but many more emerged bloody and battered from crashes.

Somehow, the Air Mail Service managed to complete 90 percent of its flights, although emergency landings were common. Pilot Dean Smith telegraphed a cryptic explanation to headquarters after his engine quit in midair, causing an unusual disaster: "Only place to land on cow. Killed cow. Wrecked plane. Scared me. Smith." While carrying the mail from Elko, Nevada, to Boise, Idaho, Paul Scott was forced to land by a broken oil line; then, followed by a pack of wolves, he walked twenty-seven miles for help. When Henry Boonstra's carburetor froze during a snowstorm, he set the plane down on a 9,400-foot-high Utah mountain, grabbed the mail, and stumbled through heavy drifts for thirty-three hours before reaching a ranch house. The resident shepherd lent him a horse, and the pilot finally reached the nearest village and phone three days later. The aviators accepted such hair-raising risks less for the salary than from the desire to hold one of the few jobs in the world that allowed them to fly. As Smith put it, "Alone in an empty cockpit, there is nothing and everything to see. It was so alive and rich a life that any other conceivable choice seemed dull, prosaic and humdrum."

Thrill-seeking behavior has a strong genetic component, and the right stuff clearly ran in the family of Katherine Stinson, the first woman authorized to fly the U.S. mail. Her parents operated a flight school in Texas, her sister Marjorie trained combat pilots in World War I, and her brother Eddie founded the Stinson Aircraft Company. The "Flying Schoolgirl" took America by storm with her loop-the-loops and skywriting, to say nothing of her leather garb and trousers, then still a rarity for women. In 1913, she amazed the crowd at the Montana State Fair by dropping mailbags from her sketchy wood-and-fabric plane, then went on to enthrall fans abroad before volunteering to be a combat pilot in 1917. She was rejected because of her sex but helped the cause by flying for pledges that brought $2 million to the Red Cross. In 1918, Stinson signed on as a regular Air Mail Service pilot and, despite a crash landing en route from Chicago to New York, managed to break a record for covering 783 miles in eleven hours. (Around 1920, tuberculosis forced her back to earth; she moved to New Mexico for her health, became a successful architect, and lived to the age of eighty-six.)

Businesses were impressed by airmail's advances and put the post under congressional pressure to offer coast-to-coast service. The first transcontinental route, completed in 1920, linked Long Island, New York, and San Francisco via stops at thirteen small airfields. At first, the mailbags had to travel by train at night because pilots couldn't fly in the dark. Planes still had no landing or navigation lights, and there were no illuminated runways, much less updated weather reports. Nevertheless, the experimental air-rail service cut nearly a day from the Railway Mail Service's cross-country delivery time. To do better, the post had to come up with the technology needed to race the mail through the dark.

Even night flight seemed possible in the inventive Roaring Twenties milieu that produced the first robot and liquid-fueled rocket, Kool-Aid and the Band-Aid. The steady improvements in illuminating a cross-country airway included hundreds of rotating beacons and floodlights that replaced runway bonfires, followed later by searchlights that sat on giant concrete directional arrows. By 1924, the post had achieved the goals of routine night flight and regularly scheduled transcontinental service. Letters sped from west to east in about thirty hours with just seven relay stops, each lasting a mere five minutes; headwinds made the reverse trip a few hours longer. Moreover, flight was becoming much safer, thanks to such technical advances as parachutes, control towers, and radio stations that provided fliers with weather forecasts; soon the Department of Agriculture began to send the bulletins, as well as stock market data, to farmers.

The post remained in the airmail business, but it did not operate its own airline for long. Indeed, one of the government-run service's major goals was to spur the development of commercial aviation and add the skies to America's transportation grid. By 1925, the department had subsidized enough infrastructure to inspire some thirty companies to test their wings. That year, Congress passed the Contract Air Mail Act, also known as the Kelly Act, which authorized the post to stimulate the young industry's growth by awarding lucrative contracts to private carriers. The bidding was competitive, but even automaker Henry Ford got some money for the "Tin Goose," his all-metal plane. The following year, Congress authorized the government to license pilots and planes, investigate accidents and safety concerns, and generally regulate the nation's newest transportation system.

The Air Mail Service's efficiency and its pilots' derring-do burnished the public image of the United States and its post. A few of its aviators, like a handful of Pony riders, became celebrities who captured the popular imagination by racing boldly through the newest frontier. Their archetype was "Wild Bill" Hopson, a former New York City taxi driver in love with speed. Fearless, genial, skilled, and movie-star handsome, he mostly got away with breaking rules as well as records and accumulating a string of forced landings and damaged planes. After one of Hopson's near-death experiences, his long-suffering supervisor, D. B. Colyer, reported: "The Pilot was only slightly injured, the mail wet in spots, and the plane practically a washout." On one occasion, Hopson found himself stranded at the airfield in Bellefonte,

Pennsylvania, while his date for the evening awaited him in Manhattan. He talked a New York City–bound pilot into allowing him to hitch a ride on one of the small plane's wings, where he clung to its guy wires for the trip's duration. In 1928, Hopson was killed at the age of thirty-eight while flying the mail and a large shipment of diamonds from New York to Cleveland over Pennsylvania's Allegheny Mountains, which were notorious for fog and tricky weather. Although untrue, the legend persisted that Wild Bill had made off to Canada with the treasure.

Postmaster General Harry New attributed at least part of the 20 percent increase in airmail volume in 1927 to an obscure twenty-five-year-old Army captain and former pilot for Robertson Aircraft, an Air Mail Service contractor. Charles Lindbergh had just become a worldwide celebrity when he flew the Ryan NYP single-engine *Spirit of St. Louis* on the first nonstop trip from New York to Paris in just thirty-three hours. Nevertheless, when asked about his future plans, he said, "I am an airmail pilot and expect to fly the mail again." Indeed, "Lucky Lindy" had mastered his craft during his earlier days on the St. Louis–to–Chicago mail route. (On one occasion, he had parachuted from a plane that had apparently run out of gas, only to have it cough back to life and spiral toward him five times as he dropped helplessly through thin air; after he and the plane landed in separate cornfields, he took the mail to the nearest post office for delivery.) Lindbergh later volunteered to do some final runs on the route between Springfield and St. Louis with his old Air Mail Service friends and recalled that "to be a pilot of the night mail appeared the summit of ambition for a flier." (Amelia Earhart, who was the first woman to solo across the Atlantic, was not an official airmail pilot, but she flew the U.S. mail at least twice.)

The post's time-honored policy of contracting with private transportation companies was a huge success for all parties involved with airmail. Postal service was greatly accelerated, which pleased the department and its customers, and by the late 1920s, the commercial aviation industry, which had been almost entirely sustained by postal subsidies, was poised to take flight on its own. The early airmail contractors evolved into major corporations—including Boeing, Pan Am, and the "Big Four" of United, Eastern, TWA, and American airlines—that were major beneficiaries of an expensive infrastructure of airfields, illuminated runways, and communications all provided by the post. Charles I. Stanton, a pilot who later headed the Civil Aeronautics Administration, summed up the Air Mail Service's impact on global as well as national development by citing the "four seeds" it planted. Airways, communications, navigation aids, and multi-engined aircraft are, he said, "the cornerstones on which our present world-wide transport structure is built, and they came, one by one, out of our experience in daily, uninterrupted flying of the mail."

No story of the early days of the Air Mail Service would be complete without mentioning its first stamp, issued in 1918, which showed a blue Jenny framed in an elaborately engraved red border. The stamp is beautiful in its own right, but a fabulous flaw, known as an invert, on one hundred of the stamps made the biplane appear to be flying upside down. This production error provided American philately with its most famous artifacts, each now worth hundreds of thousands of dollars.

Inverts occurred rarely and only during a production process involving two or more colors. The fabled Jennys were produced by a mistake of the sort that usually happened when a sheet of stamps got turned around in the course of receiving a second color. Their popularity derives not just from their great visual and human appeal—the planes appear to be mimicking the barnstormers who thrilled Americans at contemporary air shows—but also from the thrill of the chase. On the day the stamp was released, William Robey, a Washington, D.C., philatelist, went to the post office and bought the only sheet of inverts ever sold from an initially unsuspecting clerk. Intent on dodging the authorities, he sped off to hide his treasure under his mattress until he could sell it, which he did for $15,000.

. . .

DESPITE THE TRIUMPHAL ACHIEVEMENTS of airmail, the new theory that the post should be more like a company than a public service, and therefore should narrow the scope of its services, reduce its deficits, and focus on maximizing revenue from first-class mail, slowly took hold in an America that seemingly thrived under the business-oriented political ethos of the prosperous Roaring Twenties. For the first time, more people lived in cities than in small towns and on farms. Jobs were plentiful again, and upward mobility was in the air. Blue-collar youths "bettered themselves" with vocational training; women got the vote, and some enrolled in the new coed colleges. Anti-immigrant and anti-union sentiment remained high, but racism began to ebb in the cities. The people were united by the mass-produced consumer culture and enthralled by everything modern, from Art Deco design to jazz to the radios and telephones that quickly rendered the telegraph obsolete.

The sky seemed to be the limit until the stock market crashed in 1929, which triggered the Great Depression and sent the government-versus-business pendulum swinging once again. In 1932, Democrat Franklin D. Roosevelt won the White House with his promise to rescue the nation with a "new deal" based on relief for the poor, economic recovery, and reforms to prevent Wall Street's future chicanery.

Like the rest of America, the post suffered from the devastation wrought by the Depression; its revenues decreased by an unprecedented $119 million between 1930 and 1934 alone. The railroad it had depended on since the Civil War era staggered under the twin blows of the economic crisis and the increased use of automobiles, and its forced cuts in service in turn impeded the RMS. The only way in which hard times benefited the post was by greatly increasing the number of its banking customers, who soared from 770,859 in 1931 to 2,598,391 in 1935, when deposits totaled more than $1.2 billion. (These increases would continue until 1947, when the system claimed 4 million customers and more than $3 billion in deposits.)

During this extraordinarily difficult period, a Congress increasingly accustomed to thinking of the post as a troubled business rather than a public service and now strapped by the Depression put the post on what would become a long, fateful austerity diet. Over time, this starvation regimen would cause its physical facilities to deteriorate and render its technology obsolete, but President Roosevelt himself championed one of the few exceptions to this grim rule.

The New Deal's architect believed that constructing public buildings would both reduce unemployment and reassure Americans that their government *could* get things done, even during hard times. He authorized thousands of projects, including courthouses, schools, libraries, and 1,300 post offices, which after all were local representations of Washington. Moreover, at a time when the arts were mostly a privilege of the rich, these handsome new post offices were adorned with murals that celebrated average folk and their local history. As FDR explained, this artwork for the people would be "native, human, eager and alive—all of it painted by their own kind in their own country, and painted about things they know and look at often and have touched and loved." These postal murals are often attributed to the Works Progress Administration, but they were done under the aegis of the Treasury Department's Section of Painting and Sculpture, which was less concerned with employing starving artists than with boosting beleaguered America's morale.

FDR took an especially keen interest in three of six new post offices designed for New York's Dutchess County, his aristocratic family's ancestral turf. The towns of Poughkeepsie and Rhinebeck were just miles away from the Roosevelts' home in the village of Hyde Park, situated on the old thoroughfare that had first been called the King's Highway, then the Albany Post Road. The president had once served as the county historian, and he supervised every detail of these post offices, from the different vernacular styles of their architecture to the stories told by their murals, starting with the area's origin myth: Native Americans catching a first glimpse of Henry Hudson's ship *Half Moon*.

Poughkeepsie was the county seat, and its post office was accordingly built in the grand style, complete with bell tower, marble columns, mezzanine, and possibly even a secret tunnel to an armory constructed for the president's safety during World War II. One mural narrates the town's history from 1830 to 1930, showing how a small country village on a river plied by sloops (FDR complained that the sails blew in the wrong direction) had become a bustling center of commerce served by the railroad. Another painting depicts New York State's delegates solemnly ratifying the U.S. Constitution, but one charming detail was meant to amuse Poughkeepsie's children: a tiny mouse peers from its hole just beneath the central handshake between the founding fathers Alexander Hamilton and George Clinton.

The Hyde Park branch could be the poster image for America's small-town post offices. The gray fieldstone building with its pale blue wooden shutters looks more like one of the county's cozy cottages or inns than a federal facility. Its murals were painted by Olin Dows, a local historian and artist, who submitted his initial sketches to FDR for vetting. He carefully rendered the regional flora and fauna while highlighting the New Deal theme of the dignity and importance of the community's people, from the settlers constructing its first buildings to the fishermen catching a whale-like sturgeon. Even the portrayal of the picnic that FDR gave in 1939 to honor England's King George VI (who famously enjoyed his first hot dog in Hyde Park) deliberately trains the eye on the local folk, especially the fat farmer's wife hawking her homemade delicacies, rather than on the grandees off in the distance. The scene that shows the crippled FDR checking the blueprints for a new local high school from his car, which was specially equipped with hand rather than foot controls, embodies the handicapped president's optimism about the future despite great personal and social challenges.

FDR ordered the architects to model wealthy Rhinebeck's post office on the home of Henry Beekman, a prominent Dutch pioneer known by some of the president's ancestors. Dows's murals here feature the scenes of leisure and comfort that befit an affluent community, including colonists dining alfresco, skaters cavorting on a frozen pond, and even an artist sketching the landscape. In the New Deal tradition, however, the town's working people are also included, from its carpenters, who were famed for their craftsmanship, to the local slaves going about their unpaid labors.

Roosevelt had a soft spot for the bucolic Hudson Valley, but as a native son and former governor of New York, he was obliged to spread the architectural wealth. In 1935, his administration commissioned the huge four-story, block-long General Post Office in the heart of New York City's gritty borough of the Bronx. The building was designed in the popular Art Moderne style and is best known for its thirteen labor-themed murals, painted by artist Ben Shahn and his wife, Bernarda, which were inspired by Walt Whitman's democratic poetry.

Roosevelt's interest in the post as a political tool wasn't confined to its architecture. He was a passionate philatelist, and he used stamps, including some of his own design, as visual versions of the "fireside chats" that popularized his often controversial policies. A series of commemoratives that glorified his new Civilian Conservation Corps and the national parks highlighted the administration's focus on providing jobs to the unemployed and reminded Americans that even during the Depression, theirs was a spectacularly beautiful country. FDR's response to the criticism that he used stamps to promote his politics was to order new issues that honored George Washington and the White House, both icons of presidential power. His most famous philatelic contribution, however, was distinctly bipartisan: his sketch for a stamp based on James McNeill Whistler's painting titled *Arrangement in Grey and Black No. 1*, but better known as "Whistler's Mother," which appeared in 1934 in honor of all American matriarchs.

FDR was more interested in stamps and post offices than in the Post Office Department per se. He had a surprisingly cool personal relationship with James Farley, the dynamic chairman of the Democratic Party and his own postmaster general. Six-foot, four-inch "Big Jim" was the consummate wheeler-dealer and a Svengali of the spoils system. He had engineered Roosevelt's two elections as New York's governor and two victorious presidential campaigns, as well as the near-decimation of the Republican Party's clout in 1936, but the touchy president was annoyed that the talented, charismatic Farley was referred to as the Kingmaker. (Despite his many achievements, he's often remembered for unwittingly generating an unlikely corruption scandal known as "Farley's Follies." As postmaster general, he sometimes bought sheets of "preprints," or imperforate, un-gummed stamps, to give as souvenirs to the president and others, but philatelists loudly objected to this privileged access to the collectors' objects. In response, Farley had the sheets reprinted without gum or perforations for sale to the general public.) The capable postmaster general left public office before Roosevelt's third term and went on to manage a large private distribution system: Coca-Cola's international division.

Roosevelt's philatelic interests must have been a welcome distraction from the disastrous results of his response to the "Air Mail Scandal" of 1934. This imbroglio over the post's transportation contracts was rooted in events during the previous Republican administration. Walter Brown, President Herbert Hoover's postmaster general, had helped to write the Air Mail Act of 1930, also known as the McNary-Watres Act, which had greatly increased his power over postal policy. To curb the contractors' profitable practice of flying junk mail, he changed the basis of their compensation to the size of a plane's cargo space rather than the mail's weight. Partly to sweeten this bitter medicine, he also offered the carriers ten-year rather than four-year contracts. In exchange for this added security, the airlines greatly expanded their routes at no cost to the government. The act also empowered Brown to extend or consolidate airmail routes as he saw fit. When the new postal contracts were awarded to just the three large airlines, later

United, American, and TWA, that had been personally invited to attend what was dubbed the postmaster general's "Spoils Conference," the charge that the post was bankrolling cronyism and discriminating against the smaller carriers led to the sensational scandal of 1934.

In the end, the case against Brown was flawed. He certainly wanted the contracts to go to the largest, best equipped airlines that could most readily expand the nation's airways. However, announcements of meetings for all interested carriers had been published in the newspapers; smaller companies that later complained of unfairness did not attend. Partisan politics also played a role. Brown was a Republican, and Democrats eager to distract the public's attention from the Depression had sponsored the 1934 congressional investigation into the airmail contracts on the grounds that they had gone to the previous Hoover administration's friends. Years later, Brown was cleared of charges of fraud or collusion.

That same year, Roosevelt made things worse for himself and the post by voiding all of the aviation companies' domestic government contracts and calling in the U.S. Army Air Corps to deliver the mail. The private carriers by then controlled a fleet of much-improved planes that flew day and night on numerous routes, but the military and its pilots didn't have nearly the same equipment or experience. The resulting chaos included sixty-six accidents and the deaths of twelve crew members, which the legendary World War I fighter ace Eddie Rickenbacker called "legalized murder." Roosevelt was forced to reverse his order a mere month later. If the Army's terrible performance had a silver lining, it was that the bloody debacle rallied support for the development of what became the U.S. Air Force.

The Air Mail Act of 1934 restored the postal contracts to the private airlines, but it also made the bidding process more competitive, spread the federal wealth more evenly, and lowered the companies' compensation, all of which further encouraged the industry's investment in passenger service. Several small boutique aviation firms, such as Aeromarine and Chaplin, had catered to the needs of a few wealthy vacationers, but now the airlines had to figure out how to transport very large numbers of passengers—still a far-fetched idea. Americans enjoyed watching barnstormers go through their paces at air shows, but crashes such as the one that killed Notre Dame football coach Knute Rockne and six others in 1931 discouraged them from taking to the air themselves. Moreover, planes had been built for transporting cargo, not people, and until 1930, the few willing to take the risk had to wear a parachute, jounce about on a mailbag, and tolerate a maddening din. To gain the public's confidence and the necessary bank loans to convert to a new business model, the airlines developed new commercial passenger planes, such as the Boeing 247 and the Douglas DC-2, that were larger, faster, and more comfortable—and also, thanks to better navigational aids, much safer. By 1933, the Boeing 247 traveled at 155 miles per hour, and its ten passengers sat on upholstered seats in a special compartment equipped with hot water. In 1936, the Douglas DC-3, which had a quieter cabin and seats buffered by rubber, became the first popular, and profitable, passenger plane.

The mail continued to fly on the major commercial routes between big cities, but many small towns still lacked airports. By 1939, All American Aviation operated a service in a handful of eastern states that resembled an airborne version of the RMS, in that its planes both dropped off and picked up mailbags without landing. The outgoing sack was suspended on a rope between two poles, and when the pilot swooped down, a clerk caught it with a grappling hook. "Flying the pickup" was an extraordinarily demanding, risky, and expensive proposition, however, and in 1949, All American stopped the service and became a passenger carrier. In 1951, the company became Allegheny Airlines, then USAir, which is now part of American Airlines.

Air Mail continued to be a separate postal service until 1975, when planes began to carry almost all domestic intercity first-class letters for the price of a regular stamp. In 2006, the post expressed its pride in its long involvement with aviation by trademarking the term "Air Mail"— not coincidentally, if less deservedly, along with "Pony Express."

.   .   .

No sooner had America survived the Great Depression than it was thrust into World War II. The hard-pressed post, which had just returned to its previously high levels of mail volume and employment despite its austerity budget, was thrown back into crisis mode. The complexity of its wartime operations was like nothing seen in a military conflict before or since. The combination of the 11.5 million personnel at home and abroad and the vast constellation of their devoted correspondents produced a staggering number of letters to process and transport. Previously, the overseas mail had traveled on great ships such as the British *Titanic,* which sank in 1912, losing some seventeen million pieces of mail. (About a dozen letters postmarked aboard have survived, because the *Titanic* didn't head right to New York City from Southampton but stopped first at Cherbourg, in France, then at Queenstown, in Ireland; letters written early in the voyage were sent from those ports.) The huge oceangoing vessels were slow, however, and they also made tempting targets during war.

Aviation had been in its infancy during World War I, but planes could now fly overseas both faster and more securely than the big ships could sail. (The *Yankee Clipper* had carried transatlantic mail by 1939.) The problem was that the aircraft lacked adequate cargo space for bags upon bags of heavy, bulky mail. Back in 1937, the *Hindenburg,* a huge German dirigible equipped with its own post office and plenty of room for cargo as well as passengers, had represented one possibility. Mail sent from America to Europe took five to seven days to arrive by sea but just two and a half on the great airship. However, on May 6, 1937, it had caught fire and crashed in Lakehurst, New Jersey, killing thirty-six people, and of the approximately seventeen thousand letters it carried, just two hundred survived. (The National Postal Museum has exhibited an envelope, postmarked on the *Hindenburg,* that a passenger had addressed to himself so that one of his sons, a budding philatelist, could save the stamps. He and one of his four children died in the crash, but the young collector received his father's final gift in the mail.)

The debut of "Victory Mail" eliminated the problem of sending tons of bulky mailbags across the Atlantic by borrowing a technique that had been developed by Eastman Kodak for copying bank records. Soldiers and their correspondents wrote to one another on sheets of specially designed, lightweight V-Mail stationery that folded into self-contained envelopes. Next, letters from the States were opened and microfilmed, then sent on rolls holding about eighteen thousand messages apiece to military stations near the designated recipients. The film was then developed on-site to produce copies of the originals, which were delivered within a week or two to soldiers in the field. The same process operated in reverse to send V-Mail from the front back home. This communications breakthrough enabled 150,000 messages to fit into one forty-five-pound mailbag rather than the twenty-two bags previously required. As an added bonus, V-Mail that wasn't destined for overseas was light enough to travel as regular airmail.

The hundreds of millions of V-Mails that were posted during the war were subject to certain constraints. The medium couldn't accommodate regular photographs, which inspired the *Chicago Tribune* to take pictures of newborns that were then microfilmed by a special separate process and sent to their fathers overseas. Even the classic epistolary sign of affection was forbidden, because the "scarlet scourge" of lipstick kisses could gum up V-Mail's machinery. The military continued its practice of censoring all of its personnel's correspondence to obliterate any references to the location and activity of troops, as well as to monitor their morale. This unhappy task usually fell to a unit's officer, but soldiers who objected to the personal scrutiny could place their letters in a special "honor cover" that went to a larger base for a more anonymous inspection.

As in the past, war compelled the post to hire more women to replace the men at the front. In 1917, the combination of World War I and the era's labor strife had forced an urban experiment with female letter carriers, despite "a grave doubt in the minds of those familiar with the every-day work of letter carriers in the city delivery service whether women could stand the strain for any length of time without seriously impairing their health." If women were only grudgingly permitted to carry the mail on the ground, Helen Richey, the first female commercial airline pilot and the first woman to fly the mail on a regular basis, faced even more opposition during World War II. In 1935, despite her stellar record, the Air Line Pilots Association refused to admit her to its ranks, and the post cut back her flights. She quit in frustration, but during the war, she volunteered to ferry military planes around England and the United States. (Like many women, Richey found herself unemployed after peace was declared in 1945 and the men returned home, and she died at thirty-seven, an apparent suicide.) The African American women of the 6888th Central Postal Directory Battalion technically worked for the military, not the post, but they were stationed in Europe during the war to process mail for U.S. personnel overseas and served with distinction. Their efforts were the more notable considering that, as Major Charity Adams Earley, their supervisor, put it, they "were segregated two ways, because we were black and because we were women."

The post's wartime efforts were not confined to expediting military mail. The department assumed many additional burdens, including selling "war bonds," as the savings bonds sold in post offices since 1935 were then called, registering aliens, dispensing draft materials, and even helping with a livestock census; some small-town postmasters also served as military recruiters. Most of these postal efforts were predictable enough, but one made by FDR was highly imaginative. By now a master of using philatelic imagery to rouse the nation's esprit de corps, he ordered a commemorative stamp in 1942 that portrayed the seemingly odd couple of Abraham Lincoln and Sun Yat-sen, the father of the Republic of China. In the wake of Pearl Harbor, the canny president used the Chinese leader's admiration for the Great Emancipator to highlight his country's resistance to Japanese aggression.

15

MID-MODERN MELTDOWN

THE POST THAT EMERGED after World War II, like America itself, appeared to be booming as never before. The department's status was such that when the jeweler Harry Winston donated the fabled $350 million Hope Diamond to the Smithsonian Institution in 1958, he sent it by registered first-class mail from New York City to Washington, D.C., for $2.44 postage, plus a very low $142.05 for insurance. The simplest of the more objective if less colorful testimonies to the institution's standing was the most eloquent: America's already-robust mail volume actually more than *doubled* between 1945 and 1970, from almost thirty-eight billion to nearly eighty-five billion pieces—more than the rest of the world's combined.

This huge midcentury increase in mail seems surprising at first. After all, Americans now had a number of other ways to communicate and receive information. As much as they loved their radios, telephones, and televisions, however, they were still big readers and writers. They devoured morning and evening newspapers, the *Saturday Evening Post* and *Woman's Day*, and were long accustomed to communicating with letters and cards for mere pennies. Then, too, the mail had major practical advantages over the telephone for both individuals, who restricted expensive long-distance calls to emergencies and special occasions, and businesses, which needed written records of transactions. Finally, the vigorous "greatest generation" was busily creating the postwar economic and baby booms, and their new start-ups and suburbs produced much, much more mail than before, especially the bills that generated 80 percent of the first-class volume.

The glittering statistics on the sheer amount of America's mail helped to obscure a darker reality whose shadows were both existential and practical. The post that was being force-fed ever more tons of letters, parcels, and publications had been gravely depleted by a decades-long diet imposed by two global wars and the Great Depression. Its facilities were run-down, and to call its by-hand technology outdated is a dramatic understatement. The biggest problem was sorting the era's oceans of mail, and the cure was automation. The fewer times a letter or parcel has to be handled, the greater the efficiency. However, even clerks in major post offices still used the "peek and poke" sorting method familiar to Benjamin Franklin: examining a letter's address, then sticking it into the appropriate box or slot for delivery. Some insiders foresaw the catastrophic result of continuing to try to do more with less and understood that without a commitment to a massive modernization—estimated costs ranged upward from $5 billion—the issue wasn't if the post would be plunged into a crisis but when.

The urban postal palaces of the late nineteenth and early twentieth centuries, such as the Farley, that had once symbolized the institution at its peak now embodied its decline. The huge buildings, which were also major mail distribution centers, had been designed for another age. Chicago's sixty-acre Old Main Post Office, then the world's largest, served a city that was a vital rail, air, and mail hub and second only to New York as a national financial center, but its clerks struggled to do their work with only the most rudimentary tools. They raked the constant stream of incoming bags down slides into big vats, then heaved the contents onto conveyor belts that dumped the mail onto large tables for manual sorting. When letters fell off the belts, they used shovels to scoop them up and put them back. If such a system had been able to handle the prewar mail, it was completely swamped by its postwar boom.

The problem of the post's antiquated facilities was paradoxically compounded by advances in transportation. The automotive and aviation revolutions had sent the once-mighty railroad on which the department had depended for nearly a century into precipitous decline. In 1920, 80 percent of intercity travelers went by train; by 1949, that figure had dropped to 8 percent, and by 1957, to 4 percent. By 1969, America's 208,517 miles of railroad track had dwindled to some 54,000. The post office was forced to adjust, and it shifted from trains to motorized vehicles, just as it had replaced post riders with stagecoaches and stagecoaches with trains. To avoid the overcharging endemic to transportation contracts, the department even invested in its own fleet of trucks.

The decision to return to moving the mail on America's highways and byways might have been necessary, but it complicated mail processing, which could no longer easily be done simultaneously with transportation. The new Highway Post Offices that were installed inside some trucks and buses were slower, prey to traffic jams, and less efficient than the smooth-sailing Railway Post Offices had been; they swayed more, which made sorting more difficult and induced more motion sickness. The mail had to be processed *somewhere*, however, and the post was forced to return to its old hub-and-spokes circulation system centered on large regional distributing post offices.

This back-to-the-future strategy worked reasonably well in the burgeoning suburbs and exurbs, where the big trucks could sail into giant new mail processing centers that were custom-built for the purpose and conveniently positioned just off the new freeways. The gigantic urban distributing post offices, however, had been purposely built in densely developed downtown areas adjacent to the train stations through which most of the national mail had once passed; they didn't even have docking sites for the semis. The long trucks struggled to access these old postal palaces amid heavily trafficked, narrow streets dating to horse-

and-carriage days. Indeed, the department still employed some horse-drawn wagons in downtown Philadelphia until 1955.

THE QUESTION OF WHY, year after year, the government refused to address the root causes of the looming implosion of one of its largest enterprises is a complicated one. The long austerity regimen imposed by a series of national catastrophes had caused grave practical problems for the post, but it had also contributed to its quieter identity crisis. Since the reforms of the mid-nineteenth century, if not implicitly before, the simplest way to describe the institution had been something along the lines of "the system that delivers things directly to the people." In 1877, Supreme Court justice Morrison Waite had underscored the post's open-ended nature by observing that its mission of binding the nation wasn't confined to the means known to its founders—a principle boldly put to practice throughout the Progressive Era. Since the 1930s, however, the government, postal management, and the people had gradually lost touch with that traditionally flexible, expansive, forward-looking understanding of the post.

Years of national crises had accustomed postal executives to struggling along on short-term, bare-bones appropriations and steadily increasing deficits. The department's centralized operations, once models of the sublime, had become as hierarchical and ossified as the rules and regulations in its two-pound *Postal Manual.* Some forty thousand postmasters had to deal directly with Washington over the most trivial matters. Without a Montgomery Blair or John Wanamaker to supply the vision and political will needed to keep pace with change, managers followed the example set in 1930 by Postmaster General Walter Brown and fixated on increasing first-class mail volume and reducing costs—despite the fact that, without automation, the first objective made the second one impossible.

The problem of the post's lackluster leadership paled beside Congress's seeming indifference to its plight. Politicians refused to pay for the enormously costly rejuvenation the department so desperately needed largely because such a bold step was not in their self-interest. Members of Congress knew that in the new postwar global super-power, huge defense contracts trumped postal patronage. (Republican president Dwight Eisenhower famously remarked about the fact in his farewell address: "In the councils of government, we must guard against the acquisition of unwarranted influence, whether sought or unsought, by the military-industrial complex.") That said, the spoils system, though waning, still provided some political clout, which modernizing the system along more businesslike lines would necessarily end. Last but far from least, politicians heard less about the post from constituents, who, even though they generated much more mail than previous generations, took the service for granted and weren't as exclusively dependent on it. These taxpaying constituents, who now knew little of the post or its sorry state, might very well be riled by a big bill to fix it.

Instead of taking a long-term approach to the post's looming crisis, Congress repeatedly opted for the short-term solution of paying for more and more workers to cope with the skyrocketing mail volume—a huge expenditure on labor that gulped down most of the department's budget. The sacrosanct three-cent first-class postage for letters, unchanged since 1932, during the Depression, was raised three times between 1958 and 1968, to reach six cents, but the increases didn't begin to cover the rising costs of labor and transportation, much less a massive modernization. Both revenues and costs had greatly increased over time, but the fact remains that the department's total deficit for the years preceding 1930 could have seemed unremarkable for a single year in the 1950s and '60s. In a vicious circle, Congress's refusal to address the root of the post's crisis forced its managers to operate within the limits of short-term appropriations, which further discouraged foresight and innovative thinking.

Postmaster General Arthur Summerfield, an Eisenhower appointee who served from 1953 to 1961, was an exception to midcentury postal management's generally uninspired rule. This energetic son of a rural mailman had been the owner of one of the Midwest's largest car dealerships as well as the chairman of the Republican National Committee. Like Wanamaker, he was a self-made Washington outsider who understood business, salesmanship, and the importance of the latest technology. He quickly signaled his intentions to run a more modern, businesslike post by resigning his position with the committee, downplaying patronage, and hiring talented people from private enterprise.

On his second day on the job, Summerfield attempted to assess his department's condition. However, he found that no operating statement for recent months would be available for almost a year and a half, and that the huge staff did not include a single certified public accountant. The department was the world's largest buyer of transportation services, but it had not examined those costs in twenty-five years. The average post office was fifty years old, and many were older, but no money had been appropriated for their upkeep since 1938. The department's organizational chart listed the Bureau of Research and Engineering one step below what amounted to the employees' suggestion box. Worst of all, Summerfield realized, unless the post was automated, it would have to hire hundreds of thousands of additional workers to keep up with the ever-accelerating mail volume, which had climbed to forty-nine billion letters and one billion parcels that year.

The prospect of mechanizing a huge, specialized enterprise like the post was fraught with problems beyond politics, bureaucratic inertia, and even sheer astronomical expense. The institution was a monopoly, so it would be the only customer for the complex machines it needed. This fact had naturally discouraged manufacturers' interest; it also helps explain why advances in postal tools had been relatively limited in the earlier twentieth century to things like electric postage meters and stamp cancelers, stamp vending machines, and pneumatic tubes— pipelines that sped urban letters underground. Little progress had been made regarding the post's major problem of mail sorting.

Summerfield did his best to end this institutional stasis by enthusiastically experimenting with mechanizing the post. Previously, the department's own engineering staff had designed prototypes for the necessary machines, then contracted with outside companies to have the equipment built. The results were much less sophisticated than what outside industrial designers could have achieved on their own, as well as very costly. Summerfield changed the status quo by telling the private manufacturers what the post wanted its new machines to do, then letting their experts design and build them. He also reached out to posts in other nations as well as to other government agencies and private industry to develop the numerical coding systems that automated mail processing required. By 1959, the post had contracted for the first workhorses of mail automation: the Pitney-Bowes facer-canceler, which oriented letters for processing and canceled their postage, and the Burroughs Corporation's letter-position sorting machine (LSM), which helped sort them for delivery. Assured of the department's financial support, manufacturers now kept teams of engineers busy with improving the equipment. A proud Summerfield used this cutting-edge technology, which doubled clerks' efficiency, to turn Detroit's main post office into a showcase for the future.

Considering the grave problems confronting him in the here and now, Summerfield's ability to think big and far ahead is all the more impressive. In 1959 and 1960, he briefly experimented with a postal program called Speed Mail, which used the new facsimile (fax) technology to transmit documents in mere instants. The sender could dispatch a fax from his or her local post office to the recipient's, where it was printed and delivered. The service was lightning fast and potentially cheap and could even drastically reduce the volume of paper mail. The sanguine postmaster general anticipated that fax machines in every American home and business would transmit most of the nation's first-class mail. In a harbinger of the future regarding the post's forays into new communications technology, however, the promising Speed Mail project was halted in 1961. The start-up had been expensive, yet it had not been given adequate time to recover its costs. More important, air and rail mail carriers as well as Western Union had loudly voiced the traditional protests of unfair "socialistic" government competition with private industry.

Summerfield had made real progress in the post's automation, but its worsening finances limited his big plans to modernize the entire system to Detroit and a few other cities. In 1960, toward the end of his tenure in office, Summerfield, who regarded traditional post offices as "monuments in stone to political patronage, designed more for curb appeal than functionality," had the satisfaction of dedicating America's first fully mechanized mail facility, in Providence. The futuristic building's large, open bays and swooping roof anticipated Eero Saarinen's famous TWA terminal at New York City's Idlewild Airport. The work area was the size of two football fields, yet few employees were required to operate its equipment.

Much like Wanamaker, Summerfield was a strong-minded executive whose efforts to update the post were compromised by a troubled relationship with Congress, not least because of his own ego. (One day, he and James "Big Jim" Farley found themselves alone in a hallway lined with pictures of former postmasters general. When Farley observed that there had been only three great ones, Summerfield said, "Who was the other?") Something of a latter-day Comstock, he had also been ridiculed for filling a room across from his office with confiscated pornography, purportedly to educate visitors about the perceived moral menace, and for trying to ban *Lady Chatterley's Lover* from the mail long after it had been published. Many of his efforts, including a TV series called *The Mail Story: Handle with Care* and the department's jazzy new red, white, and blue graphics, were highly creative, but others ranged into the realm of science fiction. In 1959, he got the Navy submarine U.S.S. *Barbero* to transport some letters via a Regulus cruise missile, then announced, "We stand on the threshold of rocket mail." (The first high-velocity letter was quickly delivered to President Eisenhower.) Like the best of his predecessors, however, Summerfield had a robust sense of the post's mandate and its future expression, and he had literally as well as figuratively tried to propel the venerable institution into the space age.

The next postmaster general to take over the still-struggling department was J. Edward Day, a Kennedy appointee who was less interested in costly experiments in mechanization. Nevertheless, he introduced one of the midcentury post's simplest yet most important technological advances. The ZIP (zone improvement plan) code system was a more sophisticated version of the basic "zone numbering system" already used by some big cities. By adding two digits to an address—N.Y. 12, N.Y., for example—a letter could go directly to the city's mail zone No. 12, thus speeding up the delivery process. The new five-digit ZIP went further. The first three numbers identified a particular area's central mail processing facility, and the second two either a certain post office there or, in larger cities, a particular postal zone. Americans were still getting accustomed to telephone area codes, and some initially bristled at the ZIPs. Like the new, more efficient two-letter abbreviations for the states, the codes struck them as Big Brother's latest effort to turn the person into "just a number." Most people soon accepted the ZIPs, however, and this small addition to the traditional address produced a surprising number of large effects.

Because its numbers could be read by machines as well as people, the ZIP code was a giant step toward streamlining mail processing. By 1965, an early "optical character reader" helped sort letters by translating typed addresses into coding that a computer could understand. The ZIP was also a major refinement in the post's organization of America's physical and social environment, which had become much more sophisticated since the days when addresses often consisted of the name of a town or hamlet. Moreover, the new categorization system revolutionized the mass-mailing and marketing industries and greatly assisted the work of the U.S. Census Bureau, public health agencies, and other demographic research groups.

The goal of automated mail processing had been somewhat advanced by the mid-1960s, but even in the department's few mechanized oases, the work would remain brutally hard for years to come. An LSM operator had to look at a letter's ZIP code, then key in the three numbers that directed it toward its next destination—either a certain city or another LSM in that same post office; then a second operator typed in its last two numbers. Much like the RMS clerks who preceded them, these workers also had to memorize the codes for every state and country in the world, so that they could process ZIP-less mail. Moreover, they were expected to handle a letter every second; their only relief from this grueling regimen was a ten-minute break each hour, during which they carried their processed mail to a distribution station. Not surprisingly, the extraordinarily stressful work had an error rate of about 30 percent.

THE MIDCENTURY POST tried to conduct business as usual amid steadily worsening conditions, but the inevitable meltdown finally occurred in Chicago in October 1966. Ten million pieces of mail, rising in mountains and cascading into halls and basements, backed up in the enormous Old Main Post Office, which shut down for almost three weeks. The chaos also spread outside the dysfunctional facility into the city, where workers had dumped piles of undelivered mail, much of which was third-class material past its delivery date, on side streets and even in the river. (It was whispered that an assistant postmaster general had ordered all third-class mail to be burned and the postage returned to the senders, but this shocking step was never taken.) The entire nation was riveted, and appalled, as an ominous ripple effect perturbed service in other big cities, including New York, Los Angeles, Boston, and St. Louis.

The story of the Chicago debacle is not well documented, but one description that's frequently used is "perfect storm." During that era of civil rights demonstrations and urban rioting, many were quick to blame racial strife at a big-city post office where most employees were

African American. Others pointed to the rumor that the previous postmaster, who was white, had deliberately left his successor, Henry McGee, Chicago's first black postmaster, understaffed. Ethnic tensions certainly simmered there and in some other major urban facilities, but it's unlikely that race per se was the main problem. The post had long attracted many highly educated, able black career employees who lacked opportunities elsewhere, but by the 1960s, they had other options. Their replacements included many inexperienced, less skilled part-time workers, often women whose child-care responsibilities contributed to high rates of absenteeism. Chicago employed a high number of these inexpert workers, who simply couldn't handle the annual autumn onslaught of bulk advertising mail. In hindsight, such postal breakdowns in big cities at a time of "white flight" to the suburbs, where the spoils system remained stronger and service was generally good, suggests that many urban facilities no longer had the political clout to get the necessary funding, staffing, and equipment.

After the Chicago disaster, the truth about the post's desperate state was finally out. Americans wanted to know why a major government institution that was also one of the country's biggest businesses and employers suddenly seemed almost unable to function. Even Postmaster General Lawrence O'Brien, who served in the Johnson administration from 1965 to 1968, declared the department to be in a race with catastrophe. In a high-profile speech to a publishing group in April 1967, he proposed a new model for the post; the historic department should be depoliticized, removed from the cabinet, and turned into a government-owned, nonprofit business along the lines of the Tennessee Valley Association or the Federal Deposit Insurance Corporation. This new agency would be run by a board of directors and competent managers, its employees would have the right to bargain collectively, and it would be authorized to issue bonds to raise money for its modernization.

At first glance, the idea that the post—explicitly defined as a public service entitled to government support since 1851 and implicitly so long before—should suddenly be turned into a self-supporting, government-owned corporation seems startling, especially when put forward by the postmaster general himself. The concept of the post as a business, however, had been in the air since O'Brien's predecessor Walter Brown had advanced it back in 1929. Indeed, management had long focused on this formula of increasing first-class mail volume and cutting costs. Moreover, the perennial theme of "business works better than government" was back in vogue again after the end of the New Deal era. The anti-institutional culture of the 1960s teemed with protests against various powers that be. Even academics turned their attention from the state and its policies toward social dynamics, whether expressed by the civil rights movement or managerial capitalism. If government was not regarded as the outright enemy, as the opponents of the Vietnam War and others cast it, it was increasingly seen as inferior to private enterprise—a sentiment that soon helped send Republican Richard Nixon to the White House.

The post had run deficits for most of its history, more or less as a matter of course as far as Congress was concerned, despite its periodic blustering. Not even ten years before, the Postal Policy Act of 1958 had flatly stated that the post office "clearly is not a business enterprise conducted for profit or for raising general funds" but is, rather, a public service meant to promote "social, cultural, intellectual, and commercial intercourse among the people of the United States" that should be supported by the Treasury, not its own revenue. Now, however, the magnitude of its shortcomings and shortfalls, combined with society's increased pro-business orientation, cast the post's bottom line and raison d'être into high relief.

O'Brien had not been a wily political operator for presidents John Kennedy and Lyndon Johnson for nothing, and his vision for a new kind of post was soon shared at the White House. At a time when LBJ was paying for the Vietnam War and sending a man to the moon, he must have regarded the post's deficit of $1.3 billion as a real burden. The president swiftly appointed the prestigious Commission on Postal

Reorganization to analyze the department's role in a rapidly changing world and make recommendations for its future.

THE PRESIDENT'S blue-ribbon, ten-member commission faced a formidable task, if only because of the post's sheer size. Some seven hundred thousand employees handled more than seventy-nine billion pieces of mail a year in its huge network of physical facilities. The department's annual costs were $6.2 billion and its revenues, $5.1 billion—back then, enormous sums. In the private sector, only AT&T could compare with the enterprise, and it was no accident that Frederick Kappel, the former head of that company, was the postal commission's chairman. Most of its other members, including the dean of the Harvard Business School and CEOs of major corporations, shared his business-oriented perspective. The group took its responsibility seriously, and in July 1968, it issued *Towards Postal Excellence,* its 212-page report, to much fanfare.

The so-called Kappel Commission's crucial conclusion was existential in nature and a stunning reversal of historical policy that had been reaffirmed just a decade before: "Today the Post Office is a business." (This assertion was partly based on the sophistical grounds that the post was no longer "a major policy arm of the Government," because other federal departments had sharply reduced their use of it. However, these agencies had only done so when Summerfield had insisted that they pay for such services, which accounted for a hefty chunk of the post's deficit.) The report stated that like any other business, the new "government-owned corporation" should be market-driven and supported by revenue from its customers, not taxpayers.

The commission offered many recommendations regarding the details of the new postal business. It should be freed from the spoils system and depoliticized but not actually privatized—at least not yet—primarily because only the federal government could handle finances on such a scale. It should be run by a board of directors that would set postage rates in consultation with a panel of independent experts. Its employees should receive the right of collective bargaining but not to strike. Importantly, this new post should balance its budget while continuing to provide universal mail service to every American everywhere for the same low price.

Not everyone rejoiced at the prospect of turning one of the federal government's oldest institutions into a mere business. As usual, some self-interested members of Congress were in no hurry to relinquish the waning spoils system's last perquisites. Others were genuinely alarmed by the threat of cutting a public service in the name of efficiency, particularly in the rural South and West, where small, unprofitable post offices and routes abounded. Postal workers may have resented being underpaid by a penny-pinching Congress, yet many feared worse treatment from a new, even less sympathetic boss that would be more inclined to cut employment costs by mechanizing. Moreover, the Kappel Commission had glided over the fact, revealed by a Roper survey cited in its own report, that 76 percent of all Americans were "completely satisfied" with the post, and only 1 percent were "completely dissatisfied."

However, anyone who needed more convincing that something had to be done about the post found good reason in March 1970, when postal employees staged the first major strike by federal workers in American history and stopped much of the nation's mail. Their morale had been low and turnover rate high even before the urban meltdowns in the 1960s, primarily because of low wages. The average letter carrier, for example, started at barely $6,000 per year, which was significantly less than the national median income of about $7,500, and after twenty-one years made only $8,000; the poor salaries were a particular hardship in big cities, where the cost of living was higher. Then, too, although about 90 percent of the workers belonged to one of five postal unions, each of which could lobby Congress and the post, the groups couldn't bargain collectively.

Labor-management tensions peaked in the spring of 1970, when word leaked out that members of Congress were poised to give postal employees a 5.4 percent raise, contrasted to a 41 percent hike for themselves. On March 17 in New York City, Branch 36 of the National Association of Letter Carriers, fed up with low pay and worried by the looming prospect of the post's reorganization as a business, decided to take action. (Their nationwide organization of some 175,000 members, which had been founded in 1889, had grown more powerful in 1962, when Executive Order 10988 gave partial collective bargaining rights to government employee unions that did not segregate or discriminate based on race.) The New York City group broke with its parent organization to mount a wildcat strike, which quickly spread to involve perhaps a third of the post's workers in cities across the nation. Almost seven hundred post offices were shut down, including nine of the ten biggest.

The strike's devastating consequences, particularly on the business sector, shocked Americans into realizing how much the post that they took for granted actually mattered. In New York City, the stock market lurched and the draft board was unable to send notices informing nine thousand men that they had a temporary reprieve from military service. In Washington, census officials panicked over mailing their 1970 questionnaires on schedule, and declaring a national emergency, President Nixon ordered the military to deliver the mail. Postmaster General Winton Blount agreed to negotiate with the unions if their members returned to work, which they did. In exchange for a significant salary increase and other perks, labor dropped its opposition to the momentous transformation of the post proposed by the Kappel Commission.

Considering the post's long, slow, physical and philosophical erosion, proposing a radical strategy for its revival was perhaps not surprising. However, the Kappel report's central conclusion was a stunning reversal of the one given by another commission of experts gathered to assess the post's worst crisis, back in 1844. That group had concluded that, despite the post's terrible problems, it was indeed an essential public service that was necessary for creating an informed citizenry and even "elevating our people in the scale of civilization and bringing them together in patriotic affection." The days of the sweeping public service that had helped to forge American culture for almost two centuries seemed numbered, as the "true non-electric wire of government" was poised to become a "government-owned corporation."

16

THE U.S. POSTAL SERVICE

IN AUGUST 1970, an enthusiastic President Richard Nixon signed the Postal Reorganization Act, which was the most important such legislation since 1792. Loosely based on the Kappel Commission's recommendations, the law turned the founders' Post Office Department into the United States Postal Service (USPS). To mark the historic transition, the department's old-fashioned insignia of a post rider, often mistaken for a Pony Express courier, was updated to a sleekly minimalist American eagle.

This new federal agency was oddly designated as an "independent establishment of the executive branch," allegedly in order to avoid calling it a "government-owned corporation," as the Kappel report had. Remarking on the policy reversal that put a balanced budget ahead of public service, the historian Wayne Fuller wrote, "No longer was the Post Office to be the people's homespun Post Office, to be used as an instrument of government policy for whatever purposes Americans desired. Rather, it was to be a business like any other great American business."

Critics on the left and right soon zeroed in on the USPS's greatest flaw: the strange government-business hybrid incorporated disadvantages from both the public and private domains. This new post was expected to run as an independent company supported by revenue from its customers, but it was also hobbled by constraints that only AT&T

and a very few other huge businesses would accept. The most onerous were the obligations to submit to congressional oversight of its affairs and to provide universal service regardless of the price tag—a requirement sure to highlight the differences in cost efficiency between well-off areas, which generate lots of mail, and poor ones, which don't.

The post's reformulation as a kind of government-business jackalope would remain problematic, but the Postal Reorganization Act also effected some much-needed improvements. First on the list was the elimination of the scandalous spoils system, which had long compromised the post's efficiency and sullied its reputation. Since 1829, the postmaster general had been not only a cabinet member and the manager of one of the government's largest institutions but also, in most cases, the president's political crony and conduit for their party's patronage. The act ended this long, tarnished tradition by downgrading the department to an agency and removing the postmaster general from the cabinet. The USPS would be run by a board of governors, nominated by the president and confirmed by the Senate (later, with the Senate's advice and consent), which would appoint a qualified professional to serve as postmaster general and chief executive. Instead of including a legion of appointees hired and fired on the basis of partisan loyalty, the huge workforce would consist of civil service employees selected and retained on the basis of their merit.

The spoils system was already on the wane, but few politicians could relish eliminating it altogether when their own party occupied the White House. (Postmaster General J. Edward Day, a Washington neophyte when appointed by President John F. Kennedy in 1961, was amazed when Robert Kennedy, his brother's political operator, who served as attorney general rather than as postmaster general, nevertheless phoned him three times during a single afternoon about a job for one letter carrier in rural Mississippi.) However, Nixon and his postmaster general, Winton Blount, a wealthy businessman and a political appointee himself, welcomed the act's institutional reforms and were determined to turn the patronage-ridden, tax-supported Post Office

Department into a normal, revenue-supported business. They believed that depoliticizing the post was practical as well as right, partly because it would stabilize the organization and ensure that promising professionals could have a secure, long-term career.

The new USPS was no longer a federal department, but the president and Congress still retained ultimate authority over it, and it was soon apparent that the act's efforts to curb the latter's untoward interference fell short of the goal. Previously, the department had generally run at an annual average deficit of 20 percent, and congressional appropriations had made up the shortfall. Both the House and Senate had very powerful, patronage-minded committees that controlled this vital funding, as well as the department's policies, rates, wages, job appointments, transportation, pay raises, labor-management relations, and other matters, right down to the operation and fate of tiny rural post offices.

The act attempted to limit this egregious congressional meddling in several ways. Postal affairs were transferred to less powerful committees (now the Senate Committee on Homeland Security and Governmental Affairs and the House Subcommittee on Government Operations, which is part of the House Committee on Oversight and Government Reform). Postal revenues were now automatically appropriated to a new Postal Service Fund, which the USPS could use as needed without asking Congress. Moreover, the post would now propose necessary changes in postage and mail classifications to a five-member Postal Rate Commission, appointed by the president and confirmed by the Senate. This body presided over "omnibus rate case" meetings, which were formal public proceedings held to ensure transparency; the various groups that attended—big mailers such as Time Inc., smaller mailers, unions, the USPS's competitors, as well as the occasional citizen gadfly—had the opportunity to argue for favorable postage for themselves, often at the expense of other special interests. Following these complex hearings, the commission would make pricing recommendations for the board of governors' approval.

Such attempts to blunt Congress's unseemly influence gave the USPS more control over its affairs and limited legislative micromanagement on a daily basis but left it still vulnerable to political interference. The legislature remained in charge of the funding for services such as free postage on materials for the blind and overseas voters that amount to less than 0.1 percent of the budget (about $70 million in 2014). Nevertheless, Congress used this seeming loophole to control the entire post in substantive ways, from deciding which new services it could offer to which post offices it could close.

The act that at least diluted the relationship between politicians and the post also reformed its relationship to its workforce—a contentious matter that had led to the strike that had jeopardized the law's enactment. Congress, management, and labor had resolved that crisis by agreeing that employees would receive a wage increase of 8 percent, on top of a 6 percent hike for all federal employees, and would be able to reach the top of their pay grade in eight years. Now, the act also gave unions the right to bargain collectively on wages, benefits, and working conditions, although not the right to strike. (Postal salaries have continued to rise significantly, dividing public opinion along the lines foreseen by Clyde Kelly, who wrote that if the post were to become a business, the workforce "must be regarded as the devourer of revenues and every effort made to keep labor costs within the bounds of the amount derived from postage stamps.")

Finally, the Postal Reorganization Act authorized the USPS to borrow the money required to bring its buildings and equipment into the twentieth century. Within a decade, even critics would begin to acknowledge the post's technological transformation. The design and construction of the necessary buildings and machines took time, however, and throughout the 1970s, the struggling post had to deal with the exploding mail volume despite its inadequate facilities. One of its efforts to cope during this difficult period turned into a major advance in mail processing: a collaborative public-private process that's now called "work sharing."

The basic idea was not new. In 1943, the post had established a system in big cities that required bulk mailers of second- and third-class periodicals and advertising to sort their mail by zones according to the proper sequence for delivery. This policy greatly reduced the post's workload by producing what was in effect presorted mail. The introduction of the ZIP code in 1962 and affordable corporate computers that could sort mailing lists automatically in the mid-1970s laid the groundwork for even more promising cooperative efforts.

Most of America's mail is produced by businesses, and they naturally wanted to make the most of the new cost-effective, labor-saving procedures and technology. *Reader's Digest,* then a publishing behemoth, offered to presort its mail and hand it over to the post ready for delivery in exchange for a favorable "first-class bulk rate"—a classification that didn't exist then. The very notion of letting the hitherto sacrosanct first-class rates reflect the mailers' work seemed heretical at first, but Robert Cohen and some other postal executives went further, proposing that the rates of first-, second-, and third-class mail should *all* reflect the extent of presorting. Strong-willed, forward-looking William Bolger, a former mail clerk who worked his way up to the postmaster general's office in 1978 and served till 1985, agreed. To him, the controversial policy was a means both to increase mail volume and reduce the under-equipped post's workload, as well as its outlay for machines, buildings, and labor. Before long, the major publishers and the rest of the USPS's management, if not the unions, embraced the policy of work sharing, which kept service affordable, helped to double mail volume, and tacitly semiprivatized mail processing—an important yet under-remarked change that highlighted the post's role as a delivery system.

THE POSTAL REORGANIZATION ACT had addressed a crisis long avoided, but the USPS's start-up was predictably bumpy. It was not expected to become self-sufficient right away, and it got some public funding for its early years. Its deficits soared, however, and its service was dodgy, particularly regarding parcels, which gave the previously limited United Parcel Service its big breakthrough. Some impatient legislators even called for a return to the old Post Office Department, on the grounds that the public service had been more responsive to the people's needs— to say nothing of the fact that, as such, it would be back under the congressional thumb. As always, the postal reforms were more popular in the big cities, where public dissatisfaction was highest and service was most cost-effective, than in rural areas, where service was unprofitable, but people were more dependent on and happier with the post. Indeed, these historical regional tensions had nearly prevented Congress from passing the act in the first place. Texas senator Ralph Yarborough had led the opposition, evoking Old Hickory by thundering against substituting a "money corporation" for a public service that was "still the most efficient of any type of service in America." The bill arguably became law only because it was framed as a "positive" bipartisan cause during the "negative" era of Vietnam and urban riots—and because legislators, whether cheerfully or not, had finally reconciled themselves to the end of the old spoils system.

Despite dissatisfaction in some quarters, in 1977, the blue-ribbon Commission on Postal Service, a group of business, labor, and civic leaders, reported that although the USPS needed more time to become self-sufficient, it was doing a pretty good job of delivering the mail for a fair price and didn't need to be overhauled again. The group's forward-looking recommendations for improving service included cutting mail delivery to five days a week, allowing small post offices to be closed if their postmasters had relinquished their positions, appropriating $625 million to eliminate the USPS's outstanding debt from previous deficits, and allowing private carriers such as FedEx and UPS to expedite delivery of urgent letters in places where the post couldn't. In a particularly prescient, woefully overlooked observation, the commission emphasized that electronic communication was poised to decimate the volume of first-class mail on which the institution depended, and that the post must either join the digital revolution or be annihilated by it.

By the early 1980s, the USPS's modern technology was demonstrably modernizing the handling of traditional paper and parcel mail. The additional digits of the expanded ZIP+4 code, which debuted in 1978, had parsed delivery into even smaller zones, such as city blocks or corporate buildings, which cut the number of times a letter had to be handled and helped to sort mail in the right sequence for its carriers. The post needed more advanced machinery to read this more elaborate code, however, and by 1982, the first computerized optical character reader could "see" a letter just once, then print it with a bar code translated by a mechanical sorter at its destination post office. The USPS's performance standards, which clock how fast letters and parcels arrive at their destinations, improved significantly, if still unevenly, and the service mostly supported itself while supplying universal mail service at relatively stable prices and sustaining a huge middle-class workforce.

The post's productivity, which had risen in the 1970s and then flattened for a while, was surging by the early twenty-first century. The computerized system that keeps up with America's forty million changes of address per year—previously, a very labor-intensive, costly business—is one example of the mechanized marvels responsible. In the past, if John Doe moved to Denver, some of his mail was inevitably sent to his old address in San Francisco, where it would have to be redirected to his new home in Colorado. Now, when a letter mistakenly sent to him in California enters the processing system, a computer checks the post's enormous database of addresses, including those of people who have moved in the previous eighteen months, sees that Doe lives in Colorado, and sends the letter straight there—an advance that saves time, labor, and expense.

THE 1960S AND 1970S were a tumultuous era for America as well as its post, which had to keep serving the public while coping with its own crisis and reorganization. The transformation of stamps is an engaging illustration of its resilience and capacity for change even in the face of grave challenges. By the 1940s, America's philatelic iconography had begun to catch up with modern times. Stately portraits of dead presidents and war heroes occasionally gave way to those of different kinds of distinguished Americans. These high achievers included poets, scientists, artists, and inventors, as well as Booker T. Washington, an African American educator, and Jane Addams, a feminist and social reformer. By the 1950s, advances in the printing process had given artists much more latitude regarding color and the types of imagery that could be reproduced on stamps. The bright, contemporary commemoratives that resulted honored everyone and everything from the humorist Will Rogers to the American poultry industry.

Beginning in the 1960s, the post expanded its mandate to unite an increasingly culturally diverse America with stamps that celebrated widely shared themes from popular culture and promoted worthy causes. Elvis Presley remains the perennial best seller, but Robert Indiana's "Love" and the Walt Disney, *Star Wars*, and Legends of the West series also became special favorites. (In 2013, the post was criticized for going too far with the Harry Potter issue, which some perceived as both lightweight and, being of British origin, "un-American.") One stamp raised more than $79 million for breast cancer research, and although "duck stamps" are used on hunting licenses rather than mail, they have contributed $700 million to wetlands preservation. Holiday stamps expanded far beyond Christmas and Valentine's Day to include Eid al-Fitr and Kwanzaa, and popular commemoratives celebrated great national achievements, such as the exploration of space. (The USPS owns an envelope, smudged with lunar dust and postmarked on the moon in 1971, that bears a proof for the Apollo 15 stamps yet to be printed.) The new eminently collectible stamps have been a financial boon to the post, although some serious philatelists lament the shift away from intricate engraving.

Like stamps themselves, the process of choosing their subjects from among the forty thousand or so proposed each year has been thoroughly democratized. Previously, members of Congress trying to highlight their pet projects, such as dams and bridges, submitted most of the requests to the postmaster general. In 1957, however, the Citizens' Stamp Advisory Committee, an apolitical group of accomplished Americans, began to offer unbiased recommendations drawn from the enormous range of possible subjects. Until 2011, living persons were excluded, because even a seemingly sterling figure can end up tarnished, and timing remains an important consideration. Only when astronaut John Glenn had been safely pulled from the sea in 1962 did postal inspectors secretly deliver one hundred million Project Mercury stamps commemorating the event to post offices. The issue meant to honor the Moscow Summer Olympics in 1980 had been printed and distributed for circulation one day before President Jimmy Carter announced that the United States would boycott the games. The post pulled the rest of the stamps, but the disgruntled public demanded that they be put back on sale.

The USPS also responded to the turbulent American milieu of the 1960s and '70s with changes in its employment policies. The number of African Americans in its ranks increased in 1962, when Executive Order 10988 gave some collective bargaining rights to government unions that did not discriminate based on race. Efforts such as the President's Commission on the Status of Women in 1961 and the Equal Pay Act of 1963 also expanded women's employment in the postal service, and their numbers rose from just 22 percent of the workforce in the 1940s to 33 percent in the 1960s. Although the ranks of, say, female city letter carriers rose sharply, very few women still managed to become top postal executives.

In 1958, Postmaster General Summerfield had trumpeted, "With our near 16,000 women Postmasters representing close to half of our entire management staff, we believe it is fair to say the American Post Office Department . . . recognizes the management abilities of women perhaps more than any other private or governmental organization anywhere." However, his disingenuous statement tried to equate postmasters and executives. The first woman to break that glass ceiling was

Alice B. Sanger, who had been employed by Benjamin Harrison before he was elected president. He made her a clerk in the White House in 1889, which distinguished her as one of the first women to work there who wasn't a maid. She joined the Post Office Department in 1894, rose up the ladder, and in 1925 became an assistant clerk to the department's chief clerk—the first woman to hold that position. She handled a variety of clerical, budgetary, and other duties and even designed the postmaster general's official flag. In 1953, Dr. Beatrice Aitchison, a transportation specialist, became the department's first woman policy maker, and her work on more efficient, economical ways to move the mail led to significant savings.

Women executives remained seriously underrepresented in the post's top administration until 1985, when Jackie Strange became deputy postmaster general, the department's second-highest position. She was well prepared for the responsibility, having started in the department as a temporary clerk in 1946 while a college student. She ascended through the ranks, often as the first woman in various administrative positions; indeed, one of her male bosses had been fired for giving her the managerial job that was her first big break. In 2015, Megan Brennan was sworn in as America's first female postmaster general.

THE BIGGEST SURPRISE REGARDING the post's role in the Vietnam War that roiled America throughout the 1960s and early 1970s, and in subsequent wars, has been its great importance to the armed forces and their civilian supporters, despite other, more immediate means of long-distance communications. The modern phenomenon of mass correspondence between citizens concerned about the troops' welfare and unknown service members at the front began when a soldier fighting in Vietnam wrote to "Dear Abby" to say that what he and his bunkmates most wanted was mail from back home. His request loosed a flood of letters, and by Operation Desert Storm, a huge volume of mail from civilians eager to contribute to the war effort were posted to "Any Soldier."

The satisfactions of corresponding with a stranger may elude some people safe at home, but not young soldiers and sailors who might lack supportive friends and families. They want to know that America is behind them, and letters and CARE packages from concerned citizens summon thoughts of a larger community to return to. Then, too, for emotional reasons, physical letters have a special importance for military personnel. Troops stationed abroad in locations far from major bases and cities don't always have access to phone banks and computers and thus depend on paper mail. Moreover, for someone far from home and perhaps endangered, holding a letter that a loved one has written and touched is also a material comfort that's available at any time.

One big change in military mail is that most of it is now packages. Historically, the constraints imposed by transportation by sea had limited the number of parcels sent abroad. Soldiers who fought in World War II had to specify to loved ones exactly what gifts they wanted for the holidays, and then get the letters signed by their officers; back in the States, donors had to bring these letters to the post office to prove that they were sending only the requested items. During the Vietnam War, however, huge, well-publicized backlogs in San Francisco during the holiday season of 1968 changed military policy, and fleets of 747s now fly packages to troops abroad.

The whole process of delivering the military mail was streamlined in 1980, when the Department of Defense created the Military Postal Service Agency, which relieved each branch of the service from coordinating separately with the USPS. That's not to say that transporting mail to the troops is without its challenges. The military post has to negotiate with all the countries the mail will pass through, which means, for example, no alcohol or pork products in Muslim countries and no cigarettes in Italy.

THE USPS HAD MADE considerable progress in resolving some of its long-term problems in handling traditional mail, but the focus on correcting problems of the past distracted it and its congressional over-seers from its historic role in creating America and planning for the future. Such postmasters general as McLean, Blair, and Wanamaker would have anticipated the imminent digital revolution, just as Sum-merfield had more recently. They would have regarded email as the obvious evolutionary next step for paper mail and an online postal service as the logical extension of universal service. They would have insisted that the mandate to bind the nation was as readily adaptable to passwords and PINs as it had been to physical addresses, and that the post must take the lead in connecting Americans with electronic media, just as it had done with the delivery of newspapers, market data, affordable personal correspondence, and consumer goods. They would have marshaled the arguments once made for a postal telegraph on behalf of a postal Internet, maintaining that the obligation to unite the people with information and communications required making the new resource a public service rather than ceding it to private companies for their own profit.

The postal visionaries of the past would have tried to provide Americans with cheap, secure broadband access and email accounts that protect them from hackers and hucksters. They would have moved to capitalize on the post's great brand for security and privacy by offer-ing safe ways to transact business online, including a legally binding digital signature service, secure cards for paying bills and authen-ticating identity, and safe digital storage. They would have insisted that every post office in America become a neighborhood media hub equipped with a bank of computers that enabled citizens to go online for little or no expense—a service now provided by more than sixty nations around the world, to say nothing of America's own public li-braries, where people queue up or take a number for online access.

That the USPS and a Congress beset with lobbyists from special interest groups either didn't foresee or didn't respond to the digital revolution's impact on the post's traditional operations and seize upon its positive potential was a monumental failure. After all, the Internet itself was created by the federal government's own Advanced Research Projects Agency (later, Defense Advanced Research Projects Agency) and nurtured by its National Science Foundation, which funded the Computer Science Network. This convergence of federal institutions should have put the federal government's official communications-and-information system on the inside track in the race to exploit the new technology for the public good.

That certain people involved in postal affairs did grasp the digital revolution's implications only highlights the missed opportunity. Back in 1965, Summerfield had written, "How can we break the economic and time barriers of a system requiring that privately recorded messages—small pieces of paper in essence containing writing and pictures—must be passed from hand to hand in every phase of delivery from the sender to the receiver?" His visionary experiment with Speed Mail leapfrogged over traditional mail processing to the high-speed transmission of information that would climax in email. In 1977, Gaylord Freeman, the chairman of the Commission on Postal Service, had said, "Unless the Postal Service really makes a commitment, which it has not made, to electronic message transfer, they face a really bleak future." Underscoring the point with the example of the post's failure to act on a proposal from Xerox to co-launch a "daygram" service that would send faxes from one post office to another for delivery within four hours, he emphasized the commission's conclusion: "We feel quite strongly that the Postal Service doesn't recognize the seriousness of the loss of the first class mail." House Post Office and Civil Service Committee chairman James M. Hanley, a New York Democrat, agreed, observing that congressional efforts to nudge the USPS toward electronic communications had been unsuccessful: "All three Postmasters General (since the 1971 reorganization) have been reluctant to do that."

In 1982, the Office of Technology Assessment (OTA), which between 1972 and 1995 advised Congress on scientific and technological matters, published "Implications of Electronic Mail and Message Systems for the U.S. Postal Service." The report underscored that such commercial services "will increasingly compete with portions of the traditional market of the U.S. Postal Service. . . . It seems clear that two-thirds or more of the current mainstream could be handled electronically, and that the volume of USPS-delivered mail is likely to peak in the next 10 years." (First-class mail volume actually peaked in 2001, total mail volume in 2006.) Like the earlier Commission on Postal Service, the OTA urged Congress and the USPS to join the digital age before it was too late.

These warnings thrust postal management into what psychologists call an approach-avoidance conflict: a push-pull reaction to something that poses both risks and rewards. Like individuals, businesses struggle with how to balance the need to keep doing the things that produce revenue with the desire to try something new that could be either a lucrative success or a costly failure. The Postal Reorganization Act's demand that the post become a self-supporting, businesslike organization understandably weighed heavily on managers, most of whom rose through the ranks thinking more about how to move the mail and balance the books than about innovation and political maneuvering. Moreover, as an organization of insiders, the USPS had little expertise in the new world of electronic communications.

Despite the obstacles, a few top postal executives did manage to experiment with digital pilot programs. In 1982, well before the general use of email, Postmaster General Bolger launched E-COM (electronic computer-originated mail). This service enabled a computer in one post office to transmit a message to a computer in another, where it could be printed out and delivered to as many as two hundred recipients within two days—a plus in terms of both increasing speed and reducing mail handling and costs. The post struggled for several years to offer E-COM over the loud protests of such companies as International Telephone & Telegraph, Graphnet, and Telenet, which were all too aware of the logic and seeming near-inevitability of postal email. Their fears were realistic enough, considering that an enormous government enterprise like the post is better able than most businesses to lose money on launching new projects. Moreover, some eighty eclectic businesses and groups, including the Moral Majority, Merrill Lynch, and Eastern Airlines, had already signed up for E-COM, in hopes of using it for everything from bills to timely notices for just twenty-six cents per two pages.

E-COM's supporters faced the same kinds of opposition as the proponents of the postal telegraph, RFD, Parcel Post, and the Postal Savings System had experienced before them. Indeed, as recently as 1975, the USPS had bowed to pressure from Kinko's and other photocopying businesses and ordered that photocopiers be removed from post office lobbies. Allowing such a simple amenity that complemented traditional mail services had been a great convenience, especially for suburban and rural Americans, and outraged postal customers bombarded the USPS and Congress with thousands of protest letters (an effort reinforced by Xerox's media campaign to keep its own machines in place). Two years later, in a rare concession, the post reversed itself and declared that existing copiers would not be removed; however, before new ones could be installed, local postmasters had to ensure that there were no commercial alternatives nearby.

Various forces converged to doom the promising E-COM. Officials in the Commerce and Justice departments during the Reagan administration raised the possibility of violations of antitrust laws. The private companies' lawyers and lobbyists protested against government competition, found receptive ears within Congress, and initially succeeded in limiting the post's role to the physical delivery of the messages after transmission by independent firms. The final blow involved the funding. The pilot program's launch had been expensive, but E-COM had to be priced low to attract a high volume of customers; nevertheless, the post's overseers would not allow the rates to be cut. Despite the surge in electronic communications in general and its own volume in particular, which rose from two million transactions in 1982 to twenty-three million in 1984, Bolger could do nothing without Congress's approval, and E-COM was halted that year.

The precedent had been set, and later digital pilot programs faced similar obstacles. Start-up costs were high, deadlines for demonstrating profitability remained unrealistically tight, and private firms railed against government competition. When Postmaster General William Henderson, who served between 1998 and 2001, announced a secure, downloadable email service called PosteCS in 1998, UPS acted to protect its own proposed service and filed a complaint with the Postal Rate Commission. Other digital efforts around the same time, including eBillPay, Mailing Online, NetPost.Certified, and Electronic Postmark, met similar fates.

Some of the problems that plagued the post's digital pilot programs, however, were of the USPS's own making. It had little internal expertise in electronic media, and some of its efforts were poorly designed. Postal managers variously described as overly protective or arrogant made matters worse by trying to conceal details about the projects and expenses from their regulators, which cost them credibility and created bad feeling. An aggrieved Congress ordered the General Accounting Office (GAO) to examine the pilot programs' cost-revenue ratio, and its scathing report in 2000 convinced powerful politicians and even members of its own board of governors that the USPS should stop experimenting and stick to delivering traditional mail.

The GAO's grim analysis set the tone for President George W. Bush's commission on postal reform, whose 2003 report was tellingly titled *Embracing the Future: Making the Tough Choices to Preserve Universal Mail Service.* The group concluded that the post's efforts to innovate had been "largely disappointing" and had also "drained time and resources that could have been spent improving traditional postal services." The report recommended that the USPS be required to focus on its core mission, described as providing "products and services related to the delivery of letters, newspapers, magazines, advertising mail, and parcels"; it should not even provide other government services, such as expediting passports, unless they covered their own costs.

. . .

THE NEWLY NARROW DEFINITION of postal service was soon reified by the Postal Accountability and Enhancement Act (PAEA) of 2006, a major piece of legislation that made 150-odd changes to the Postal Reorganization Act of 1970. Those who wish to see mail service privatized lament that the law fell short of their ultimate goal. Others believe that it imposed enormous financial burdens on the USPS while simultaneously obstructing its efforts to modernize, thus consigning it to a slow death by a thousand cuts.

The gravest of the wounds dealt by the PAEA—and the single most important reason for the post's recent crisis—concerns a serious labor issue. Despite mechanization, employees' wages and benefits still account for 80 percent of the USPS's operating expenses, which is significantly more than private carriers' 60 percent, although the latter's lower costs also reflect their ownership of their means of transportation. However, meeting the payroll of the current workforce is less worrisome for the post and many other organizations, both public and private, than the obligation of covering retirees' health care and other benefits, which are already costly and projected to rise steeply. The PAEA required the post to prefund the retiree health care benefits already earned by its employees, although the money will not be used until they actually retire—a complicated formulation that's often abbreviated as prefunding for the next seventy-five years. Starting in 2007, at the onset of the major recession, the post was ordered to pay the Treasury, via the Retiree Health Benefit Fund, $5.5 billion annually for ten years. The service began to report huge annual deficits beginning that same year, even though the USPS's actual operations have recently been profitable.

The PAEA's draconian retiree health care benefits burden was soon widely criticized as outlandish and unfair, but Congress refused to ameliorate it. The official explanation was that the massive prefunding protected taxpayers from an eventual bailout, but the real reason was political: the need to keep the larger federal budget "neutralized." That is, because the post's payments to the Treasury count as a revenue "plus," any relief from them, according to the Balanced Budget Act of 1997, would have to be offset by equivalent tax increases or cost cutting—steps sure to annoy some lobbies and constituents somewhere. Since 2011, the post has simply defaulted on the payments, and efforts to reduce them to a more manageable level have been complicated by various legislators' insistence on attaching political strings to potential solutions.

The PAEA also replaced the Postal Rate Commission with the Postal Regulatory Commission, which was charged with monitoring the USPS's performance in important respects. The most controversial is ensuring that postage rates are capped according to the Consumer Price Index regardless of the post's increased costs—an unreasonable demand that no private business would accept. Finally, the act took a very hard line regarding innovation and ordered the USPS to conform to a very tight definition of postal service, namely "the delivery of letters, printed matter, or mailable packages, including acceptance, collection, sorting, transportation, or other functions ancillary thereto."

Back in 2002, already worried that the post suffered from "oversight blight," Murray Comarow, the Kappel Commission's executive director and a major architect of the USPS, had anticipated the PAEA and its effect on postal management: "If the nation's best executives occupied every top postal position, they would find themselves at a loss to run an organization that has only marginal influence over how much it pays its people, how much it charges its customers, or whether it can make sensible service changes without political or union resistance."

WHILE AMERICA WENT ONLINE, the USPS and Congress remained intent on improving and increasing what the people already called "snail mail." Although it had become much more efficient in performing its traditional paper and parcel functions by the early twenty-first century, the nation's official communications and information system had failed to join the revolution that had already transformed modern life.

Moreover, the post's image in the minds of average Americans remained stuck in the era of its midcentury meltdown. A soggy magazine or a letter that takes a week to arrive is a relatively infrequent occurrence, considering each person's hundreds of deliveries per year, but people stubbornly if unfairly continued to regard such occasional lapses as characteristic of the whole enterprise. Just as most hadn't realized that the price of a stamp previously covered just part of the cost of actually delivering a letter, most didn't understand that, as of 1971, the stamp was supposed to cover the entire expense. When postage prices necessarily climbed, they were vexed, even though rates remained relatively stable when adjusted for inflation. Very few appreciated that between the early 1980s and 2007, the USPS had supported itself without any tax dollars while continuing to provide universal service at reasonable rates—an achievement that would have impressed Benjamin Franklin and every postmaster general since. Perhaps most important, Americans and their elected representatives had by now long taken the post for granted and largely expected it to function without their interest or input. The transformation of the Post Office Department into the United States Postal Service seemed to erase the last vestiges of their awareness of the dynamic institution described by Congressman Clyde Kelly, who had anticipated and fought against its slow decline:

> Throughout all past history, whatever political party
> was in control of the Government . . . conservative or
> progressive, the Post Office has been used in new ways
> for the promotion of the general welfare. . . . When new
> conditions arose where additional benefits could be
> extended through this nation-wide enterprise, there was
> no hesitation in following the path of national progress.

===================

WHITHER THE POST?

ANYONE WHO TROUBLES TO LEARN about the post's long, eventful past must also take an interest in its present and future. Even without the benefit of hindsight, a few things are clear. The post is in trouble again, but to paraphrase, the reports of its death have been greatly exaggerated. The $68.9-billion-per-year enterprise is the world's most productive postal system, handles 40 percent of its mail, and charges its lowest rates. If it were a private company, the USPS would rank in the top tenth of the Fortune 500. Its enormous assets, which are distributed across 3.5 million square miles, include a phenomenal physical delivery system built over more than two centuries, the nearly thirty-two thousand post offices, and the nation's second-largest civilian workforce (after Walmart). Moreover, the post visits more than 154 million addresses almost daily and, in a dangerous, unpredictable world, continues to be a bulwark of the democracy as well as the economy. As Postmaster General Arthur Summerfield said, "We live by communications, and at any moment we may find that we survive because of them."

Predictions that the post's end is nigh are hardly new and were more justified during its crises in the 1840s and the 1960s and '70s. The recent jeremiad began in 2007, when the USPS reported a seriously alarming deficit just as the great recession began. The common wisdom blames its ongoing financial crisis on the Internet's decimation of first-class mail volume, which has indeed decreased by 25 percent since its peak in 2004. Better-informed observers add a highly politicized Congress's pattern of inaction alternating with interference, particularly in the form of such legislation as the Postal Accountability and Enhancement Act of 2006, which imposed the staggering Retiree Health Benefit Fund payments that mostly account for the USPS's recent deficits.

Everyone agrees that "something must be done about the post office," which can't operate indefinitely without enough money. Determining exactly *what* should be done is a political decision that only Congress can make, yet legislators have been in no particular hurry to act. Some of their reluctance reflects pressure from the powerful lobbies that pay for political campaigns and benefit from maintaining the postal status quo. The labor unions want to keep members' jobs. The mass mailers strive to preserve their cheap rates, regardless of increasing costs. The private carriers support the post's commitment to serving nearly every address in the country six days a week, because they often pay the USPS to do the "last mile," or final stretch, of their deliveries for them, particularly outside metropolitan areas.

If certain paradoxical postal policies reflect the influence of special interest groups, others arise from politicians' efforts to please their constituents. The fate of unprofitable post offices, most of which are in rural or low-income areas, is a good example. Budget hawks since the Early Republic have griped that there are too many of them, but most were established back in the days when people had to walk, ride a horse, or drive a wagon to get their mail. The number of post offices peaked in 1901 at about 76,000, rapidly diminished with the advent of Rural Free Delivery and the automobile, and continues to decline. Of America's 31,800 post offices, stations, and branches in 2014, slightly more than 3,000 of the largest brought in 46 percent of the post's total "walk-in" revenue. Many of the rest are either underperforming urban offices that could be consolidated with others nearby or among the half that are still in rural places.

A private company would simply close the unprofitable retail facilities—a logical move for any revenue-driven enterprise. Indeed, the USPS management has already shut down half of its major distribution centers, with consequent delays in mail delivery that are particularly noticeable in rural states. It has also eliminated 10,000 jobs, mostly by attrition, and reduced hours at 13,000 small post offices, which prevented many from closing. However, of the 3,700 unprofitable facilities the postmaster general proposed shutting down in 2011, only about 140 were actually terminated. What prevents the USPS from further pruning its operations is the opposition from postal unions as well as aggrieved citizens and legislators from vulnerable, mail-dependent areas, who stress the post's public service dimension over mere business considerations. They also observe that closing more rural offices wouldn't make much of dent in the postal deficit at the cost of compromising the national infrastructure and a part of daily life that's important to many citizens—also a rational point of view.

Coming up with a consistent policy for resolving the fate of small post offices would require Congress to consider these two legitimate choices—prioritizing cost-effectiveness or public service—and make a principled decision. Legislators, however, are well aware of the venerable maxim that one of the few things your congressman can do for you is to save your post office. Some politicians argue for preserving them in general, but others who loudly lament their financial toll will fight like tigers to keep the unprofitable post offices in their own fiefdoms. In short, both Republican and Democratic politicians share an unusually bipartisan view of the matter: "I think it's smart to close post offices that aren't cost-effective—but not in my district or state."

Congress may deserve the lion's share of the blame for their dysfunctional relationship, but the USPS contributes to it as well. The fracas over Saturday mail delivery in 2013 is a good example. Legislators bewailed the post's net losses of $45 billion since 2007 and once again insisted that something must be done. Postmaster General Patrick Donahoe eagerly agreed and offered to slash billions in costs by taking various steps, which included, in a historic reversal, *slowing down* first-class mail delivery by a day or more—sometimes much more, particularly outside cities. He also proposed stopping Saturday letter delivery, which alone would save $2 billion per year. The majority of Americans have favored this sensible economy since 1977, when the Commission on Postal Service found that most people said they could easily live with five-day-a-week letter mail. While Congress was debating the idea, the Government Accountability Office stepped in to contest the postmaster general's claim that Saturday service was no longer legally mandated, and the Postal Regulatory Commission questioned the size of the alleged savings. Instead of rising to these challenges, however, the USPS withdrew its own plan, allegedly because of backstage lobbying by the unions, which want to maximize jobs and work hours, and mass mailers, which want Saturday advertising to encourage weekend shoppers. Thus, despite the opinion of the public over almost forty years and at least some of the USPS's top management, costly six-day letter delivery continues.

POLITICS CONTRIBUTES TO THE USPS's current predicament, but its fundamental challenge is existential: What should—and could—America's information and communications system be in the twenty-first century?

One reason why answering that question is difficult is that the post is not a one-size-fits-all operation. It must serve a huge geographically and socioeconomically diverse population whose members have very different needs and are spread over a vast, various terrain stretching from Key West, Florida, to Barrow, Alaska. It delivers mail in the canyons of Wall Street and to the bottom of the Grand Canyon, reached by mule, and even operates a boat service for Great Lakes ships in transit. Urban and rural Americans, the young and the old, house-holders and businesses, the healthy and the disabled, the well-off and the disadvantaged—all have different expectations of the post.

The briefest consideration of the post office's role in community life is enough to convey the difficulty of setting postal policy for the whole nation. Most Americans now live in metropolitan areas, where they enjoy an array of media services as well as easy access to consumer goods and mass entertainment. They generally like their letter carriers but go only when they must to their big, crowded, impersonal post offices. As population density decreases, however, this dynamic changes dramatically. Some 20 percent of Americans live in rural areas, which are concentrated in the Midwest and West but exist all over the coun-try; indeed, at 82.6 percent, Vermont has the highest proportional per-centage of country and small-town folk. These less populous places also have the largest share of small post offices, which are often vital social and commercial hubs. A trip to the P.O. tends to be an enjoyable break that's part of life's rhythm and an opportunity for spontaneous interactions—so much so that many country people who could have home delivery prefer to pick up their mail.

Even among Republicans and Democrats, opinions about the post and its future are not as predictable as might be assumed. As regard-ing the federal government in general, conservatives are more inclined to want to scale it back, progressives to preserve it. The post has histor-ically enjoyed significant bipartisan support, however, and there are many exceptions to the rule on both sides, notably Republicans who represent large swaths of the rural population that's more dependent on mail. Even postal management harbors different perspectives on the institution's future, particularly regarding innovation.

That said, there are three basic schools of thought about the post's future. Those who dispute the government's right to monopolize a ser-vice that business could provide want to privatize it. They observe that the nation is increasingly bound by commercially supplied electronic communications, and they assert that the post should simply close down and cede any traditional mail operations that can turn a profit to the independent carriers.

The cause of postal privatization has attracted ideologues since James Hale and Lysander Spooner back in the mid-nineteenth century and has echoed periodically in the halls of the Capitol since. In the 1970s, Senator Jesse Helms, Republican of North Carolina, argued to end the postal monopoly on the grounds that it was just a matter of time until companies would turn to electronic billing, which would cut the revenue from first-class mail. Senator James Buckley, a Conservative/Republican from New York, proposed to "liberalize" the postal market by opening it to competition from independent carriers and granting them access to private mailboxes, which federal law prohibited. In 1979, the Private Express Statutes were suspended to allow rival companies to compete with the post for the delivery of "extremely urgent" letters.

The privatizers raise some good points, particularly regarding the post's labor issues and what amounts to its encouragement of junk mail. They note that a number of European nations that have de-monopolized their posts have seen some improvements regarding innovation and cost. (Indeed, the USPS took some steps in that direction long ago by adopting the principle of work sharing and making concessions regarding urgent letters.) However, privatizers gloss over the major reason for the different bottom lines of businesses and public services, even a hybrid like the USPS: the latter do the difficult, unprofitable work that the former eschew, such as providing universal mail service to every American everywhere for the same low price.

If the post were privatized, or even turned into a regulated private industry like the airlines and railroads, management would naturally place revenue over the commonweal. Postage between big cities, such as Boston and Los Angeles, might remain low, but a profit-oriented business would legitimately demand higher rates per mile in less cost-efficient areas that are off the beaten track. As of 2015, the USPS charged forty-nine cents to send a first-class letter from Deposit, New York, to American Falls, Idaho, but a private carrier, like an airline, would ask much more, thus effectively compromising universal service.

Then, too, many of those who blithely say "just privatize the post office" are unfamiliar with the way the nation's delivery system actually operates in the twenty-first century. FedEx and UPS are most profitable in metropolitan areas and would risk bankruptcy in trying to handle the enormous volume of the entire nation's mail. Moreover, during the past several decades, dealing with each other and practical realities on the ground has nudged the post and the independent carriers to become "co-opetitors" that are bound by the former's last-mile service. Parcel delivery is not a significant added expense for the USPS, which carries the mail door-to-door six days a week anyway. Neither of the major independent carriers, however, could make those exhaustive rounds without subsidization. Just as FedEx and UPS pay the post for help with this final phase of their deliveries, the post pays the private firms for transportation services. In the latest iteration of the public-private collaboration that the post has engaged in since the days of the stagecoach, FedEx's planes carry the U.S. mail by day and the company's own freight by night.

The privatizers' bold rhetoric lends itself to iconoclastic opinion pieces and letters to the editor in newspapers, but it has not won over the great majority of American households and businesses. The national delivery system has evolved over time, and though it might not be the Platonic ideal, it works pretty well. The independent carriers and the post both benefit from their symbiotic relationship, as do consumers, because the post's lower rates keep the private companies' prices in check. Moreover, surveys show that while most people accept that the post, like the rest of world, must change with the times, they don't think that the Internet has made it obsolete, any more than planes eliminated boats or TV killed radio. They don't see why they must choose between public and private services, digital and physical media, if they don't have to.

. . .

ADVOCATES OF THE second and third schools of thought on the post's role in the twenty-first century agree on a number of important principles. Both the more liberal and conservative of these supporters value the post's great reputation for security and privacy—the same old-fashioned virtues in which the Internet is seriously deficient—its tremendous infrastructure, and its state-of-the-art technology for processing traditional mail. They believe that Congress is arguably the USPS's worst enemy and that the post must be freed from legislative oversight blight. (One provocative proposal for effecting that change is based on the fact that, unlike most huge businesses, the USPS has no shareholders. However, if it were to pay taxes on its revenue, as a normal company does, the Treasury would become a powerful vested interest with a strong incentive to push Congress for the reforms necessary to make the post solvent. Near the top of that list would be the elimination of the price caps imposed by the PAEA in 2006 that prevent the post from raising its low charges to cover its high costs.) These groups ask, "Why not keep a public asset that offers dependable, inexpensive services, receives no tax dollars for its operations, belongs to the citizens, and is important to many of them, some vitally so? Who would benefit from privatizing it?" Although the post's left- and right-leaning supporters agree on some big things, they divide over others, particularly whether the USPS should emphasize its business or public-service nature and whether it should cut back its services or expand into new areas.

The post's progressive supporters allow that its failure to go digital was a serious lapse but argue that it can still make up for the missed opportunity. They want to retrofit the meaning of "postal service" and the founders' information-based postal commons for a world in which, as the saying goes, if it can be digital, it will be digital. They want the post to provide Americans with broadband access and a secure electronic "home base" that would unify their scattered online lives, link their digital and physical addresses, and provide hack-proof services, such as an electronic mailbox, a lockbox for important private data, and verification and authentication for legal and business transactions. They question why the government that gives financial support to Wall Street companies despite their baroque abuses can't help a benign and popular public institution modernize its services, as it has in the past.

The nation's growing problem of financial inequality could provide the post with an opportunity to run a digital experiment based on a century-old precedent. About a quarter of Americans are effectively barred from the private banking system by low income, which leaves them prey to overpriced, unscrupulous payday lenders, check cashers, and pawnshops. The duties of the USPS's Office of Inspector General include investigating opportunities for generating revenue, and its research suggests that the post could respond to this unmet need with an electronic update of postal savings banking, which ended in 1966: the basic financial services provided by a "nonbank bank"—the awkward term for an institution that doesn't handle *both* loans and deposits. Customers would receive a postal card that they could use for purchasing, withdrawing from an ATM, depositing and cashing checks, paying bills, and making international money transfers. The post would charge a fraction of what the predatory vendors do, while also producing substantial revenue for itself. The banking industry's objections about the specter of unfair competition, first made a century ago, and Congress's recent restrictions on new "nonpostal" services pose formidable obstacles, but the post's long history of issuing money orders might enable the USPS to test the plan without congressional approval.

Going online is not the only way in which the post could modernize. Its huge workforce, which moves house-by-house through America's neighborhoods nearly every day, could provide more services, such as checking on the elderly and infirm and contributing to "big data" on air pollution, traffic patterns, and other public concerns. Better use could be made of the nation's nearly thirty-two thousand post offices by allowing them to handle state and local matters, such as processing traffic tickets, driver's licenses, car registrations, and hunting and fishing licenses. As in many nations, they could become community information hubs that offer computers, Internet access, and even simple rooftop aerials that provide free or low-cost local "intranet" web and phone service. The local Starbucks or Dunkin' Donuts could even move into the post office, space permitting. This type of public-private collaboration could attract more customers for both enterprises; help maintain a town's identity, ZIP code, and gathering place; save on new construction; and preserve architectural landmarks, some of which the USPS has already sold to private developers amid significant controversy.

The first hurdle to expanding postal services in the twenty-first century would be convincing Americans and their elected representatives that such a thing is still possible. Congress would have to reassess fifty years of policy that has prioritized traditional mail and discouraged postal innovation and confront strenuous opposition from lobbyists deploying the same arguments that their predecessors used against the postal telegraph, RFD, the Postal Savings System, and Parcel Post. To make a major investment in America's telecommunications infrastructure, the legislators would also have to bet on the equivalent of the tremendous return on bipartisan funding for interstate highways and rural electrification in the 1950s and '60s. On one hand, the timing is currently favorable for such a step, because the government could borrow the money at low long-term interest rates; on the other, the nation's current center-right politics constrains federal spending.

THE POST'S MORE conservative supporters believe that, like the federal government in general, it is simply too big and ambitious. Like postmasters general Benjamin Franklin, Ebenezer Hazard, Albert

Burleson, and Walter Brown before them, they narrow their eyes on the bottom line. Considering the decline in the first-class mail that has traditionally been its main source of revenue, they conclude that the post must bow to Congress's directives, act more like a business, and offer only traditional services that are profitable or at least self-supporting, notably the delivery of parcels and advertisements. They maintain that by acknowledging the changed times and downsizing gracefully, the post can continue to deliver America's hard copy and endure as a national resource.

The conservatives' leaner, meaner post would scale back its workforce and facilities and become the general contractor for a public-private delivery system. The businesses that produce at least three-quarters of the nation's mail would handle all the "upstream" activity that precedes delivery, such as sorting, bar-coding, and transporting it to large distribution stations, as many firms already do. From those facilities, the post's carriers would depart on their routes with their bags mostly presorted—again, as many do now. In short, the USPS would become a public utility that, aside from doing some collection, was primarily a delivery system of carriers.

Most scenarios for such a stripped-down USPS emphasize the revenue to be reaped from a kind of gold-plated version of Parcel Post. The same Internet that reduced first-class mail's volume also significantly increased that of packages, which rose by 50 percent between 2010 and 2015, making the post a cornerstone of America's delivery-and-returns-dependent electronic marketplace. (With its reputation for security and connections with mail systems abroad, the post could also benefit from the international e-commerce boom, which is plagued with such difficulties as authenticating buyers and sellers across borders and deciphering foreign taxes and customs duties.) To make the most of the parcel boom, which helped account for the $1.1 billion increase in postal revenues between 2014 and 2015, however, the USPS must improve its retail services. It must also do more to cultivate the

tech-empowered tough customers who are accustomed to online merchants' cosseting and impatient with any friction that interferes with
their purchasing pleasure. To win over more of these consumers, the
post must provide more individualized treatment, almost-instant delivery, and round-the-clock, no-wait pickups and returns.

The conservatives' no-frills model of the post comes at a price. The
universal-service requirement could be modified if not eliminated.
Mailing could become more expensive, especially in out-of-the-way
places and for such amenities as quicker service. Local post offices
would disappear, and the postal workforce would be significantly reduced. Buying stamps and sending letters and parcels would be handled in drug or convenience stores by retail workers who earn less than
postal clerks. (Indeed, the USPS has already taken steps in this direction. Like the private employees who staff postal service counters in
stores such as Staples, shop owners enrolled in the Village Post Office
program sell stamps and ship flat-rate packages. Moreover, they can do
so during hours when post offices are closed—practices critics con-
demn as further jeopardizing full-service post offices.) Such a pared-
down USPS might be cost-effective, but it would not be the dynamic,
evolving communications and information system envisioned by the
founders and steadily amplified into the twentieth century.

SHOULD THE POST OF the twenty-first century devolve into a private
industry? Update its historical mandate, as it has in the past, and bind
the nation with digital services? Become a bare-bones version of the
current government-business hybrid that focuses on paying its way, especially by delivering parcels?

Any discussion of the post and its value takes place in the context
of much larger issues and questions, starting with: What is the value of
government itself? The United States and its post were creations of the
Age of Enlightenment. More than two centuries later, reason no longer necessarily produces agreement, and the principles of universality

and equality that are intrinsic to the post are questioned in practice if not theory. Since the 1960s, institutions in general have been reflexively seen as obstacles to progress rather than its potential agents. The idea that government should not do what private business could do instead, which has ebbed and flowed in American life since the early nineteenth century, is widely tolerated if not accepted.

The effort to assess a huge, complex institution that in its nearly two and a half centuries has been both advanced and backward, principled and corrupt, brilliant and dysfunctional, also requires what F. Scott Fitzgerald called "first-rate intelligence," which he defined as "the ability to hold two opposed ideas in the mind at the same time, and still retain the ability to function." Then, too, the post's future is in the hands of citizens and their elected representatives who are mostly unaware of its history, which tells America's story from creating the democracy's educated electorate to expanding the small Atlantic nation to the Pacific to adding the skies to its transportation grid.

The post office is the least remarked and most misunderstood of the nation's original great institutions, but it's the one that did the most to create America's expansive, forward-looking, information- and communications-oriented culture. In need of drastic reform, it almost went out of business in the 1840s, only to be resurrected and reach its zenith a few decades later. Before deciding its future, it behooves Americans and their leaders to reflect on what the post has accomplished over the centuries and what it could and should contribute in the years to come.

ACKNOWLEDGMENTS

The history of America's post spans more than two centuries, and this book would not have been possible without the help of many postal scholars, employees, and enthusiasts. Anyone who studies American communications in general and the post office in particular stands on the shoulders of historian Richard R. John. His erudition is matched only by his generosity and enthusiasm in sharing it with others. I'm very grateful to the historians James McPherson, Richard Kielbowicz, and Philip Rubio, who also kindly read my manuscript and offered their comments and corrections. Any errors are mine alone.

The Smithsonian National Postal Museum is a wonderful resource that belongs on the agenda of any tourist visiting Washington, D.C. I thank Allen Kane, its director; Cheryl Ganz, emerita curator of philately; and Nancy Pope and Lynn Heidelbaugh, curators in its history department, for sharing their insights, as well as Marshall Emery, who supplied many of the book's images from the museum's archives. I'm also grateful for the help of John Fleckner, senior archivist at the Smithsonian National Museum of American History; F. Robert van der Linden, chairman of the Aeronautics Department of the Smithsonian Institution's National Air and Space Museum; and Jeremy Johnston, curator and historian at the Buffalo Bill Center of the West.

I thank Jennifer Lynch, the USPS historian, particularly for her research on the post's women and minority employees. I'm grateful to David C. Williams, the Inspector General of the USPS, and especially to Renee Sheehy and Mohammad Adra at the Office of Inspector General. Former postal executive Robert Cohen was an invaluable help in researching the institution's modern history. Comments from former Deputy Postmaster General John Nolan and John Pickett and John Waller, also from the Office of Inspector General, were also most helpful.

I'm grateful to Steve Hutkins and his friends at the Save the Post Office website; Matthew Liebson, president of the Ohio Postal History Society; Frank Scheer, the energetic founder of the Railway Mail Service Library; and philatelist Richard C. Frajola. Historians Robert Allison and Nathaniel Sheidley introduced me to the colonial post in Boston, and Michael Schragg offered a personal tour of the U.S. Postal Museum, in Marshall, Michigan. Diane DeBlois and Robert Dalton Harris, who live in what might be a postal museum outside Albany, New York, shared their stories and scholarship as well as their treasures. The sponsors of PostalVision 2020 invited me to a conference, and the American Philatelic Society to an annual meeting, where Ken Martin directed me to my first collectible: a beautiful twenty-nine-cent Grace Kelly, the last of America's engraved stamps.

Finally, I thank Kristine Dahl, my agent, Ann Godoff, my editor, and the team at Penguin Press, especially Will Heyward and Casey Rasch, and copy editor Candice Gianetti, who kept the long journey to this book running on steel wheels.

NOTES

1: Inventing the Government: B. Free Franklin

8 **"was by the Endeavour made a better and a happier Man than I otherwise should have been"**: Benjamin Franklin, *Benjamin Franklin's Autobiography*, eds. Leo Lemay and P. M. Zall (New York: Norton, 1986), p. 73.

8 **"it is finer and more godlike to attain it for a nation"**: Aristotle, in William D. Ross, *The Nicomachean Ethics of Aristotle* (London: World Library Classics, 2009), p. 6.

9 **"If man could have half his wishes, he would double his troubles"**: Benjamin Franklin, *Poor Richard's Almanack: Selections from the Apothegms, and Proverbs, with a Brief Sketch of the Life of Benjamin Franklin* (Waterloo, IA: The U.S.C. Publishing Co., 1914), p. 30.

9 **"To-morrow, every fault is to be amended; but that to-morrow never comes"**: Ibid., p. 56.

9 **"The noblest question"**: Ibid., p. 49.

9 **"Well done is better than well said"**: Ibid., p. 57.

10 **"It would be a very strange Thing"**: Benjamin Franklin to James Parker, 20 March 1751. http://founders.archives.gov/documents/Franklin/01-04-02-0037.

11 **"within the compass of a nut shell"**: Max Farrand, ed., *The Records of the Federal Convention of 1787*, vol. 3 (New Haven, CT: Yale University Press, 1911), p. 540n.

11 **The simple drawing showed:** *Pennsylvania Gazette* (Philadelphia). May 9, 1754, p. 2. http://www.history.org/history/teaching/enewsletter/volume5/november06/primsource.cfm.

11 **optical telegraph relayed coded messages:** The optical telegraph (the word "telegraph" comes from the Greek for "writing at a distance") that preceded the electrical version was first used in France in the nineteenth century. It also expedited shipping in Boston, New York City, and San Francisco, notably on Telegraph Hill.

12 **"It is said that as many days"**: Herodotus, *The Histories*, ed. and trans. A. D. Godley, vol. 4, book 8, verse 98 (Cambridge, MA: Harvard University Press, 1924), pp. 96–97.

12 **"perhaps the only mercantile project"**: Adam Smith, *An Inquiry into the Nature and Causes of the Wealth of Nations*, ed. John Ramsay McCulloch (Edinburgh: A & C Black, 1863), p. 368.

13 **"all letters which are brought from beyond the seas"**: H. T. Peck, Selim H. Peabody, and Charles F. Richardson, eds., *The International Cyclopaedia: A Compendium of Human Knowledge*, vol. 12 (New York: Dodd, Mead, 1892), p. 72.

14 **"Your kinde lines I received"**: John Endicott to John Winthrop, 1639. Katherine Grandjean, *American Passage: The Communications Frontier in Early New England* (Cambridge, MA: Harvard University Press, 2015), p. 47.

14 **Few colonists could afford to use the Crown post**: Ian K. Steele, *The English Atlantic, 1675–1740: An Exploration of Communication and Community* (New York: Oxford University Press, 1986).

15 **"enter into a close correspondency"**: John Romeyn Brodhead, *History of the State of New York*, vol. 2 (New York: Harper & Brothers, 1853). Quoted in William Smith, *History of the Post Office in British North America* (Cambridge, UK: Cambridge University Press, 1920), p. 197.

15 **A witty journal kept by sharp-eyed "Madam" Sarah Kemble Knight**: Sarah Kemble Knight, *The Journal of Madam Knight* (Boston: David R. Godine, 1972).

Knight's journal wasn't published for more than a century after her death, but her droll account would have delighted her contemporaries, who were increasingly interested in what their neighbors in other colonies were up to. An enthusiastic traveler, she relishes "neet and handsome" lodgings, steaming cups of "Chocolett," and the customs of the natives, tribal and British alike.

Many Bostonians, Philadelphians, and New Yorkers would have chuckled over Knight's report of customs in Connecticut, where the Indians "marry many wives and at pleasure put them away"—a free and easy approach to matrimony that also prevailed "among the English in this (Indulgent Colony) as their records plentifully prove." They would have been amused by her account of a woman who told some visiting Quakers, who were "humming and singing and groneing after their conjuring way," to "take my squalling Brat of a child here and sing to it . . . [for] I can't get the Rogue to sleep." Some would have been shocked to hear that Connecticut's residents were "too indulgent (especially ye farmers) to their slaves . . . permitting them to sit at Table and eat with them, (as they say to save time,) and into the dish goes the black hoof as freely as the white hand."

16 **"a stout fellow, active and indefatigable"**: Francis Lovelace to John Winthrop, 27 December 1672, in Brodhead, *History of the State of New York*, vol. 2, p. 6.

Some post riders exhibited a strong entrepreneurial streak, quitting the service to set up as independent express carriers or encouraging illegal tipping, hustling lottery tickets, or toting parcels on the side. A British postal inspector once discovered hearty seventy-two-year-old Ebenezer Herd, a Crown courier for forty-six years, preparing to deliver a pair of oxen to a customer along with the mail.

16 **"very bad, Incumbered with Rocks"**: Knight, *Journal of Madam Knight*, p. 17.

16 **"what cabbage I swallowed"**: Ibid., p. 5.

16 **"got a Ladd and Cannoo"**: Ibid.

17 **"Clamor of some of the Town topers"**: Ibid., p. 9.

17 **"tyed by the Lipps to a pewter engine"**: Ibid., p. 2.

17 **"It being one chief project of that old deluder"**: Nathaniel B. Shurtleff, ed., *Records of the Governor and Company of the Massachusetts Bay in New England*, vol. 2 (Boston: William White, 1853), p. 203.

18 **"or if any Glut of Occurrences happen, oftener":** http://nationalhumanities
center.org/pds/amerbegin/power/text5/PublickOccurrences.pdf.

18 **The authorities almost immediately shut down:** Ibid.

19 **"But being still a boy":** Benjamin Franklin, *Memoirs of Benjamin Franklin*, vol. 1
(Philadelphia: McCarty & Davis, 1834), p. 8.

20 **"facilitated the correspondence":** Benjamin Franklin, *The Autobiography of
Benjamin Franklin* (Boston: Houghton Mifflin Company, 1923), p. 167.

22 **"You must obey this now for a Law":** Captaine John Smith, *The Generall Historie of
Virginia, New-England, and the Summer Isles* (London: I.D. and I.H. for Michael
Sparks, 1624).

22 **"Let all men have as much freedom":** John Smith, *The Journals of Captain John
Smith: A Jamestown Biography*, ed. John Milliken Thompson (Des Moines, IA:
National Geographic Books, 2007), p. 139.

22 **"I am obnoxious to each carping tongue":** Anne Bradstreet, "The Prologue," *The
Works of Anne Bradstreet, in Prose and Verse*, ed. John Harvard Ellis (Charlestown,
MA: Abram E. Cutter, 1867), p. 101.

23 **so-called revenue stamps:** The first display in the Smithsonian National Postal
Museum's "Gems of American Philately" section contains a proof of the revenue
stamp mandated by the Crown's 1765 Stamp Act. The colonists' collective outrage
over this form of taxation, which led to their first unified step on the long path to
independence, helps to explain the hated item's rarity.

24 **"They will not find a rebellion":** Benjamin Franklin, *The Papers of Benjamin
Franklin*, vol. 13, eds. Leonard W. Labaree, Helen C. Boatfield, and James H.
Hutson (New Haven, CT: Yale University Press, 1969), p. 142.

24 **"an abridgment of what are called English liberties":** Quoted in James K.
Hosmer, *The Life of Thomas Hutchinson* (Boston and New York: Houghton Mifflin
1896), appendix, p. 436.

25 **"Were any Deputy Post Master to do his duty":** Hugh Finlay, *Journal Kept by
Hugh Finlay, Surveyor of the Post Roads on the Continent of North America*, ed. Frank
H. Norton (Brooklyn, NY: Norton, 1867), p. 32.

26 **"letters are liable to be stopped":** William Goddard's petition to the Continental
Congress, September 29, 1774, in the collection of the National Postal Museum,
Washington, D.C.

27 **"His name was familiar to government and people":** John Adams, *Diary and
Autobiography*, vol. 1, ed. L. H. Butterfield (Cambridge, MA: Harvard University
Press, 1961) p. 245.

28 **"If you would not":** Franklin, *Poor Richard's Almanack*, p. 32.

2: BUILDING THE POSTAL COMMONS

30 **"The disinclination of the individual States to yield":** George Washington to
Benjamin Harrison, January 18, 1784, The George Washington Papers at the
Library of Congress, 1741–1799, Series 2: *Letterbooks 1754–1799*, Library of
Congress, Manuscript Division. http://teachingamericanhistory.org/library
/document/letter-to-benjamin-harrison/.

31 **"Is there a doubt whether a common government"**: George Washington, "Farewell Address," September 17, 1796, ibid., and http://avalon.law.yale.edu /18th_century/washing.asp.

31 **"The importance of the post office and post roads"**: George Washington to Congress, October 25, 1791, ibid., and http://avalon.law.yale.edu/18th_century/ washs03.asp.

31 **"the only means of carrying heat and light"**: Benjamin Rush, "Address to the People of the United States," *American Museum* (January 1787), p. 8.

31 **In 1790, the system:** Statistics on post offices and routes from United States Postal Service, "Universal Service and the Postal Monopoly," http://about.usps.com /who-we-are/postal-history/universal-service-postal-monopoly-history.txt.

33 **"the sole and exclusive right"**: *The Articles of Confederation; the Declaration of rights; the Constitution of the Commonwealth, and the Articles of the Definitive Treaty between Great-Britain and the United States of America* (Richmond, VA: Dixon and Holt, 1784).

33 **"establish Post Offices and post Roads"**: Constitution of the United States, Article 1, Section 8, Clause 7.

36 **"a communications revolution that was as profound"**: Richard R. John, *Spreading the News: The American Postal System from Franklin to Morse* (Cambridge, MA: Harvard University Press, 1995), p. vii.

36 **"There is no resource so firm"**: George Washington, "Fifth Annual Address," 1793, in James Richardson, ed., *Compilation of the Messages and Papers of the Presidents, 1789-1917,* 53rd Congress, 2nd session, 1907, H. Misc. Doc. 210 (serial 3265), vol. 1, p. 142 (Washington, D.C.: U.S. Government Printing Office, 1896–99).

37 **"His own mind was in a perpetual state of exaltation"**: Oliver Wendell Holmes, *Currents and Counter-Currents in Medical Science with Other Addresses and Essays* (Boston: Ticknor and Fields, 1861), p. 26.

38 **"principles, morals, and manners of our citizens"**: Rush, "Address to the People of the United States," ibid., p. 10.

39 **"the true non-electric wire of government"**: Benjamin Rush, "On the Defects of the Confederation," in Dagobert D. Runes, ed., *The Selected Writings of Benjamin Rush* (New York: The Philosophical Library, 1947), p. 29.

39 **"among the surest means of preventing the degeneracy"**: James Madison, "Address of the House of Representatives to the President," 1792, in Robert A. Rutland et al., eds., *Papers of James Madison, Congressional Series,* vol. 14, 6 April 1791–16 March 1793 (Charlottesville: University of Virginia Press, 1983), p. 404.

40 **"a better man than Rush"**: Quoted in Carl Binger, M.D., *Revolutionary Doctor: Benjamin Rush, 1746–1813* (New York: W. W. Norton, 1966), p. 296.

40 **"as a man of Science"**: Ibid.

41 **"suffer any person, but such as you entrust"**: Timothy Pickering, "Instructions to the Deputy Postmasters" (1792), in Richard R. John, ed., *The American Postal Network, 1792–1914,* 4 vols. (London: Pickering & Chatto, 2012), vol. 1, p. 4.

41 **"so frequent and great an evil"**: Quoted in Wayne E. Fuller, *The American*

Mail: Enlarger of the Common Life (Chicago: University of Chicago Press, 1972), p. 241.

42 **"I know of but one effectual Security"**: Timothy Pickering to John Hargrove, August 8, 1794, National Archives Microfilm Publication 601, *Letters Sent by the Postmaster General, 1789–1836*, roll 3, 372–33. Quoted in Deanna Boyd and Kendra Chen, "The History and Experience of African Americans in America's Postal Service," http://postalmuseum.si.edu/AfricanAmericanhistory/p1.html.

42 **the lively society of the Early Republic**: For an excellent survey of this era, see Daniel Walker Howe's Pulitzer prize–winning *What Hath God Wrought: The Transformation of America, 1815–1848* (New York: Oxford University Press, 2009).

44 **"more dangerous than standing armies"**: Thomas Jefferson to John Taylor, May 28, 1816, in Paul Leicester Ford, ed., *The Writings of Thomas Jefferson*, vol. 10 (New York: G. P. Putnam's Sons, 1892–99), p. 31.

45 **"metaphysical abstractions"**: Quoted in Joseph J. Ellis, *After the Revolution: Profiles of Early American Culture* (New York: Norton, 2002), pp. 202, 206.

45 **"Our fellow citizens in the remote parts of the Union"**: Archives of the United States Post Office Department, Letterbooks of the Postmaster General, Book C, 1793, p. 54. American Historical Association, *Annual Report of the American Historical Association* (Washington, D.C.: U.S. Government Printing Office, 1911), p. 144.

3: MOVING THE MAIL

47 **"an infant people, spreading themselves"**: Quoted in Albert J. Beveridge, *The Life of John Marshall*, vol. 1 (New York: Houghton Mifflin, 1916), p. 250.

47 **"great travellers; and in general better acquainted"**: Morris Birkbeck, *Notes on a Journey in America from the Coast of Virginia to the Territory of Illinois* (London: James Ridgway, 1818), p. 34.

49 **"large stage chair, with two good horses"**: Quoted in Oliver W. Holmes and Peter T. Rohrbach, *Stagecoach East: Stagecoach Days in the East from Colonial Period to the Civil War* (Washington, D.C.: Smithsonian Institution Press, 1983), p. 11.

49 **"so artful that the postmaster cou'd not detect them"**: Finlay, *Journal Kept by Hugh Finlay*, p. 18.

49 **"the establishment of stages"**: Quoted in Clyde Kelly, *United States Postal Policy* (New York: D. Appleton, 1931), pp. 30–31.

50 **Hazard had used his travels**: Ebenezer Hazard, *Historical Collections: Consisting of State Papers and Other Authentic Documents; Intended as Materials for an History of the United States of America* (Philadelphia: T. Dobson, 1792).

51 **"carrying and delivering of any letters"**: *The Articles of Confederation; the Declaration of rights.*

52 **"It is extremely to be lamented"**: George Washington, letter to John Jay, *The Writings of George Washington from the Original Manuscript Sources, 1745–1799, Volume 30: June 20, 1778–January 21,1790*, ed. John C. Fitzpatrick (Washington D.C.: U.S. Government Printing Office, 1931), p. 16.

54 **"every Monday morning at five o'clock"**: Dallas Bogan, "Warren County Local

History, Part 1: Early Ohio Postal Systems and Post-Riders," September 4, 2004. http://www.rootsweb.ancestry.com/~ohwarren/Bogan/bogan248.htm.

55 **"persons of integrity, sound health, firmness":** Ibid.

55 **The territory's first regular overland route:** Ibid., "Part 2: Profiling Ohio's Postal Routes and Carriers."

56 **"All teams and vehicles were prompt":** Ibid.

56 **treed by a pack of wild hogs:** Ibid.

56 **Still another escaped from an Indian attack:** Ibid.

59 **"I traveled along a portion of the frontier":** Alexis de Tocqueville, *Democracy in America*, ed. J. P. Mayer, trans. George Lawrence (Garden City, NY: Doubleday, 1971), p. 303.

60 **"Frightful roads. Perpendicular descents":** Quoted in George Wilson Pierson, *Tocqueville in America* (Baltimore: Johns Hopkins University Press, 1938), p. 579.

61 **"counteract every tendency to disunion":** John Caldwell Calhoun, "Speech to the House of Representatives," February 4, 1817, in Richard Kenner Crallé, ed., *The Works of John C. Calhoun: Speeches Delivered in the House of Representatives and in the Senate of the United States* (New York: D. Appleton, 1864), p. 190.

61 **"covered with advertisements of elections":** John Fowler, *Journal of a Tour through the State of New York in the Year 1830* (New York: A.M. Kelley, 1970; reprint of 1831 original), p. 72.

62 **"It's a great constitutional question":** Quoted in Pierson, *Tocqueville in America*, p. 653.

62 **"There isn't anyone who does not recognize":** Quoted in ibid., p. 590.

4: THE POLITICIZED POST

63 **"to increase the ease of communication":** Pierson, *Tocqueville in America*, pp. 589–90.

64 **"astonishing circulation of letters":** Tocqueville, *Democracy in America*, p. 283.

65 **"If it were possible to communicate":** *The Express Mail*, 1827. McLean Papers, Library of Congress, Washington D.C., quoted in John, *Spreading the News*, p. 86.

66 **"On all the principles of fair dealing":** Ibid., p. 85.

68 **"To the victor belong the spoils":** William Learned Marcy, remarks in the Senate, January 25, 1832, *Register of Debates in Congress*, vol. 8, col. 1325, quoted in I. D. Spencer, *The Victor and the Spoils* (Providence, RI: Brown University Press, 1959), pp. 59-60.

69 **"should be rejected from his position":** An Ex-Clerk, "Seven Years in the Boston Post Office" (1854), in John, *American Postal Network*, vol. 1, p. 182.

70 **"what the veins and arteries are to the natural body":** Andrew Jackson, "First Annual Message to Congress," December 8, 1829, in *Inaugural Addresses of the Presidents of the United States* (Washington, D.C.: U.S. Government Printing Office, 1989).

70 **The first postmaster general to be empowered:** For more information on the decade's changes, see Robert Dalton Harris Jr., "The Three Postal Networks of

the United States in the 1830s," Business History Conference 2004. http://www
.thebhc.org/sites/default/files/Harris_0.pdf.

72 **"reliable men for confidential work"**: Quoted in Louis Melius, *The American
Postal Service* (Washington, D.C.: National Capital Press, 1917), p. 48.

73 **"very strange, that such a provision"**: Jeremiah Evarts, "An Account of
Memorials . . . Praying that the Mails May not be Transported, Nor Post-
Offices Kept Open, on the Sabbath" (1829), in John, *American Postal Network*,
vol. 3, p. 5.

74 **"it does me no injury"**: Thomas Jefferson, *Notes on the State of Virginia*,
ed. Frank Shuffelton (New York: Penguin, 1998), p. 165.

74 **"Is it not necessary"**: Barnabas Bates, "An Address . . . on the Memorials to
Congress to Prevent the Transportation of the Mail . . . and the Opening of the
Post Offices on Sunday" (1829), in John, *American Postal Network*, vol. 3, p. 102.

76 **"tyrants" are prone to single out**: Cincinnatus, "Freedom's Defense: Or a Candid
Examination of Mr Calhoun's Report on the Freedom of the Press" (1836), in ibid.,
vol. 1, p. 149.

5: CRISIS AND OPPORTUNITY

79 **"I get along very well"**: Quoted in Kathryn Burke, "Letter Writing in America,"
http://postalmuseum.si.edu/letterwriting/lw03.html.

81 **"It is the care and duty of the Post Office Department"**: Franklin, "An
Examination of the Probable Effect of the Reduction of Postage" (1844), in John,
American Postal Network, vol. 3, p. 125.

81 **they carried a very substantial portion**: In *The Crying of Lot 49*, Thomas Pynchon
evokes the postal crisis of the 1840s and the rise of private mail services in the saga
of Oedipa Maas, a Californian who gets caught up in a mystery upon becoming
coexecutor of a former suitor's estate. The dead man's extensive philatelic
collection includes some stamps possibly linked to an underground postal service
called the Tristero, which had seemingly been vanquished by its Thurn und Taxis
rival in the eighteenth century. The book's title may refer to the California Gold
Rush of 1849, when poor communications in the West became a vital national
concern and encouraged private postal services.

82 **"a current of affection"**: James Simmons, *Remarks of Mr. Simmons, of Rhode Island,
in Support of His Proposition to Reduce Postages to a Uniform Rate of Five Cents for a
Single Letter, for All Distances* (Washington, D.C.: J. & G. S. Gideon, 1845), p. 12.

82 **"exceedingly onerous and unjust"**: Amasa Walker, "Cheap Postage, and How to
Get It" (1845), in John, *American Postal Network*, vol. 3, p. 135.

82 **"Lower unit cost through the increased volume"**: Kelly, *United States Postal Policy*,
pp. 88–89.

82 **"a striking figure—tall"**: "Death of Pliny Miles, the American Advocate of Cheap
Postage," *New York Times*, May 4, 1865.

83 **"the constitution expresses, neither in terms"**: Lysander Spooner, *The
Unconstitutionality of the Laws of Congress, Prohibiting Private Mails* (New York:
Tribune Printing Establishment, 1844), p. 1.

84 **"seizes upon the lightning itself"**: James De Bow, *The Cause of the South: Selections from "De Bow's Review," 1846–1867,* eds. Paul F. Paskoff and Daniel J. Wilson (Baton Rouge: Louisiana State University Press, 1982), p. 71.

85 **"it would suffer as all enterprizes suffer"**: Quoted in Fuller, *American Mail,* p. 174.

85 **"superseded in much of its important business"**: Annual Report of the Postmaster General, 1846. Quoted in United States Postal Service, https://about.usps.com/who-we-are/postal-history/telegraph.pdf.

86 **"elevating our people in the scale of civilization"**: Quoted in Gerald Cullinan, *The United States Postal Service* (New York: Praeger, 1973), p. 57.

86 **"the people's post office"**: Fuller, *American Mail,* p. 42.

86 **Congress shored up the post's finances in other important ways**: For more information on the postal monopoly, see Richard R. John, "The Postal Monopoly and Universal Service: A History," School of Public Policy, George Mason University. http://www.journalism.columbia.edu/system/documents/704 /original/Appendix_D.pdf.

89 **"Far more than other government policies or actions"**: Richard B. Kielbowicz, *News in the Mail: The Press, Post Office, and Public Information, 1700–1860s* (Westport, CT: Greenwood Press, 1989), p. 1.

6: THE PERSONAL POST

91 **David Henkin calls "the postal age"**: David M. Henkin, *The Postal Age: The Emergence of Modern Communications in Nineteenth-Century America* (Chicago: University of Chicago Press, 2006).

92 **"My dearest Ella"**: Letter from the private philatelic collection of Matthew Liebson.

94 **The lid of this "Victorian laptop"**: Catherine J. Golden, *Posting It: The Victorian Revolution in Letter Writing* (Gainesville: University Press of Florida, 2009), p. 116.

95 **precocious fifteen-year-old Carrie Deppen**: Diane DeBlois and R. D. Harris, "Connections of a Lady Telegrapher," *The Congress Book 2009* (Philadelphia: American Philatelic Congress, 2009).

95 **"Three weeks ago I received thy letter"**: Lucretia Mott, *Selected Letters of Lucretia Coffin Mott,* eds. Beverly Wilson Palmer et al. (Champaign: University of Illinois Press, 2002), p. 233.

98 **"Oh, could I hear thee once declare"**: Thomas Cooke, *Universal Letter Writer* (New York: Thomas Nelson and Sons, 1855), p. 222.

98 **"Weddings now are all the go"**: http://www.mtholyoke.com/pcsite/pcs/images38 /Howland11.jpeg.

99 **Many were simply mean or sarcastic**: Quoted in "The Days of the 'Vinegar Valentines,'" http://www.dailymail.co.uk/femail/article-2277508 /The-days-Vinegar-Valentines-How-cards-1900s-used-tell-suitors-DIDNT -fancy-them.html.

99 **the hobby of philately**: Philately's open-ended, democratic, do-it-yourself quality helps explain its enduring global popularity. Stamp collecting has no rules that must be followed and no particular requirements of time or money. The salesclerk who collects stamps of birds and the Silicon Valley mogul who hunts for costly

arcana can both enjoy the same pleasures of learning new things, making exciting discoveries, and contributing to philatelic knowledge. Like Microsoft's Bill Gates, Dell's Michael Dell, and Symantec's Gordon Eubanks, many begin as children, almost all of whom collect *something* for a while. Those who take up the hobby later in life do so for many reasons, which include relief from workaday stress. A small minority pursues expensive rarities, but most collectors gravitate toward stamps that connect in some way to their personal lives. Some trace their families' histories in America or abroad and others complement their interests in a particular sport, celebrated figure, or historic period. Philately attracts the young and old, rich and poor, but men predominate. King George V of England passed the world's largest, finest stamp collection to his granddaughter Queen Elizabeth II, who is the most famous woman philatelist today. (Other famous collectors have included Amelia Earhart, Yul Brynner, Jasha Heifetz, and John Lennon.)

101 **"we have substituted the Head of Franklin"**: Quoted in "The First Postage Stamp Honoring Benjamin Franklin," http://postalmuseum.si.edu /collections/object-spotlight/franklin.html.

7: Growing the Communications Culture

105 **"the visible form of the Federal Government"**: United States Post Office Department, *Report of the Postmaster-General* (Washington, D.C.: Government Printing Office, 1889), p. 3.

106 **Many small rural and frontier settlements came and went:** According to resident and local historian Cheryl O'Brien, the first white settlers of the Upper Wind River region of northwest Wyoming, who arrived in the 1870s and '80s, were ranchers. They were followed by homesteaders, gold miners, and the Scandinavian "tie hackers" who lumbered the vast pine forests to build the railroad. A community needed fifty residents to get a post office, and in 1889, the town of Dubois, which had first proposed to call itself Tibo (Shoshoni for "white man"), had the area's earliest, which was 200 miles from a railroad. The first postmaster was Charlie Smith, a legendary explorer and rancher who was celebrated in the diary of Owen Wister, author of the best seller *The Virginian* and friend of Teddy Roosevelt. After moving from place to place, the Dubois post office settled down for a while in Welty's general store, presided over by postmaster Alice Welty, the first of several women to fill the position. This sociable Victorian matron, who has a cameo in *Rising from the Plains*, John McPhee's book on the region's geology and characters, was known for her enjoyment of the latest gossip and inclination to have a gander at her customers' letters as she handed them over.

The Upper Wind River area had ten other early post offices, each with a story to tell. Mary Rhodes, the postmaster at Leesdale, was a good friend of the outlaw Butch Cassidy, who worked on a ranch nearby; he even left her a ring. (She may have been among the many locals who reported seeing him around long after his alleged death in South America.) The short life of the log-cabin Tipperary post office, named for the still-popular World War I song, ended in 1940, after the white homesteaders' grazing rights on tribal land, granted in the early 1900s, were revoked. The town of Lenore—named for the first postmaster's daughter and consisting of ten buildings, a cemetery, and a stagecoach stop—had been founded on optimistic speculation about an imminent railroad spur that had never materialized. After the main highway was relocated, Lenore's post office closed in 1942, but the small community lived on and is known as the onetime home of Charles Henry King, its postmaster, who was a grandfather of President Gerald Ford. (Presentation for the Dubois Outreach Center of the Central College of Wyoming, February 9, 2013.)

106 **The books were published five times as frequently:** For more information about these surveys, see Diane DeBlois and Robert Dalton Harris, "Using the Official Registers: Local Sources of Postal Revenue," Winton M. Blount Symposium on Postal History, November 4, 2006, National Postal Museum. http:// postalmuseum.si.edu/research/pdfs/Harris_paper.pdf.

106 **To re-create a sense of what:** The general store–post office of Headsville is now located in Bellefonte, Pennsylvania, next to the American Philatelic Center and its legendary library of twenty thousand books, which was formerly housed at nearby Penn State University. The charming Victorian town lies in the heart of central Pennsylvania's iron country, and its ironworks cast the cannons for Admiral Perry's fleet in the War of 1812 and, later, much of the Brooklyn Bridge. A beacon of commercial and social progress, Bellefonte was one of the first places in the world to have electricity, and its skilled workforce in the mid-nineteenth century included hundreds of former slaves eager to find jobs. Its prominent residents have included five governors of Pennsylvania.

107 **Some were slapdash shanties:** Carl Scheele, *The American Philatelist,* October 1971.

107 **"He is a Democrat in politics":** Quoted in Marshall Cushing, *Story of Our Post Office: The Greatest Government Department in All Its Phases* (Boston: A. M. Thayer & Co., 1893), p. 462.

110 **"I am sensible that the emolument":** Quoted in United States Postal Service, "Women Postmasters," July 2008. http://about.usps.com/who-we-are /postal-history/women-postmasters.pdf.

110 **"a doubt has been suggested":** Ibid.

111 **"has not been the practice of the Department":** Ibid.

111 **as "dark as a pocket":** "Brave Polly Martin, Who Used to Drive the Attleboro Mail," *Boston Daily Globe,* May 5, 1884. Quoted in United States Postal Service, "Women Mail Carriers," June 2007. http://about.usps.com/who-we-are /postal-history/women-carriers.pdf.

8: Linking East and West

114 **"all honest, because there was nothing to steal":** *The Quarterly of the Oregon Historical Society,* Portland, Oregon, June 1904, p. 174.

116 **Her much-publicized epistolary accounts:** Narcissa Prentiss Whitman, *The Letters of Narcissa Whitman, 1836–1847* (Fairfield, WA: Ye Galleon Press, 1986).

117 **"I never was so contented":** Narcissa Whitman to Harriet and Edward Prentiss, 3 June 1836, ibid., p. 16.

117 **"There is one manner of crossing":** Narcissa Whitman, journal entry, 13 August 1836, ibid., p. 27.

118 **"We must clean after them":** Narcissa Whitman to Clarissa Prentiss, 2 May, 1840, ibid., p. 93.

118 **"fraught with as much promise":** Samuel Parker, *Journal of an Exploring Tour Beyond the Rocky Mountains* (Ithaca, NY: Mack, Andrus & Woodruff, 1840), p. 329.

118 **"My dear Mother, I have been thinking":** Narcissa Whitman to Clarissa Prentiss, 5 December, 1836, ibid., p. 44.

118 **"I do not know how many":** Narcissa Whitman to Clarissa Prentiss, 2 May, 1840, ibid., p. 96.

118 **"My Dear Mother, I cannot describe":** Narcissa Whitman to Clarissa Prentiss, 2 May, 1840, ibid., p. 93.

119 **"This country is destined":** Narcissa Whitman to Stephen and Clarissa Prentiss, 9 October, 1844, ibid., p. 181.

119 **"once here I think":** Narcissa Whitman to Stephen and Clarissa Prentiss, ibid., p. 184. Mrs. Whitman did not date this letter, but it appears in *The Letters of Narcissa Whitman* between letters dated October 9, 1844, and February 10, 1845.

119 **"Can the aged mother read":** Henry H. Spalding to Stephen and Clarissa Prentiss, 6 April, 1848, quoted in William A. Mowry, *Marcus Whitman and the Early Days of Oregon* (New York: Silver, Burdett and Company, 1901), p. 329.

120 **"Go west young man":** John Babson Lane Soule, editorial, *Terre Haute* [Indiana] *Express*, 1851.

123 **"So little confidence have we":** Quoted in David Nevin, *The Expressmen* (New York: Time-Life Books, 1974), p. 24.

125 **"a glorious triumph for civilization":** Quoted in Arthur Chapman, *The Pony Express* (New York: G. P. Putnam's Sons, 1932), p. 71.

125 **"No one who has not seen":** Quoted in Nevin, *The Expressmen*, p. 53.

126 **"an imposing cradle on wheels":** Mark Twain, *Roughing It* (Hartford, CT: American Publishing Company, 1886; orig. publ. 1872), p. 25.

127 **even Captain Sir Richard Francis Burton:** See Richard F. Burton, *The City of the Saints* (New York: Harper & Brothers, 1862).

127 **"I now know what Hell is like":** Waterman L. Ormsby, *The Butterfield Overland Mail: Only Through Passenger on the First Westbound Stage*, eds. Lyle H. Wright and Josephine M. Bynum (San Marino, CA: Henry E. Huntington Library and Art Gallery, 2007; orig. publ. 1942), pp. viii, 167, 173.

128 **"Here I lay me down to sleep":** Quoted in Frederick Nolan, *The Wild West: History, Myth & the Making of America* (London: Arcturus, 2003), p. 131.

9: THE MAIL MUST GO THROUGH

132 **The Pony's most important tools:** The horse played a role in America's rural life—and in the popular mind and heart—well into the modern age. Just as Henry Ford's Model T's were rolling off the assembly line in Detroit, Bud and Temple Abernathy, ages nine and five, rode their horses from their home in Oklahoma to

New York City. During their month-long trip, Orville Wright offered them a plane ride, and President William Howard Taft greeted them at the White House. Parading alongside Teddy Roosevelt and the Rough Riders, they were cheered by more than a million New Yorkers. In the summer of 1911, the Abernathys broke their own record, riding nearly four thousand miles, from New York to San Francisco, in sixty-two days.

133 **"Wanted: Young, skinny fellows"**: Laura Ruttum, "The Pony Express: History and Myth," http://www.nypl.org/blog/2010/02/01/pony-express-history-and-myth.

133 **"a little bit of a man"**: Twain, *Roughing It*, p. 70.

134 **"I . . . do hereby swear"**: http://www.xphomestation.com/facts.html#J.

134 **"setting aside the chance of death"**: Burton, *The City of the Saints*, pp. 5, 460.

135 **"The mail must go through!"**: Quoted in Ralph Moody, *Riders of the Pony Express* (Lincoln: University of Nebraska Press, 2004), p. 24.

139 **"'HERE HE COMES!' Every neck"**: Twain, *Roughing It*, p. 184.

10: WAR CLOUDS, SILVER LININGS

141 **"should deem their letters safe"**: Timothy Pickering to John Hargrove, August 8, 1794, *Letters Sent by the Postmaster General*, roll 3, pp. 372–73. Quoted in Boyd and Chen, "The History and Experience of African Americans in America's Postal Service," http://postalmuseum.si.edu/AfricanAmericanhistory/p1.html.

141 **"especially as it came within my knowledge"**: Joseph Habersham to Isaac E. Gano, postmaster of Frankfort, Kentucky, April 1801, ibid., roll 10, p. 321.

142 **"most active and intelligent"** slaves: *The American Annual Cyclopaedia and Register of Important Events*, vol. 4 (New York: D. Appleton, 1865), p. 236. Quoted in ibid.

142 **"no other than a free white person"**: *The Public Statutes at Large of the United States of America from the Organization of the Government in 1780 to March 3, 1845*, vol. 2 (Boston: Charles C. Little and James Brown, 1850), p. 191. Quoted in ibid.

142 **After he escaped from bondage**: "True Tale of Slavery," *The Leisure Hour: A Family Journal of Instruction and Recreation*, February 1861, p. 85.

143 **"The mails, unless repelled, will continue"**: Abraham Lincoln's First Inaugural Address. http://avalon.law.yale.edu/19th_century/lincoln1.asp.

143 **the Confederacy censored the mail**: For more information, see Diane DeBlois and Robert Dalton Harris, "Newspapers and the Postal Business of the Confederacy," *Postal History Journal*, No. 156, October 2013.

144 **"If I owned four millions of slaves"**: Quoted in Robert M. Poole, *On Hallowed Ground: The Story of Arlington National Cemetery* (New York: Walker & Company, 2009), p. 15.

145 **the quiet county seat of Elmira**: Alan Parsons, "How the Post Office in Elmira, NY Met the Challenges of the American Civil War," presentation, 7th Annual Postal History Symposium, American Philatelic Society, November 2–3, 2012. http://stamps.org/2012-Papers-and-Presentations.

145 **Writing to the folks back home**: The American Philatelic Society's 2012 symposium, titled "The Blue & Gray," featured a handsome exhibition of Confederate generals' letters and covers from 1861 to 1865. Stonewall Jackson and

Jeb Stuart were represented, of course, but so were many of their less familiar peers. Among them was Adam "Stovepipe" Johnson, who got his nickname when he tricked a Union town into surrendering by threatening them with his impressive artillery, which closer inspection revealed to be a faux cannon cobbled together from two pieces of stovepipe and some wheels. Admiral *and* General Raphael Semmes was the only officer in either army to hold both ranks. Stand Watie, a Cherokee chief born in Georgia, had the double distinction of being the war's only Indian general, North or South, as well as the last general to surrender to the Yankees. That so many of these officers met untimely deaths on the battlefield adds poignancy to the messages addressed to their mothers, wives, and sweethearts.

149 "a tall, lean man": Quoted in William Howard Russell, *My Diary North and South* (Baton Rouge: Louisiana State University Press, 2001; orig. publ. 1863), p. 43.

149 "I knew nothing of the postal service": Quoted in Dorothy Fowler, *The Cabinet Politician* (New York: Columbia University Press, 1943), p. 107.

154 They successfully redirected a letter: James H. Bruns, "Remembering the Dead," *EnRoute* 1, no. 3 (July–September 1992). http://postalmuseum.si.edu/research/articles-from-enroute/remembering-the-dead.html.

154 "more faithful in the performance": United States Postal Service, "A Brief History of Women at Postal Service Headquarters," 2008, quoted in Abbey Teller and Christina Park, "Women in the U.S. Postal System," http://postalmuseum.si.edu/womenhistory/women_history/history_19century.html.

155 "immoral things are sometimes found": Letter to the Editor, "Women as Government Clerks," *New York Times,* February 18, 1869, p. 2.

156 In 1881, the obituary: United States Postal Service, "African-American Postal Workers in the 19th Century," https://about.usps.com/who-we-are/postal-history/african-american-workers-19thc-2011.pdf.

157 Isaac Myers, the first known: *African Methodist Episcopal Church Review* 7, no. 4 (April 1891), pp. 354–55, quoted in ibid.

157 A position as a clerk: William Cooper Nell, *The Colored Patriots of the American Revolution* (Charleston, SC: Nabu Press, 2010; orig. publ. 1855).

158 "Boys, the old flag": Ronald S. Coddington, "The Old Flag Never Touched the Ground," *New York Times,* July 19, 2013.

11: FULL STEAM AHEAD

161 One such train, traveling: Carl H. Scheele, *A Short History of the Mail Service* (Washington, D.C.: Smithsonian Institution Press, 1970), p. 104.

161 Most correspondence traveled within a radius of fifty miles: The English novelist Anthony Trollope, who had a long career with the Royal Mail, traces the complicated journey of a letter during the heyday of railway mail, in both the U.S. and Great Britain, in a charming passage from *Framley Parsonage* that also refers to the etiquette of Sabbath mail: "And now, with my reader's consent, I will follow the postman with that letter to Framley; not by its own circuitous route indeed, or by the same mode of conveyance; for that letter went into Barchester by the

Courcy night mail-cart, which, on its road, passed through the villages of Uffey and Chaldicotes, reaching Barchester in time for the up-mail from London. By that train, the letter was sent towards the metropolis as far as the junction of the Barset branch line, but there it was turned in its course, and came down again by the main line as far as Silverbridge; at which place, between six and seven in the morning, it was shouldered by the Framley footpost messenger, and in due course delivered at the Framley Parsonage exactly as Mrs Robarts had finished reading prayers to the four servants. Or, I should say rather, that such would in its usual course have been that letter's destiny. As it was, however, it reached Silverbridge on Sunday, and lay there till the Monday, as the Framley people have declined their Sunday post. And then again, when the letter was delivered at the parsonage, on that wet Monday morning, Mrs Robarts was not at home." (Anthony Trollope, *Framley Parsonage*, chapter 5, pp. 58–59, http://www.online-literature.com /anthony-trollope/framley-parsonage/5/.)

162 **"The midnight train is whining low"**: Hank Williams, "I'm So Lonesome I Could Cry," 1949.

163 **"On his memory, accuracy, and integrity"**: Quoted in Cushing, *Story of Our Post Office*, p. 173.

163 **"Any indications of derangement"**: Ibid., p. 83.

170 **"of all existing departments"**: Quoted in Fuller, *American Mail*, p. 2.

170 **"The public be damned"**: "Vanderbilt in the West; The Railroad Millionaire Expresses Himself Freely," *New York Times*, October 9, 1882.

174 **A carrier recorded only as "Stringer"**: Cushing, *Story of Our Post Office*, p. 40.

175 **"As soon as the ice begins to form"**: Quoted in United States Postal Service, "Star Routes," November 2012. https://about.usps.com/publications/pub100/pub100_017.htm.

175 **In 1900, the economist H. T. Newcomb**: Quoted in Richard John, *History of Universal Service and the Postal Monopoly*, http://www.journalism.columbia.edu /system/documents/704/original/Appendix_D.pdf.

176 **The history of communications in Yellowstone National Park**: Each year, the world's first national park postmarks roughly one piece of mail for each of its four million visitors. Yellowstone's main post office, in the village of Mammoth Hot Springs, was constructed in 1937 and has a certain modernist elegance in a part of the country better known for rustic log cabins. The two large Art Deco bear sculptures that flank its entrance might have been inspired by the jeweler Cartier. In summer, when many vacationers as well as personnel receive letters and parcels, five postal employees sort the mail into old-fashioned pigeonhole racks behind the well-appointed lobby's service windows and wall of postal boxes. In winter, the park's population shrinks to mostly rangers and other employees, and the perks of its two postal workers include cozy apartments over the shop.

177 **a feast that was "a beaut"**: Letter from Edwin Kelsey, December 3, 1898, in *Fort Yellowstone Historic District Tour Guide: The Army Years, 1886–1918* (Yellowstone National Park, WY: Yellowstone Association, 2010).

178 **"$1.25 a day above horsefeed"**: Unpublished material from files of the USPS Historian. Records indicate that Wyeth was a mail carrier on a "special" supply route that served post offices that were too new and remote to be served by regular routes.

Wyeth's pictures later appeared in *Century, Harper's Monthly, Ladies' Home Journal, McClure's, Outing,* and *Scribner's* magazines. He also illustrated Western novels, such as *Arizona Nights* by Stewart Edward White and the original Hopalong Cassidy tales by Clarence E. Mulford. On February 1, 2001, the U.S. Postal Service issued a sheet of stamps commemorating twenty American illustrators and selected Wyeth's illustration of Captain Billy Bones from *Treasure Island* to represent his life's work.

12: THE GOLDEN AGE

182 **"our whole economic and political system"**: Quoted in John Joseph Lalor, ed., *Cyclopaedia of Political Science, Political Economy, and of the Political History of the United States,* vol. 3 (New York: C. E. Merrill & Company, 1893), p. 310.

182 **"enormous, resistless, inconceivable"; "we beat the world"**: Cushing, *Story of Our Post Office,* pp. 17, 18.

185 **"is for the transmission of intelligence"**: Quoted in Henry Martyn Field, *The Story of the Atlantic Telegraph* (New York: Charles Scribner's Sons, 1898), p. 100.

186 **"that most subtle and universal"**: U.S. Congress, House Executive Documents for 1873, "Report of the Postmaster-General," vol. 3 (43rd Cong., 1st sess.), (Washington, 1874), quoted in "Republican Mass Meeting—Speech of Mr. Creswell," *Baltimore American,* October 18, 1873.

186 **"There must be a limit"**: Quoted in Fuller, *American Mail,* pp. 180–81.

186 **"Let us adhere, as closely"**: Leonidas Trousdale, "The Postal Telegraph System" (1869), in John, *American Postal Network,* vol. 4, p. 42.

186 **"It is not contended"**: Gardiner Hubbard, "The Proposed Changes in the Telegraphic System," *North American Review* 117, no. 240 (July 1873), pp. 80–107.

187 **"the greatest business organization"**: Charles Emory Smith, "Greatest Business Organization in the World: The United States Postal Service" (1899), in John, *American Postal Network,* vol. 1, p. 393.

189 **"I do not think it essential"**: Cushing, *Story of Our Post Office,* p. 898.

189 **"See if each one does not commend itself"**: Ibid., p. 1001.

191 **Most drove their own horse-drawn wagons**: Since 1987, Michael Schragg, the founder and curator of the U.S. Postal Museum, in Marshall, Michigan, where he long served as postmaster, has assembled its more than two thousand postal artifacts that offer an enchanting, educational window into the lost world of turn-of-the-century rural America and the great improvements wrought by RFD and Parcel Post. Along with an array of mail buggies, postal ledgers, and hand-stamps, the collection includes a photograph of a carrier from Stella, Kentucky, grinning widely atop his horse and wearing a peculiar apron equipped with numbered

pockets. The man was illiterate, but the district was desperate for a carrier during World War II, so the postal clerks sorted the mail for him and put it in the pouches, whose numbers he could read.

The museum is housed in Marshall's splendid copper-roofed Greek Revival post office, which befits a prosperous town founded in 1830 and auspiciously named for John Marshall, the Supreme Court's second Chief Justice, while he still lived. Rumor had it that the town would become the new state's capital, but tiny Lansing got that honor. By the 1840s, Marshall was a bustling, politically progressive postal and railroad hub, which later helped it achieve notoriety as the capital of wildly popular if bogus patent medicines of the sort described as "snake oil" or "pink pills for pale people." The nearby clinic of Dr. John Harvey Kellogg, the inventor of corn flakes and the modern cereal industry, drew devotees eager to follow his regimen of vegetarianism, sexual abstinence, exercise, and enemas.

192 **"insanity is on the decrease"**: "Meyer's Postal Plans: Radical Changes Advocated by Postmaster General," *Washington Post*, October 13, 1907, p. 3, cited in United States Postal Service, "Universal Service and the Postal Monopoly: A Brief History," October 2008. https://about.usps.com/universal-postal-service /universal-service-and-the-postal-monopoly-history.pdf.

192 **"financial ruin, general demoralization"**: Abraham D. Hazen, "The Post Office Before and Since 1860, Under Democratic and Republican Administrations" (1880), in John, *American Postal Network*, vol. 1, p. 342.

195 **"Though modest in manner"**: Cushing, *Story of Our Post Office*, p. 449.

195 **Of the country's some 67,000 postmasters**: Ibid., p. 443.

195 **"unlike any other feminine artist"**: Ibid., p. 453.

195 **"And yet while there are no monuments"**: George B. Cortelyou, "The Postmistress," *The Delineator* 67 (January 1906), p. 71. Quoted in Teller and Park, "Women in the U.S. Postal System," http://postalmuseum.si.edu/WomenHistory /women_history/history_reconstruction.html.

196 **Viola Bennett, of Suwanee, Georgia**: "Resolute Georgia Girl Is Rural Mail Carrier," [Atlanta] *Constitution*, September 13, 1904. "Woman Mail Carrier Hurt. Horse Throws Miss Viola Bennett from Her Buggy," ibid., April 29, 1906. Quoted in "Women Mail Carriers," June 2007. https://about.usps.com/who-we-are/postal -history/women-carriers.pdf.

196 **As Cushing put it, they "fill places"**: Cushing, *Story of Our Post Office*, p. 681.

197 **"a Scotchman, a bachelor"**: Quoted in ibid., p. 715.

197 **"Every time a woman is appointed"**: "Women Not Wanted," *New York Times*, November 9, 1902, p. 3. Quoted in United States Postal Service, "Women of Postal Headquarters," https://about.usps.com/who-we-are/postal-history/women- at-headquarters.pdf.

197 **wives should "stay at home"**: Quoted in "Women Clerks Who Wed," *Washington Post*, November 25, 1902, p. 2. Quoted in ibid.

197 **This official bias against married women**: Will Hays's tenure as postmaster general lasted just one year before he left in 1922 to become the first president of the Motion Picture Producers and Distributors of America (later the Motion

Picture Association of America). The organization was founded to sanitize Hollywood's image after the trial of Roscoe "Fatty" Arbuckle, in which he was accused, and later found not guilty, of raping and murdering a woman in his home. In 1930, the Presbyterian deacon and former chairman of the Republican Party implemented the "Hays Code," which forced studios to remove any potentially offensive material from their movies and seriously dampened artistic expression in film until 1960, when the current age-based movie rating system was created.

198 **"Mrs. Minnie Cox, Postmistress":** *Cleveland Gazette*, February 7, 1903, cited in Boyd and Chen, "The History and Experience of African Americans in America's Postal Service."

13: REDEFINING "POSTAL"

202 **The elegant Palladian structure:** After the Post Office Department moved to new quarters in 1897, the beautiful marble building was used by various government agencies. It gradually fell into such a state of disrepair that even a rescue by the Smithsonian Institution was judged to be too expensive. The building was eventually bought by the Kimpton Hotels chain and opened in 2002 as a chic boutique hotel.

202 **"We doubt if there is a building":** *Harper's New Monthly Magazine*, December 1859.

206 **"Express companies extend their business":** *Harper's Weekly*, December 7, 1889.

206 **"The effect of such a law":** C. A. Hutsinpillar, "The Parcels Post" (1904), in John, *American Postal Network*, vol. 4, p. 262.

206 **"our great cooperative express company":** James L. Cowles, "A United States Parcels Post," in ibid., p. 236.

207 **"educating energy augmented by cheapness":** Ralph Waldo Emerson, *Society and Solitude* (Boston: Houghton, Mifflin, 1870), p. 26.

209 **"so trashy and wishy-washy":** James Britt, "Second Class Mail Matter: Its Uses and Abuses" (1911), in John, *American Postal Network*, vol. 4, p. 470.

210 **"As long as the people":** Wilmer Atkinson, "Guessing and Figuring Having Failed, Try a Few Ounces of Common Sense" (1911), in John, *American Postal Network*, vol. 4, p. 455.

210 **"most majestic system of public education":** Edward Everett Hale, "A Public Telegraph," *Cosmopolitan*, December 1891, pp. 249, 251.

210 **postal service had become "a great university":** *Congressional Record*, 59th Congress, 1st sess., 5081, April 11, 1906. Quoted in United States Postal Service, "Universal Service and the Postal Monopoly," October 2008, https://about.usps.com/universal-postal-service/universal-service-and-postal-monopoly-history.text.

211 **Theft continued to be the most common crime:** In one notorious case of postal fraud, Roy DeWelles was sentenced to ten years in prison in 1965 after using mail solicitations to make more than $500,000 from bogus health services and his $2,500 Detoxacolon machine, which he sold to chiropractors and alternative healers. He was finally apprehended for mailing false advertising to ten thousand people. In 1988, postal inspectors arrested televangelist Jim Bakker for mail fraud

amounting to $158 million in charitable donations used for personal gain, for which he was sentenced to forty-five years in prison.

211 **"Comstockery is the world's standing joke"**: George Bernard Shaw, Letter to the Editor, *New York Times,* September 26, 1905, p. 1.

211 **an "Irish smut dealer"**: "Who's Bernard Shaw? Asks Mr. Comstock," *New York Times,* September 28, 1905, p. 9.

212 **"Shall the right to mail service"**: Louis Post, "Our Despotic Postal Censorship," in John, *American Postal Network,* vol. 1, p. 407.

212 **"Good men must not obey the laws"**: Ralph Waldo Emerson, "Politics," *Essays: Second Series* (Boston: James Munroe, 1844). Quoted in https://emersoncentral.com /politics.htm.

214 **If there's a physical symbol of what the combination of the post at its peak:** The Farley Post Office continues to play an important role in the preservation of New York City's historic buildings. The demolition of Pennsylvania Station, its glorious companion building across the street, in 1963 was the impetus for the establishment of the New York City Landmarks Preservation Commission in 1965. In 2007, New York State bought the Farley building from the post and plans a massive renovation that will create a multi-use, public-private facility meant to rejuvenate Midtown West. The Farley post office's lobby and public service area will be meticulously restored to its original grandeur circa 1912.

Mail formerly processed at the Farley is now handled by the Morgan Annex between 28th and 30th Streets on 9th Avenue. Following the terrorist attacks of 9/11, however, the Farley took over some operations from the damaged Church Street post office located across the street from the World Trade Center.

214 **The quotation, paraphrased from Herodotus:** Herodotus, *The Histories,* ed. and trans. A. D. Godley, pp. 96–97.

216 **"Congress was building on the policy"**: Kelly, *United States Postal Policy,* p. 88.

14: STARVING THE POST

217 **make the world "safe for democracy"**: Woodrow Wilson, speech to the 65th Cong., 1st Sess., Senate Document No. 5. https://www.ourdocuments.gov/doc .php?flash=true&doc=61.

217 **"You are not here to make a living"**: Woodrow Wilson, speech at Swarthmore College on October 25, 1913, in *Selected Addresses and Public Papers of Woodrow Wilson,* ed. Albert Bushnell Hart (New York: Boni and Liveright, 1918), p. 15.

219 **"willfully utter, print, write"**: "The Espionage Act of 1917," University of Houston Digital History. http://www.digitalhistory.uh.edu/disp_textbook .cfm?smtID=3&psid=3904.

220 **a return to "normalcy"**: Warren G. Harding, "Back to Normal: Address Before Home Market Club," Boston, Massachusetts, May 14, 1920, in Warren Harding and Frederick Schortemeier, *Rededicating America* (Indianapolis: Bobbs-Merrill, 1920).

221 **"The great postal highway"**: Kelly, *United States Postal Policy,* p. 255.

221 **"the Post Office has been used"**: Ibid., pp. 168–69.

221 **"The greatest single difference"**: Ibid., p. 120.

222 "a very safe airplane": Quoted in "The Early Years of Air Transportation," https://airandspace.si.edu/exhibitions/amercia-by-air/online/early_years03.cfm.

223 "just something to clutter up the cockpit": Quoted in Donald Dale Jackson, *Flying the Mail* (Alexandria, VA: Time-Life Books, 1982), p. 92.

224 "Only place to land on cow": Quoted in ibid., p. 6.

224 "Alone in an empty cockpit": Quoted in ibid.

226 "The Pilot was only slightly injured": D. B. Colyer, *News Letter*. Week Ending September 26, 1925, Air Mail Service, Omaha, Nebraska, Record Group 28, National Archives and Records Administration.

227 "I am an airmail pilot": Quoted in Jackson, *Flying the Mail*, p. 148.

227 "to be a pilot of the night mail": Ibid.

228 citing the "four seeds": Quoted in United States Postal Service, "Airmail," https://about.usps.com/publications/pub100/pub100_026.htm.

230 "native, human, eager and alive": Franklin D. Roosevelt, "The Freedom of the Human Spirit Shall Go On," Address at the Dedication of National Gallery of Art, Section of Fine Arts, March 17, 1941, Special Bulletin, National Archives, Record Group 121, Entry 122.

234 Rickenbacker called "legalized murder": Edward Rickenbacker, *Rickenbacker: An Autobiography* (Upper Saddle River, NJ: Prentice-Hall, 1967), p. 186.

238 "a grave doubt in the minds": "Capital City Tries Women as Letter Carriers," *The Postal Record: A Monthly Journal of the National Association of Letter Carriers* 30, no. 12 (December 1917), p. 399. Cited in Teller and Park, "Women in the U.S. Postal System," http://postalmuseum.si.edu/womenhistory/women_history/history_streets.html.

238 "were segregated two ways": Quoted in Jennifer Lenhart, "Six Military Women and Six U.S. Wars; Charity Adams Earley; World War II," *Washington Post*, October 18, 1997.

15: Mid-Modern Meltdown

243 "In the councils of government": Dwight D. Eisenhower, Farewell Address, January 17, 1961, Box 38, Speech Series, Papers of Dwight D. Eisenhower as President, 1953–61, Eisenhower Library; National Archives and Records Administration.

246 "monuments in stone to political patronage": Arthur E. Summerfield, *U.S. Mail: The Story of the United States Postal Service* (New York: Holt, Rinehart & Winston, 1965), p. 205.

246 "Who was the other?": Ibid., p. 230.

246 "We stand on the threshold": Quoted in United States Postal Service, "Missile Mails," July 2008. http://about.usps.com/who-we-are/postal-history/missile-mail.pdf.

250 "clearly is not a business enterprise": Postal Policy Act of 1958, *U.S. Statutes at Large*, 72, pp. 134, 135.

250 O'Brien had not been a wily political operator: Not a flower born to blush unseen, Larry O'Brien later became the chairman of the Democratic National Committee, and the burglary of his office by political opponents in 1972 set off the

Watergate scandal, which led to President Richard Nixon's resignation. He went on to serve as the commissioner of the National Basketball Association.

251 The group took its responsibility: *Towards Postal Excellence: The Report of the President's Commission on Postal Reorganization* (Washington, D.C.: U.S. Government Printing Office, 1968).

254 "elevating our people in the scale of civilization": Quoted in Melville Clyde Kelly, *The Community Capitol: A Program for American Unity* (Pittsburgh: Mayflower Press, 1921), p. 207.

16: THE U.S. POSTAL SERVICE

255 In August 1970, an enthusiastic President Richard Nixon: Postal Reorganization Act of 1970, U.S. Statutes at Large, 84 (1970).

255 "independent establishment": http://www.21cpw.com/wp-content /uploads/2015/05/Postal-Reorganization-Act-1970.pdf.

255 "No longer was the Post Office": Fuller, *American Mail*, p. 331.

256 However, Nixon and his Postmaster General: Winton Blount's admirable efforts included the policy of recruiting able African Americans executives, such as John Strachan, who managed the huge New York Metropolitan Postal Center that ran operations in both Manhattan and the Bronx.

The dynamic Blount was followed by Postmaster General Elmer Klassen, a former president of the American Can Company, who was initially touted as a labor relations expert. Before long, however, he was criticized by influential political columnist Jack Anderson and others for giving away enormous benefits to the postal unions during a period of high inflation.

Postmaster General Marvin Runyon, who served between 1992 and 1998, had a unique view of postal employment issues. The no-nonsense Texan had been a Ford assembly-line worker before becoming an auto executive and head of the Tennessee Valley Authority. "Carvin'" Marvin got his nickname after downsizing the post's workforce by firing 23,000 bureaucrats in order to hire more mail handlers.

258 "must be regarded as the devourer": Kelly, *United States Postal Policies*, p. 190.

259 The very notion of letting the hitherto sacrosanct: For more information, see Coleman Hoyt and Robert Cohen, *Postal Worksharing: An Irreverent History* (Woodstock, VT: private publisher, 2011).

260 substituting a "money corporation": Quoted in Fuller, *American Mail*, p. 338.

263 The number of African Americans in its ranks: The ranks of the post's most interesting African American employees must include Kermit Oliver, who began working nights as a clerk in the Waco, Texas, post office in 1978. The reclusive artist, who is the son of a black cowboy, is renowned for paintings that depict Native Americans and regional flora and fauna, such as prickly pear cacti, wild turkeys, and mustangs, surrounded by elaborate decorative borders. His pictures sell in the five figures, and he also designs highly sought-after $400 scarves for

Hermès, the French luxury goods firm. However, Oliver kept his nocturnal version of the artist's day job. (See Jason Sheeler, "Portrait of the Artist as a Postman: The Strange and Secret World of Kermit Oliver," *Texas Monthly*, October 2012.)

263 "With our near 16,000 women Postmasters": Postmaster General Arthur Summerfield, Post Office Department press release, February 3, 1958, quoted in United States Postal Service, "Women Postmasters," July 2008. https://about.usps.com/who-we-are/postal-history/women-postmasters.pdf.

267 "How can we break": Summerfield, *U.S. Mail*, p. 205.

267 "Unless the postal service really makes": "Postal Study Proposes Five-Day Mail Delivery Increased Federal Subsidies to Mail Service," *CQ Quarterly Almanac* 1977, pp. 547–50.

267 "All three Postmasters General": Ibid.

268 "compete with portions of the traditional market": Office of Technology Assessment Reports Collection. http://govinfo.library.unt.edu/ota/Ota_4 /DATA/1982/8214.PDF.

270 had been "largely disappointing": President's Commission on the United States Postal Service, *Embracing the Future: Making the Tough Choices to Preserve Universal Mail Service*, August 2003. http://govinfo.library.unt.edu/usps/offices /domestic-finance/usps/pdf/freport.pdf.

271 was soon reified: Postal Accountability and Enhancement Act of 2006, U.S. Statutes at Large, 120 (2006). https://www.gpo.gov/fdsys/granule /STATUTE=120/STATUTE=120=Pg3198/content-detail.html.

272 "the delivery of letters": Title 39 U.S. Code §102. https://www.law.cornell.edu/ uscode/text/39/102.

272 "If the nation's best executives": Murray Comarow, "The Future of the Postal Service," in Thomas H. Stanton and Benjamin Ginsberg, *Making Government Manageable: Executive Organization and Management in the Twenty-First Century* (Baltimore: Johns Hopkins University Press, 2004), p. 95.

273 "Throughout all past history": Kelly, *United States Postal Policy*, pp.168–69.

AFTERWORD: WHITHER THE POST?

275 "We live by communications": Summerfield, *U.S. Mail*, p. 165.

278 It delivers mail in the canyons of Wall Street: In 1999, Michael Schragg, the founder and director of the U.S. Postal Museum, in Marshall, Michigan, fulfilled a lifelong dream: delivering mail by boat to the great freighters traveling along the Detroit River to the Great Lakes. The post's transportation contractor for the nation's only floating ZIP code—48222—is the Westcott Company, which also delivers supplies such as light bulbs and toilet paper to the big ships. The freighters don't stop to get their mail, which would be a costly delay. Instead, the small mail boat pushes itself into the ship's side, which rises eight to ten stories above, then the freighter's crew lowers down a bucket for the mail.

281 **it has not won over the great majority:** Office of Inspector General, USPS, "What Postal Services Do People Value the Most? A Quantitative Survey of the Postal Universal Service Obligation," Report No. RARC-WP-15-007, February 23, 2015. https://www.uspsoig.gov/sites/default/files/document-library-files/2015/rarc-wp-15-007_0.pdf.

This large survey published in collaboration with Gallup, shows that most respondents—both households and businesses—still strongly value traditional mail, particularly door and curb delivery, access to post offices, and universal service at a uniform first-class rate.

282 **state-of-the-art technology:** The process for a single first-class letter works something like this: When the letter arrives at a local post office, it's sent to a large regional processing plant, where it's placed with others on a conveyor belt. Mechanical wands smooth out and level the mail stream, so that each piece is unobstructed. Conventional letters are separated from thick or odd-sized ones, then are screened for biohazards. Next, an advanced face-canceler system zeroes in on the letter's front side, so that a digital camera can snap its address. An optical character reader then scans that bit of information so that a computer can compare it to the post's database of 154 million addresses.

The letter gets sprayed with a bar code that gives a city, state, street, house number, and the now-expanded ZIP code plus 6, which sequences the carrier's route properly. Then the bar-coded envelope is fed into a "delivery input/output subsystem" machine, which directs it toward a processing center near its final destination within or outside the state. The letter is dispatched via the most efficient, cost-effective route, whether on a plane leaving Miami for Atlanta or a truck going from New York City to Newark, New Jersey. When it reaches a sorting facility near its destination, another machine reads its bar code and directs the envelope to the proper receptacle for its trip to the recipient's local post office, properly sequenced for delivery. (For more information, http://postalmuseum.si.edu/research/pdfs/ZIP_Code_rarc-wp-13-006.pdf.)

284 **As in many nations, they could become community information hubs:** In 2012, during the chaos following Superstorm Sandy in New York City, some technologists demonstrated the advantages of an intranet by setting up a web of aerials in Brooklyn's hard-hit waterfront neighborhood of Red Hook. Residents deprived of electricity and cell service were thus able to keep informed about flooding, transportation, and other vital issues.

287 **called "first-rate intelligence":** F. Scott Fitzgerald, "Pasting It Together," *Esquire*, March 1936.

SUGGESTED READINGS

BOWYER, MATHEW J. *They Carried the Mail: A Survey of Postal History and Hobbies.* New York: Robert B. Luce, 1972.

BRUNS, JAMES H. *Great American Post Offices.* New York: John Wiley & Sons, 1998.

CHAPMAN, ARTHUR. *The Pony Express.* New York: G. P. Putnam's Sons, 1932.

CULLINAN, GERALD. *The United States Postal Service.* New York: Praeger, 1973.

CUSHING, MARSHALL. *The Story of Our Post Office: The Greatest Government Department in All Its Phases.* Boston: A. M. Thayer & Co., 1893.

DAY, J. EDWARD. *My Appointed Round: 929 Days as Postmaster General.* New York: Holt, Rinehart & Winston, 1965.

FINLAY, HUGH. *Journal Kept by Hugh Finlay, Surveyor of the Post Roads on the Continent of North America, during His Survey of the Post Offices between Falmouth and Casco Bay in the Province of Massachusetts, and Savannah, in Georgia: Begun the 13th Septr. 1773 & Ended 26th June 1774,* ed. Frank H. Norton. Brooklyn, NY: Norton, 1867.

FOWLER, DOROTHY GANFIELD. *The Cabinet Politician: The Postmasters General, 1829-1909.* New York: Columbia University Press, 1943.

——. *Unmailable: Congress and the Post Office.* Athens: University of Georgia Press, 1977.

FULLER, WAYNE E. *The American Mail: Enlarger of the Common Life.* Chicago: University of Chicago Press, 1972.

——. *RFD: The Changing Face of Rural America.* Bloomington: Indiana University Press, 1964.

——. *Morality and the Mail in Nineteenth-Century America.* Urbana and Chicago: University of Illinois Press, 2003.

GANZ, CHERYL R. *Every Stamp Tells a Story: The National Philatelic*

Collection. Washington, D.C.: Smithsonian Institution Scholarly Press, 2014.

HENKIN, DAVID. *The Postal Age: The Emergence of Modern Communications in Nineteenth-Century America*. Chicago: University of Chicago Press, 2006.

HOLMES, DONALD B. *Air Mail: An Illustrated History, 1793–1981*. New York: Clarkson N. Potter, 1981.

HOLMES, OLIVER W., AND PETER T. ROHRBACH. *Stagecoach East: Stagecoach Days in the East from the Colonial Period to the Civil War*. Washington, D.C.: Smithsonian Institution Press, 1983.

HOWE, DANIEL WALKER. *What Hath God Wrought: The Transformation of America, 1815–1848*. New York: Oxford University Press, 2009.

JACKSON, DONALD DALE. *Flying the Mail*. Alexandria, VA: Time-Life Books, 1982.

JOHN, RICHARD R. *Spreading the News: The American Postal System from Franklin to Morse*. Cambridge, MA: Harvard University Press, 1995.

———. *Network Nation: Inventing American Telecommunications*. Cambridge, MA: Harvard University Press, 2010.

———, ed. *The American Postal Network, 1792–1914*. 4 vols. London: Pickering & Chatto, 2012.

KELLY, CLYDE. *United States Postal Policy*. New York: D. Appleton, 1931.

KIELBOWICZ, RICHARD B. *News in the Mail: The Press, Post Office, and Public Information, 1700–1860s*. Westport, CT: Greenwood Press, 1989.

KNIGHT, SARAH KEMBLE. *The Journal of Madam Knight*. Boston: David R. Godine, 1972.

LONG, BRYANT ALDEN, AND WILLIAM JEFFERSON DENNIS. *Mail by Rail: The Story of the Postal Transportation Service*. New York: Simmons-Boardman, 1951.

MIKUSKO, M. BRADY, AND F. JOHN MILLER. *Carriers in a Common Cause: A History of Letter Carriers and the NALC*. Washington, D.C.: National Association of Letter Carriers, 1989.

RUBIO, PHILIP F. *There's Always Work at the Post Office: African American Postal Workers and the Fight for Jobs, Justice, and Equality*. Chapel Hill: University of North Carolina Press, 2010.

SCHEELE, CARL H. *A Short History of the Mail Service*. Washington, D.C.: Smithsonian Institution Press, 1970.

SHAW, CHRISTOPHER W. *Preserving the People's Post Office*. Washington, D.C.: Essential Books, 2006.

STEELE, IAN K. *The English Atlantic, 1675–1740: An Exploration of Communication and Community*. New York: Oxford University Press, 1986.

SUMMERFIELD, ARTHUR E. *U.S. Mail: The Story of the United States Postal Service*. New York: Holt, Rinehart & Winston, 1965.

TERRELL, JOHN UPTON. *The United States Post Office Department: A Story of Letters, Postage, and Mail Fraud*. New York: Meredith, 1968.

UNITED STATES POSTAL SERVICE. *An American Postal Portrait: A Photographic Legacy*. New York: HarperResource, 2000.

VAN DER LINDEN, F. ROBERT. *Airlines and Air Mail: The Post Office and the Birth of the Commercial Aviation Industry*. Lexington: University Press of Kentucky, 2002.

WEB SITES

Smithsonian National Postal Museum:
http://postalmuseum.si.edu/

For research on philately and postal operations:
http://arago.si.edu/

United States Postal Service:
United States Postal Service: "Who We Are"
http://about.usps.com.http://about.usps.com/who-we-are/postal-history
/welcome.htm
Publication 100: *The United States Postal Service: An American History, 1775–2006*
http://about.usps.com/publications/pub100.pdf

Save the Post Office:
http://www.savethepostoffice.com/

Railway Mail Service Library:
http://www.railwaymailservicelibrary.org/

INDEX